COLOR ATLAS OF TURFGRASS WEEDS

Golf Courses, Lawns, Roadsides, Sports Fields, Recreational Areas, Commercial Sod, Cemeteries, Pastures

---

L. B. (Bert) McCarty,
Coordinating Author
Professor of Horticulture,
Clemson University, Clemson, SC.

John W. Everest,
Professor of Agronomy and Soils,
Auburn University, Auburn AL.

David W. Hall
David W. Hall Consultant, Inc., Gainesville, FL.
Formerly with KBN Engineering, Inc.,
and University of Florida, Institute of Food and Agricultural Sciences,
and Florida Museum of Natural History.

Tim R. Murphy,
Professor of Crop and Soil Sciences,
The University of Georgia, Griffin, GA.

Fred Yelverton,
Associate Professor of Crop Science,
North Carolina State University, Raleigh, NC.

Ann Arbor Press

This book represents information obtained from authentic and highly regarded sources. Reprinted material is quoted with permission, and sources are indicated. A wide variety of references are listed. Every reasonable effort has been made to give reliable data and information, but the author and publisher cannot assume responsibility for the validity of all material or for the consequences of their use.

Ann Arbor Press
310 North Main Street
P.O. Box 20
Chelsea, MI 48118
www.sleepingbearpress.com
Ann Arbor Press is an imprint of Sleeping Bear Press

Printed and bound in Canada.
10 9 8 7 6 5 4 3 2 1

Library of Congress Cataloging-in-Publication Data

Color atlas of turfgrass weeds / L.B. (Bert) McCarty ... [et al.].
            p. cm.
ISBN 1-57504-142-1
1. Turfgrasses-Weed control. 2. Weeds-Identification. 3. Turf management. I. McCarty, L. B. (Lambert Blanchard), 1958- II. Title.
SB608.T87 C645 2000
635.9'64295--dc21
            00-01267

ACKNOWLEDGMENTS

Appreciation is extended to the following individuals: Photographers, Mr. Vic Christ, Mr. Jim Strawser, Dr. Tommy Willard, Dr. Joe Neal, Dr. John Boyd, and Dr. Ford Baldwin; and Dr. Danny Colvin and Dr. Ray Dickens for their technical assistance.

AUTHORS

L. B. (Bert) McCarty, is a Professor of Horticulture at Clemson University in Clemson, South Carolina.

John W. Everest, is a Professor of Agronomy and Soils at Auburn University in Auburn, Alabama.

David W. Hall. David W. Hall Consultant, Inc., Gainesville, FL. Formerly with KBN Engineering, Inc., Gainesville, FL, and with the University of Florida's, Institute of Food and Agricultural Sciences and Florida Museum of Natural History.

Tim R. Murphy, is a Professor of Crop and Soil Sciences at The University of Georgia in Griffin.

Fred Yelverton, is an Associate Professor of Crop Science at North Carolina State University in Raleigh.

SERIES PREFACE

Color Atlas of Turfgrass Weeds by Dr.'s Bert McCarty, John Everest, David Hall, Tim Murphy and Fred Yelverton is a comprehensive, authoritative source of information on problem weeds in the turfgrass environment, that is specifically oriented to the turfgrass manager's needs. It is the second in a four-set **Color Atlas** that encompases diseases, weeds, insects, and environmental stresses of turfgrasses. The authors have called upon their many years of experience in research and education to prepare this practical text. Identification guidelines for the important weeds of turfgrasses in North America are described in the text and illustrated by numerous color photographs. Each weed is described along with its means of propagation, its distribution in North America, and the control strategies. This book is a welcome, key addition to the *Turfgrass Science and Practice Series*.

CONTENTS

CONTRIBUTORS

The authors express gratitude to the following corporations and companies who provided grants that facilitated the development of this publication. These grants were used to partially offset the travel expenses and photography supplies associated with this publication.

American Cyanamid Company (Now, BASF Corporation)
Dow AgroSciences

INTRODUCTION

A weed can be defined as a plant growing where it is not wanted. For example, tall fescue is considered a weed when grown in a pure stand of bermudagrass but is highly desirable when grown in a monoculture such as a golf course rough. In addition to being unsightly, weeds compete with turfgrasses for light, soil nutrients, soil moisture, and physical space. Weeds also are hosts for pests such as plant pathogens, nematodes, and insects. Certain weeds are also irritants to humans when allergic reactions to pollen or chemicals occur.

One of the most undesirable characteristics of weeds in turf situations is the disruption of visual turf uniformity. This may be due to the leaf width or shape, growth habit, or color differences between weeds and a turfgrass species. Many broadleaf weeds such as dandelion, plantains, and pennywort have a wider leaf than the preferred turf species. They also have a different leaf shape. The growth habit of smutgrass, goosegrass, dallisgrass, and quackgrass results in clumps or patches of these species which also disrupt turf uniformity. In addition, large clumps are difficult to mow effectively and increase maintenance problems. The lighter green color and presence of seedheads typically associated with certain weeds such as annual bluegrass in a golf green often distracts from the playing surface.

Weeds often are symptomatic of a weakened turf, not the cause of it. Understanding this helps to explain the major reason for weed encroachment into a turf area (e.g., thin turf density, bare spots, and poor growth). Reasons for weak or bare turf areas are numerous. These include: (a) improper selection of a turf species not adapted to local environmental conditions; (b) damage from turfgrass pests such as diseases, insects, nematodes, and animals; (c) environmental stresses such as excessive shade, drought, heat, and cold; (d) improper turf management practices such as misuse of fertilizer and chemicals, improper mowing height and/or frequency, and lack of soil aeration; and (e) physical damage and compaction from concentrated or constant traffic. Unless factors which contribute to the decline of a turf area are corrected, problems with weed infestations should be expected to continue.

Developing a Weed Management Program

Weed management is an integrated process where good cultural practices are employed to encourage desirable turfgrass ground cover as well as the intelligent selection and use of herbicides. A successful weed management approach involves the following:

1. proper weed identification
2. prevention of weed introduction
3. proper turfgrass management or cultural practices
4. if necessary, the proper selection and use of a herbicide.

Weed Identification

The first step to successful weed management is proper identification, which is the primary focus of this book. Traditionally, plant identification has been based on the recognition of floral and reproductive structures. The reproductive features of plants are less variable than the vegetative structures; however, in well-maintained turfgrasses, mowing continually removes the floral parts and seedheads of many weed species. Turfgrass managers must be able to identify weeds on the basis of the appearance and form of the primary vegetative structures, such as ligules, leaves, and stems, in order to institute timely and efficient control practices. Turf managers should be able to identify each weed to genus and preferably to species in order to select the appropriate control technique. Weed identification also is the first step in understanding why weeds occur and how to control them. For instance, most sedges prefer moist, wet areas while sandspur species prefer drier sites (Table 1).

Table 1. Weeds as Indicators of Specific Poor Soil Conditions

Soil Condition	Indicator Weed(s)
Low pH	Red sorrel, broomsedge
Compacted soil	Goosegrass, prostrate knotweed, annual bluegrass, slender rush
Low soil nitrogen levels	Legumes (clover, chickweed, black medic, lespedeza), speedwell, bitter sneezeweed, broomsedge, chicory
High soil nitrogen levels	Moss, ryegrass, annual bluegrass
Poor (sandy) soils	Poorjoe, sandspur, quackgrass, spurges, black medic, prostrate knotweed, yellow woodsorrel
Droughty soils	Bahiagrass
Poor drainage	Sedges, alligatorweed, annual bluegrass, barnyardgrass, pennywort, rushes
Surface moisture	Algae, moss
High pH	Plantains
High nematodes	Spurges, Florida pusley, prostrate knotweed
Low mowing	Algae, annual bluegrass, chickweeds, pearlwort
High or infrequent mowing	Bull thistle, chicory, clover

Continued problems with the species shown in Table 1 can be expected until the conditions limiting turfgrass growth are corrected.

Basic identification of a problem species begins with classifying the weed type. *Broadleaf* species or dicotyledonous plants, have two cotyledons (young seed leaves) at emergence and have net-like veins in their true leaves. Broadleaf weeds often also have colorful flowers. Examples include clovers, spurges, lespedeza, plantains, henbit, Florida pusley, beggarweed, and matchweed (or mat lippia). *Grasses* or monocotyledonous plants, only have one cotyledon present when seedlings emerge from the soil. Grasses have two-ranked leaves and hollow, rounded stems with nodes (joints), and parallel veins in their true leaves. Leaf sheaths are usually open (not fused). Most grass species have ligules, a projection at the inside junction of the leaf blade and collar. Ligules may be membrane-like, a membrane with hairs on top, or in some species, totally absent (Table 2). Examples include crabgrass, goosegrass, dallisgrass, thin (bull) paspalum, and annual bluegrass.

Table 2. Distinguishing Characteristics of Monocots Compared to Dicots

Characteristic	Monocot	Dicot
Seedling cotyledons	one	two
Leaf veination	parallel	netted
Leaf attachment	directly on stems	usually on short stalks called petioles
Ligules	present, rarely absent (grasses, sedges, rushes)	absent
Vascular bundles	scattered	distinct (arranged in a ring of bundles surrounding a central pith)
Vascular tissue growth	only primary	primary & secondary, thus can become woody
Meristems	basal	terminal
Root system	fibrous without cambium layer	taproot with a cambium layer
Flowers	not showy (grasses, sedges, rushes)	usually showy
Flower parts	group of 3s	usually group of 4s or 5s

Sedges generally favor a moist habitat, have a closed leaf sheath, usually three-ranked leaf arrangements, ligules mostly absent, and have stems which are either triangular-shaped and solid. Rushes also are mostly found in moist to wet habitats, have an open leaf sheath, often have a ligule and have round and solid stems. Table 3 lists some of the distinguishing characteristics between grasses, sedges, and rushes.

Table 3. Distinguishing Characteristics between Grasses, Sedges, and Rushes

Character	Grasses	Sedges	Rushes
Stem	usually hollow, round, or flattened	usually 3-sided, pithy, rarely hollow	round and filled with sponge-like pith
Nodes	very noticeable	indistinct	indistinct
Leaf arrangement	2-ranked	3-ranked	3-ranked
Leaf sheath	usually split	usually closed	usually open
Leaf blade	flat, often folded, hairy or smooth	flat, usually smooth	round or flat, usually smooth, often with visible partitions
Leaf margin	smooth, rough hairy, or sharp	usually rough	usually smooth
Collar	often a distinct band	indistinct	indistinct
Auricles	present or absent	absent	present or absent
Ligule	present, rarely absent	absent or only weakly developed	absent or only weakly developed

Plant Life Cycles

Weeds complete their life cycles in either one growing season (**annuals**), two growing seasons (**biennials**), or three or more years (**perennials**). Annuals that complete their life cycles from spring to fall are generally referred to as **summer** or **warm-season annuals**, and those that complete their life cycles from fall to spring are **winter** or **cool-season annuals**. Summer annual grasses, as a class, are generally the most troublesome in turf.

Control Options

Maintaining today's modern, multimillion dollar turf complexes at the desired level of aesthetics requires knowledge of specific weeds, their biology, and available control measures. The following discusses current selective weed control options turf managers have at their disposal. Weed control should be a carefully planned and coordinated program instead of being a hit-or-miss operation. Understanding how and why weeds are present on a site is more important than knowing what control options are available once the weed is present.

Herbicides

Herbicides may be classified according to chemistry, method of application, timing of application, persistence, selectivity, and mode-of-action.

1. **Selective**. A selective herbicide controls or suppresses certain plant species without seriously affecting the growth of another plant species. Selectivity may be due to differential absorption, translocation, morphological and/or physiological differences between turfgrasses and weeds. The majority of herbicides used in turfgrasses are selective in nature. For example, 2,4-D (several trade names) is used for selective control of many broadleaf weeds, such as dandelion, without significant injury to turfgrasses.

2. **Nonselective**. Nonselective herbicides control plants regardless of species. These are primarily used to control all plants as in the renovation or establishment of a new turf area, "spot treatments," or a trimming material along sidewalks. Glyphosate (Roundup Pro) and diquat (Reward) are examples of nonselective herbicides. Herbicides such as atrazine (Aatrex, others) or MSMA (Bueno 6, others) can be nonselective at rates in excess of those used for selective control.

3. **Systemic**. Systemic herbicides are extensively translocated (moved) in the plant's vascular system. The vascular system translocates the nutrients, water, and other materials necessary for normal growth and development. In contrast to the quick kill observed with contact herbicides, systemic herbicides require several days or even a few weeks to be fully translocated throughout the plant's vascular system, and therefore, require a longer period of time before kill. Systemic herbicides are also classified as selective or nonselective. Glyphosate is a nonselective, systemic herbicide while 2,4-D, dicamba (Vanquish), imazaquin (Image), and sethoxydim (Vantage) are examples of selective, systemic herbicides.

4. **Contact**. Contact herbicides only affect the portion of green plant tissue contacted by the herbicide spray. These herbicides are not translocated in the vascular system of plants or only are to a limited extent. Therefore, underground plant parts such as rhizomes or tubers are not killed. Usually repeat applications are needed with contact herbicides to kill regrowth from these underground plant parts. Adequate spray volumes and thorough coverage of the weed foliage are necessary for effective control. These herbicides kill plants quickly, often within a few hours of application. Contact herbicides may be classified as selective or nonselective. Bromoxynil (Buctril) and bentazon (Basagran T&O) are classified as selective, contact herbicides. Diquat (Reward) and glufosinate (Finale) are nonselective, contact herbicides.

Herbicides from the same class of chemistry are grouped into families in much the same way plants are grouped into genera and species. In general, members of the same herbicide family are similarly absorbed and translocated and have similar mode-of-actions.

Timing of Herbicide Application

Herbicides also are classified as preemergence or postemergence, depending on the time the chemical is applied in respect to turfgrass and/or weed seed germination. Although the majority of herbicides may be classified into one category, atrazine (AAtrex), simazine (Princep), dithiopyr (Dimension), and pronamide (Kerb) are notable exceptions. They are used as both preemergence and postemergence herbicides.

Preplant herbicides. These are applied before turfgrass is established, usually to provide nonselective, complete control of all weeds present. Soil fumigants, such as metam-sodium (Vapam), methyl bromide (Terrogas, Dowfume, Bromogas, others), and dazomet (Basamid), and nonselective herbicides such as glyphosate (Roundup) may be used as nonselective preplant herbicides.

Preemergence herbicides. Preemergence (PRE) herbicides are applied to the turfgrass site prior to weed seed germination and form a barrier at, or right below, the soil surface. Most preemergence herbicides prevent cell division during weed-seed germination as the emerging seedling comes into contact with the herbicide. Weeds that already have emerged (visible) at the time of application are not controlled consistently by preemergence herbicides because their primary growing points escape treatment.

Postemergence herbicides. Postemergence (POST) herbicides are applied directly to emerged weeds. In contrast to preemergence herbicides, this group of herbicides provides little, if any, soil residual control of weeds. A complete chemical weed control program can be accomplished with postemergence herbicides, provided multiple applications are used throughout the year. However, due to the necessity of repeat applications and temporary turfgrass injury, most turfgrass managers use postemergence herbicides in conjunction with a preemergence weed control program. Postemergence herbicides are useful to control perennial grasses and broadleaf weeds that are not controlled by preemergence herbicides. Certain postemergence herbicides also may be used on newly established turfgrasses.

Refer to the Appendix for listing of turfgrass species' tolerance to various preemergence and postemergence herbicides. Also listed are effectiveness ratings for various preemergence and postemergence herbicides for troublesome grasses, broadleaf weeds, and sedges.

Weed Identification Format

The weeds shown in this book are arranged alphabetically by family and scientific name within family. For each species, the Weed Science Society of America (WSSA)-approved family, common, and scientific name is shown. Alternative common and scientific names are listed below the WSSA-approved names. The following example demonstrates the arrangement of genus and species used in this book.

Family Name (Common Family Name)
Weed Common Name

Synonyms:

Species: [Alternative Scientific Names]

Description:

Propagation:

Distribution:

Control Strategies:

Disclaimer

This book contains information on the use of specific herbicides for weed control in turfgrasses. However, herbicide labels constantly change. It is the responsibility of the reader to follow all directions and precautions shown on the label before use. Herbicides suggested for use are based on the herbicide label, land grant university data, and/or the opinion of the authors. Trade or brand names are included only for information. Neither the authors nor the publisher guarantee or warrant published standards on any product mentioned nor does the use of a trade name imply approval of any product to the exclusion of others which also may be suitable.

GRASS AND GRASS-LIKE PLANTS

Amaryllidaceae = Liliaceae (Amaryllis or Lily Family)
Spring Starflower

Synonyms:
Star-of-Bethlehem

Species:
Ipheion uniflorum (Lindley) Raf.

Description:
Escaped, cultivated cool-season perennial from a central bulb. Leaves flat, linear, somewhat fleshy. Plant emits onion-like odor when crushed. Solitary, fragrant, white to lavender flowers on long stalks. Midribs of petals usually darker colored than petals. Mature fruit not seen. Flowers in early spring. Occurs in lawns, gardens, and other disturbed sites.

Propagation:
Primarily by tubers (bulbs).

Distribution:
North Carolina, through panhandle Florida and Texas. Native to Argentina.

Control Strategies:
Postemergence applications of 2,4-D, imazaquin, or atrazine/simazine. Apply 2,4-D or imazaquin in late fall and again in late winter. Repeat this sequence for two years. Avoid moving or using soil contaminated with tubers. Refer to the Appendix for additional control information. Check the herbicide label for specific application rates and turfgrass tolerance before use.

Spring Starflower flowers

Darker midribs of flower petals

Spring Starflower habit

Mature Spring Starflower bulbs

Commelinaceae (Spiderwort Family)
Spreading Dayflower

Synonyms:
Common Dayflower

Species:
Commelina diffusa Burm. f.

Description:
Freely-branched, reclining summer annual lily-like herb
which can be a weak perennial in warmer climates, with
smooth stems. Leaves parallel-veined, alternate, broadly
lance-shaped, with closed sheaths; sheaths short with a few
soft hairs on the upper margin. Flowers with three blue
petals, in leaf-like enclosure which is open on the margins,
usually solitary. Asiatic dayflower (*C. communis* L.) is similar except its flowers have two blue and one smaller white
petal extending below. Flowers last one day, hence, the
common name. Flowers late summer until frost. Found in
most moist habitats along forest edges and right-of-ways.

Spreading Dayflower habit

Propagation:
Seed and stem fragments.

Distribution:
Massachusetts, Missouri, Indiana, south into Florida and
west to Texas, Kansas, and Oklahoma. Also in the West Indies, Mexico, Central and South America, Tropical Africa,
Asia, Taiwan, Japan, and Malaysia.

Control Strategies:
Postemergence applications of three-way mixtures containing 2,4-D, dicamba, MCPP, or MCPA. Repeat this application in 7 days. Atrazine/simazine, bentazon, and metribuzin
plus MSMA or DSMA also provide postemergence control.
Refer to the Appendix for additional control information.
Check the herbicide label for specific application rates and
turfgrass tolerance before use.

Spreading Dayflower flower

Spreading Dayflower leaves

Commelinaceae (Spiderwort Family)
Doveweed

Synonyms:
Naked Stem Dewflower

Species:
Murdannia nudiflora (L.) Brenan; [*Aneilema nudiflorum* (L.) Kunth]

Description:
Summer annual with fleshy, creeping stems, rooting at nodes. Leaves fleshy, alternate, narrowly lanced-shaped. Leaf sheaths short with soft hairs on upper margins. Flowers in somewhat open clusters, blue to purple. Flowers summer until frost. Occurs in turf areas and moist woods.

Propagation:
Seed and possible stem fragments.

Distribution:
North Carolina through Florida, west into Texas. Also in Asia.

Control Strategies:
Postemergence applications of three-way mixtures containing 2,4-D, dicamba, MCPP, or MCPA. Repeat this application in 7 days. Atrazine/simazine and metribuzin plus MSMA or DSMA also provide postemergence control. Refer to the Appendix for additional control information. Check the herbicide label for specific application rates and turfgrass tolerance before use.

Doveweed habit

Doveweed flower heads

Doveweed flower

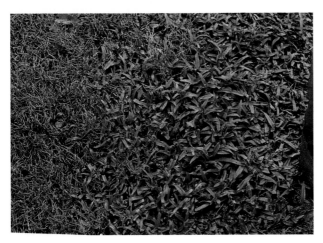
Doveweed in turf

5

Commelinaceae (Spiderwort Family)
Common Spiderwort

Synonyms:
Bluejacket; Ohio Spiderwort

Species:
Tradescantia ohiensis Raf.

Description:
Tufted, erect perennial herb 20 to 60 cm tall with waxy, succulent stems. Long, alternate, grass-like linear-shaped leaves; upper leaves usually narrower than lower ones. Leaves hairless and waxy. Multiple, three-petaled blue flowers on drooping stalks borne at the end of the stem. Flowers usually last only one day. Flowers midspring through early summer. Found in lawns, sandy roadsides, ditches, fence rows, and waste areas.

Propagation:
Seed and root fragments.

Distribution:
In states east of the Mississippi River south to central Florida and west to Texas, Oklahoma, Kansas, and Missouri. Also found in Ontario and Quebec. Native to North America.

Control Strategies:
Postemergence applications of three-way mixtures containing 2,4-D, dicamba, MCPP, or MCPA. Repeat this application in 7 days. Atrazine/simazine and metribuzin plus MSMA or DSMA also provide postemergence control. Refer to the Appendix for additional control information. Check the herbicide label for specific application rates and turfgrass tolerance before use.

Common Spiderwort habit

Common Spiderwort leaves

Common Spiderwort flower

Cyperaceae (Sedge Family)
Annual Sedge

Synonyms:
Water Sedge; Poorland Flatsedge

Species:
Cyperus compressus L.

Description:
Summer annual, with a few long leaves at the top of a bare stem. Seedhead with clusters of flat spikes on short to long stalks. Spikes greenish, sometimes shining, up to 1 inch (2.5 cm) long. Withstands mowing heights on golf greens. Fruits summer until frost. Found in sandy, moist, disturbed areas.

Propagation:
Seed.

Distribution:
Minnesota, Ohio, and New York south through Florida and west to Texas. Also in Bolivia, Ecuador, and Brazil.

Control Strategies:
Control soil moisture, as excessive amounts encourage most sedges including kyllinga species. Preemergence control with either metolachlor, atrazine/simazine, or oxadiazon. Post-emergence control with repeat applications of atrazine/simazine, MSMA/DSMA, bentazon, halosulfuron, imazaquin alone or with MSMA/DSMA. Refer to the Appendix for additional control information. Check the herbicide label for specific application rates and turfgrass tolerance before use.

Annual Sedge seedhead cluster

Annual Sedge habit

Annual Sedge seedhead

Cyperaceae (Sedge Family)
Globe Sedge

Synonyms:
Baldwin's Flatsedge

Species:
Cyperus croceus Vahl; [*Cyperus globulosus* Aublet]

Description:
Perennial with densely tufted stems. Leaf blades flat, smooth, dense, bright green. Seedhead branches at top of stem. Seeds in loose globe-like clusters. Occurs commonly in turf and other moist to dry sandy habitats. Fruits summer into early fall.

Propagation:
Seed.

Distribution:
Virginia south into Florida and west to Texas, Oklahoma, and Missouri. Also in the West Indies, Central and South America, Indonesia, Thailand, Japan, and China.

Control Strategies:
Control soil moisture, as excessive amounts encourage most sedges including kyllinga species. Preemergence control with metolachlor. Postemergence control with repeat applications of bentazon, halosulfuron, imazaquin alone or with MSMA/DSMA. Refer to the Appendix for additional control information. Check the herbicide label for specific application rates and turfgrass tolerance before use.

Globe Sedge seedhead cluster

Globe Sedge seedhead cluster

Globe Sedge habit

Cyperaceae (Sedge Family)
Yellow Nutsedge

Synonyms:
Yellow Nut-grass; Chufa Flatsedge, Chufa, Ground Almond, Earth Almond, Rush Nut

Species:
Cyperus esculentus L.

Description:
Rapidly spreading, perennial grass-like herb with three-ranked basal leaves. Leaves flat or slightly corrugated, usually as long or longer than flowering stem, with long attenuated tip. Seedhead yellowish-brown or straw-colored, formed at end of triangular stem. Tubers round, lacking hairs and formed at ends of whitish rhizomes. Does not form chains of tubers. Tubers slightly sweet to taste; often planted for wildlife food. Fruits midsummer into fall. Occurs in most moist to dry cultivated and otherwise disturbed habitats.

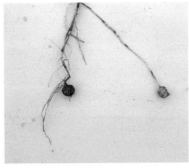

Yellow Nutsedge terminal tubers

Propagation:
Primarily by tubers.

Distribution:
Throughout the United States. Also in Canada, the West Indies, Mexico, Central and South America, Europe, Africa, Asia, and Hawaii. Native to Europe.

Control Strategies:
Control soil moisture, as excessive amounts encourage most sedges including kyllinga species. Preemergence control with metolachlor. Postemergence control with repeat applications of bentazon, halosulfuron, imazaquin alone or with MSMA/DSMA. Refer to the Appendix for additional control information. Check the herbicide label for specific application rates and turfgrass tolerance before use.

Yellow Nutsedge pointed leaf tip, left;
Purple Nutsedge leaf tip, right.

Yellow Nutsedge seedhead

Purple Nutsedge seedhead, left; Yellow Nutsedge seedhead, right.

Cyperaceae (Sedge Family)
Purple Sedge

Synonyms:
Saw Sedge; Swamp Flatsedge

Species:
Cyperus ligularis L.

Description:
Tufted, large, coarse perennial, waxy to purple in color, with a hard base and triangular stems. Leaf sheaths also waxy to purple. Leaf blades originating from the base of the plant, waxy, thick, stiff and with sharp, finely toothed margins and midrib. Seedhead with five to twelve leaf-like rays and several dense, head-like, usually lobed, oblong spikes. Some spikes on short to long stalks. Fruits during warm months. Found in disturbed areas, pinelands, coastal hammocks and swamps.

Propagation:
Seed.

Distribution:
In central and southern peninsula of Florida. Also in the West Indies, Mexico south into Brazil, and in Tropical Africa.

Control Strategies:
Control soil moisture, as excessive amounts encourage most sedges including kyllinga species. Maintain a routine mowing schedule. Postemergence control with repeat applications of bentazon, halosulfuron, imazaquin alone or with MSMA/DSMA. Refer to the Appendix for additional control information. Check the herbicide label for specific application rates and turfgrass tolerance before use.

Purple Sedge habit

Purple Sedge seedhead cluster

Mature Purple Sedge seedhead cluster

Cyperaceae (Sedge Family)
Texas Sedge

Synonyms:
Mangspike Flatsedge

Species:
Cyperus polystachyos Rottb. var. *texensis* (Torr.) Fern.

Description:
Summer annual with stems of varying heights. Leaf blades reddish-brown to greenish-brown. Seedhead branches tightly clustered to open and diffusely spreading. Seeds in long, very narrow, flattened, yellowish to reddish-brown spikes. Fruits midsummer through early fall. Occurs in dry to moist to wet sandy soils, frequently in turf.

Propagation:
Seed.

Distribution:
Massachusetts to Missouri, south into Florida and west to Texas. Cosmopolitan in the tropics, the West Indies and Central America, Europe, Asia, and Hawaii.

Control Strategies:
Control soil moisture, as excessive amounts encourage most sedges including kyllinga species. Maintain a routine mowing schedule. Postemergence control with repeat applications of bentazon, halosulfuron, imazaquin alone or with MSMA/DSMA. Refer to the Appendix for additional control information. Check the herbicide label for specific application rates and turfgrass tolerance before use.

Texas Sedge seedheads and leaves

Texas Sedge seedhead

Texas Sedge, left; Yellow Nutsedge, right

Cyperaceae (Sedge Family)
Cylindric Sedge

Synonyms:
Pinebarren Flatsedge

Species:
Cyperus retrorsus Chapm.

Description:
Grass-like perennial with densely tufted stems. Leaf blades
flat, smooth, bright green. Seedhead branches at top of
stem. Seeds usually point down and are in tight cylindrical
clusters. Clusters green, turning brown to black at maturity.
Fruits summer into fall. May form weak rhizomes. Occurs
commonly in turf and most other sandy habitats from moist
to very dry.

Propagation:
Seed.

Distribution:
New York to southern Florida, west to Texas and Oklahoma,
inland to Arkansas and Tennessee. Native to North America.

Control Strategies:
Control soil moisture as excessive amounts encourages most
sedges including kyllinga species. Preemergence control with
metolachlor. Postemergence control with repeat applications
of bentazon, halosulfuron, imazaquin alone or with
MSMA/DSMA. Refer to the Appendix for additional control information. Check the herbicide label for specific application rates and turfgrass tolerance before use.

Mature Cylindric Sedge seedhead

Cylindric Sedge seedhead

Globe Sedge, left; Cylindric Sedge, right

Cyperaceae (Sedge Family)
Purple Nutsedge

Synonyms:
Purple Nut-grass; Nutgrass, Coco-sedge, Coco-grass

Species:
Cyperus rotundus L.

Description:
Rapidly-spreading, deep-green perennial with three-ranked basal leaves. Leaves mostly basal, flat or slightly corrugated, usually shorter than flowering stem, abruptly tapering at tip. Flowers are terminal radiating cluster of spikes from a whorl of leaf-like bracts. Seedhead purple to reddish brown, formed at end of triangular stem. Tubers, oblong, covered with hairs, and found in chains connected by brown, wiry rhizomes. Tubers bitter to taste. Fruits midsummer through fall. Occurs in most moist to dry cultivated and otherwise disturbed habitats. Considered one of the world's worst weeds.

Propagation:
Primarily by tubers.

Distribution:
Throughout the southern USA states north to Kentucky and West Virginia, west to Central Texas, and in southern California. Also in the West Indies, Mexico, Central and South America, Europe, Africa, Asia, and Hawaii.

Control Strategies:
Control soil moisture, as excessive amounts encourage most sedges including kyllinga species. Postemergence control with repeat applications of halosulfuron, imazaquin alone or mixed with MSMA/DSMA. Refer to the Appendix for additional control information. Check the herbicide label for specific application rates and turfgrass tolerance before use.

Purple Nutsedge seedhead

Yellow Nutsedge, left; Purple Nutsedge, middle; Globe Sedge, right.

Purple Nutsedge habit

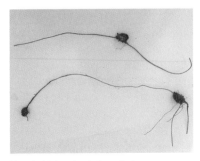

Purple Nutsedge tuber chains

13

Cyperaceae (Sedge Family)
False Nutsedge

Synonyms:
September Sedge; Strawcolored Flatsedge

Species:
Cyperus strigosus L.

Description:
Perennial from short rhizomes. Many large leaves at top of bare triangular stem under the seedhead. Narrow greenish-yellow spikelets massed on short to long stalks in congested to open, large seedheads. Flowers summer into fall. Found in ditches, marshes, and other moist to wet areas including turf.

Propagation:
Seed.

Distribution:
From Maine, Minnesota, South Dakota, south into Florida, west to Nebraska, Kansas, Oklahoma, and Texas. Also in California, Oregon, Washington, and Quebec. Introduced into Italy.

Control Strategies:
Control soil moisture, as excessive amounts encourage most sedges including kyllinga species. Maintain a routine mowing schedule. Postemergence control with repeat applications of bentazon, halosulfuron, imazaquin alone or with MSMA/DSMA. Refer to the Appendix for additional control information. Check the herbicide label for specific application rates and turfgrass tolerance before use.

False Nutsedge seedhead

Cyperaceae **(Sedge Family)**
Surinam Sedge

Synonyms:
Tropical Flatsedge

Species:
Cyperus surinamensis Rottb.

Description:
Perennial from short rhizomes. A few long leaves at top of the triangular stem under the seedhead. Stem with downward curving prickles, rough to the touch when rubbed upward. Seedhead with numerous tightly congested clusters of spikes on long stalks. Flowers late spring until frost. Found in ditches, marshes, and other moist to wet sites including turf.

Propagation:
Seed.

Distribution:
South Carolina south into Florida and west to Texas. Also found in Central America, Bolivia, and Argentina.

Control Strategies:
Control soil moisture, as excessive amounts encourage most sedges including kyllinga species. Routine mowing reduces its persistence. Postemergence control with repeat applications of bentazon, halosulfuron, imazaquin alone or with MSMA/DSMA. Refer to the Appendix for additional control information. Check the herbicide label for specific application rates and turfgrass tolerance before use.

Surinam Sedge seedheads

Surinam Sedge seedhead cluster

15

Cyperaceae (Sedge Family)
Hurricanegrass

Synonyms:
None reported.

Species:
Fimbristylis cymosa R. Br.; [*Fimbristylis spathacea* Roth.]

Description:
Tufted perennial from a rhizomatous crown. Triangular stems erect, one to several per tuft, unbranched to the seedhead. Leaves very narrow, flat to rolled, point in all directions. Leaves immediately below seedhead, shorter than seedhead. Seedhead a dense cluster of flowers. Scales of flowers brown with a papery margin. Flowers during warm months. Found in turf in brackish areas and dry waste areas.

Propagation:
Seed.

Distribution:
Central and southern peninsula of Florida. Also in the West Indies, Mexico, Central America, South America, and the Old World Tropics.

Control Strategies:
Control soil moisture, as excessive amounts encourage most sedges including kyllinga species. Postemergence control with repeat applications of atrazine/simazine, bentazon, halosulfuron, or imazaquin alone or with MSMA/DSMA. Refer to the Appendix for additional control information. Check the herbicide label for specific application rates and turfgrass tolerance before use.

Hurricanegrass seedhead

Hurricanegrass with St. Augustinegrass stolon

Hurricanegrass habit

Cyperaceae (Sedge Family)
Green Kyllinga

Synonyms:
Perennial Kyllinga; Shortleaf Spike Sedge

Species:
Kyllinga brevifolia Rottb; [*Cyperus brevifolius* (Rottb.)
Hassk.; *Kyllinga brevifolius* Rottb.]

Description:
Mat-forming perennial to 6 inches (15 cm) tall from reddish
purple rhizomes. Leaves and stems, dark green. Seedhead
usually a simple single roundish congested head, pale-green
in color initially, often turning brown at maturity, nearly
round or oblong, usually with three short leaves just below.
Seed scales with teeth on keel. Spikelets lance-oblong, compressed. Fruits during warm months. Found in low areas or
in turf where moisture is in excess.

Propagation:
Seed and rhizomes.

Distribution:
Sporadic occurrence from Delaware and Rhode Island
south through the Carolinas. Common from Georgia into
south Florida, west to Texas and California. Also in
Hawaii, Mexico, Central and South America, the West Indies, Africa, Asia, Indonesia, Australia, and Europe.

Control Strategies:
Control soil moisture, as excessive amounts encourage most
sedges including kyllinga species. Low, routine mowing
heights reduce its persistence. Postemergence control with
repeat applications of halosulfuron, MSMA/DSMA, imazaquin alone or with MSMA/DSMA. Refer to the Appendix
for additional control information. Check the herbicide
label for specific application rates and turfgrass tolerance
before use.

Green Kyllinga spike

Green Kyllinga runner

Green Kyllinga in bermudagrass turf

17

Cyperaceae (Sedge Family)
False Green Kyllinga

Synonyms:
Pasture Spike Sedge, Smooth Green Kyllinga

Species:
Kyllinga gracillima Miq.; [*Cyperus brevifolius* (Rottb.) Endl. ex Hassk. var. *leiolepis* (Franch. & Savigny) T. Koyama; *Cyperus brevifolioides* Thieret & Delahoussaye; *Kyllinga brevifolioides* (Thieret & Delahoussaye) G. Tucker, *nom. illeg.*]

False Green Kyllinga habit

Description:
Rhizomatous mat-forming perennial with ability to fruit under most turfgrass mowing heights. Single inflorescence (seedhead) a round spike, 8–10 mm in diameter. Bracts spreading below. Spikelets 3.5 to 4.6 mm long and 1.2 to 1.3 mm wide. Seed lens-shaped with smooth edges. Nutlets obovate (egg-shaped). Appears very similar to green kyllinga (*Kyllinga brevifolia*) but seedhead development appears to be daylength-dependent, fruiting mainly in late August until frost, while green kyllinga fruits during all warm months. Occurs in moist to wet turf, ditches, pond banks, and other poorly drained or excessively wet areas.

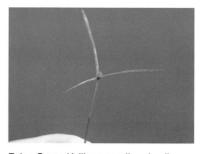

False Green Kyllinga seedhead spike

Propagation:
Seed and rhizomes.

Distribution:
In USA from Pennsylvania through Florida westward into eastern Texas. Also in California. Pantropical species apparently introduced into continental United States from Asia.

False Green Kyllinga, left; Green Kyllinga with seedheads, right.

Control Strategies:
Control soil moisture, as excessive amounts encourage most sedges including kyllinga species. Low, routine mowing heights reduce its persistence. Postemergence control with repeat applications of halosulfuron, MSMA/DSMA, imazaquin alone or with MSMA/DSMA. Refer to the Appendix for additional control information. Check the herbicide label for specific application rates and turfgrass tolerance before use.

False Green Kyllinga seedhead, left; Green Kyllinga seedhead, right.

Cyperaceae (Sedge Family)
White Kyllinga

Synonyms:
Botoncillo, Espartillo

Species:
Kyllinga nemoralis (J. R. & G. Forst.) Dandy ex Hutchinson & Danziel; [*Cyperus kyllingia* Endl.; *Kyllinga monocephala* Rottb.; *Kyllinga intermedia* R. Br.]

Description:
Mat-forming, tufted perennial, pantropical plant to 6 inches (15 cm) tall. Inflorescence a simple, single white-colored, terminal seedhead, nearly round or oblong, usually with three short leaves below. Spikelets 2.7 to 3.5 mm long, 1.5 mm wide. Leaves 2 to 4 mm wide. Flowers during warm months. Found in low, wet areas including turf. Appears similar to *Kyllinga brevifolia* except for its distinguishable white colored seedhead.

Propagation:
Seed and rhizomes.

Distribution:
Currently found only in Hawaii in the USA. Common in Old World tropics, Cuba, Indonesia, Africa, Australia, Singapore, Japan, Taiwan, Philippines, China, and Central America

Control Strategies:
Control soil moisture, as excessive amounts encourage most sedges including kyllinga species. Low, routine mowing heights reduce its persistence. Postemergence control with repeat applications of halosulfuron, imazaquin alone or with MSMA/DSMA. Refer to the Appendix for additional control information. Check the herbicide label for specific application rates and turfgrass tolerance before use.

White Kyllinga habit

White Kyllinga runner

White Kyllinga seedhead spike

19

Cyperaceae (Sedge Family)
Tufted Kyllinga

Synonyms:
Low Spike Sedge

Species:
Kyllinga pumila Michx.; [*Cyperus tenuifolius* (Steud.)
Dandy; *Cyperus densicaespitosus* Mattf. & Kukenth. ex
Kukenth.; *Cyperus densicaespitosus* Mattf. & Kukenth. ex
Kukenth. var. *major* (Nees) Kukenth.; *Kyllinga tenuifolia*
Steud.]

Description:
Densely tufted summer annual or possibly a short-lived
perennial in warm climates. Inflorescence consists of 1 to 3
heads, oval. Bracts spreading. Spikelets 1.8 to 3.3 mm long,
0.5 to 1.1 mm wide. Seed lens-shaped, edges have small angular teeth-like projections (denticulate) and require magni-
fication to see. Nutlets narrowed to short stipe-like base.
Fruits midsummer until frost. Found in moist to wet turf,
ditches, pond banks, and other poorly drained or excessively wet areas. Resembles green kyllinga (*Kyllinga brevifolia*) in size and seedhead shape but lacks rhizomes and has a
tufted (clumping) growth habit whereas green kyllinga produces rhizomes and forms mats.

Propagation:
Seed.

Tufted Kyllinga seedhead spike

Tufted Kyllinga habit

Green Kyllinga, left; Tufted Kyllinga,
right.

Distribution:
Throughout Eastern United States from Pennsylvania and Kansas to Florida westward to Oklahoma and eastern Texas. Also in the West Indies, eastern and central Mexico, Central America to Argentina, and tropical Africa. Native to continental United States.

Control Strategies:
Control soil moisture, as excessive amounts encourage most sedges including kyllinga species. Postemergence control with repeat applications of halosulfuron, imazaquin alone or with MSMA/DSMA. Low, routine mowing heights reduce its persistence. Refer to the Appendix for additional control information. Check the herbicide label for specific application rates and turfgrass tolerance before use.

Tufted Kyllinga seedhead, left; Cocks-Comb Kyllinga seedhead, right.

Cyperaceae (Sedge Family)
Fragrant Kyllinga

Synonyms:
Annual Kyllinga

Species:
Kyllinga sesquiflorus (Torr.) Mattf. & Kuekenth.; [*Kyllinga odorata* Vahl; *Cyperus sesquiflorus* (Torr.) Mattf. & Kuekenth.]

Description:
Summer annual or perennial with a bunch-type growth habit and single elongate-rounded, sometimes lobed seedhead. Head subtended by three or four leaves at the top of a bare stem. Seed scale smooth on keel. Seedheads whitish-cream colored. Emits sweet aroma when leaves are mowed or crushed. Fruits midsummer until frost. Found in moist disturbed areas including turf.

Propagation:
Seed.

Distribution:
From North Carolina and Arkansas, south to Florida and west to eastern Texas. Also in Mexico, Central America, Uruguay, and the West Indies.

Control Strategies:
Control soil moisture, as excessive amounts encourage most sedges including kyllinga species. Low, routine mowing heights reduce its persistence. Postemergence control with repeat applications of halosulfuron, imazaquin alone or with MSMA/DSMA. Refer to the Appendix for additional control information. Check the herbicide label for specific application rates and turfgrass tolerance before use.

Fragrant Kyllinga seedhead spike

Tufted Kyllinga, left; Fragrant Kyllinga, middle; Cocks-Comb Kyllinga, right.

Fragrant (Annual) Kyllinga habit

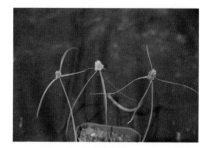

Tufted Kyllinga seedhead, left; Fragrant Kyllinga, middle; Cocks-Comb Kyllinga, right.

Cyperaceae (Sedge Family)
Cocks-Comb Kyllinga

Synonyms:
Asian Spike Sedge, Metz's Sedge

Species:
Kyllinga squamulata Thonn. ex Vahl; [*Cyperus metzii* (Hochst. ex Steud.) Mattf. & Kukenth. ex Kukenth.]

Description:
Tufted summer annual or possibly a short-lived perennial in warm climates. Number of inflorescence (heads) usually 1 (rarely to 3), 6–10 mm in diameter. Bracts spreading. Spikelets 2.5 to 4.5 mm long and 0.8 to 1.6 mm wide. Seed edges (keels) are "cockscomb" shaped. Fruits midsummer until frost. Found in moist to wet turf, ditches, pond banks, and other poorly drained or excessively wet areas. Pantropical species and apparently introduced into continental United States from Asia and Africa.

Propagation:
Seed.

Distribution:
Coastal southeastern USA from North Carolina through Florida throughout the tropics.

Control Strategies:
Control soil moisture, as excessive amounts encourage most sedges including kyllinga species. Low, routine mowing heights reduce its persistence. Postemergence control with repeat applications of halosulfuron, imazaquin alone or with MSMA/DSMA. Refer to the Appendix for additional control information. Check the herbicide label for specific application rates and turfgrass tolerance before use.

Cocks-Comb Kyllinga seedhead spike

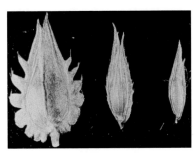

Seed of Cocks-Comb Kyllinga, left; *Kyllinga brevifolia*, center; *Kyllinga pumila*, right

Cocks-Comb Kyllinga habit

Tufted Kyllinga seedhead, left; Cock's-Comb Kyllinga, right.

23

Gramineae = Poaceae (Grass Family)
Quackgrass

Synonyms:
Creeping Quackgrass

Species:
Agropyron repens (L.) Beauv.; [*Elytrigia repens* (L.)]

Description:
A green- to silvery-colored perennial with long, sharp rhizomes. Leaves with flat blades, usually sparsely hairy on the upper surface, with clasping auricles. Leaf blades rough on the upper surface, smooth below and pointed. Rolled venation. Very short, membranous ligule. Seedhead is a stiffly erect spike of many several-flowered spikelets. Fruits in summer. Found in moist disturbed sites.

Propagation:
Seed and rhizomes.

Distribution:
Northern one-half of the United States, north of a line that extends through North Carolina, Oklahoma, Colorado, and California. Also in Europe, Asia, Canada, Alaska, Hawaii, the Middle East, India, Japan, Australia, and South America.

Control Strategies:
Postemergence control for most grass weeds includes repeat applications of MSMA or DSMA, fenoxaprop, fluazifop, sethoxydim, asulam, quinclorac, or metribuzin. Refer to the Appendix for additional control information. Check the herbicide label for specific application rates and turfgrass tolerance before use.

Quackgrass spiked seedhead

Quackgrass habit with silvery-colored leaves

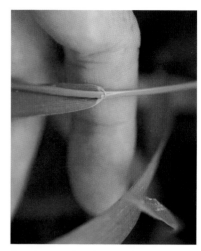

Quackgrass clasping auricles

Gramineae = Poaceae (Grass Family)
Bushy Bluestem

Synonyms:
Bushy Broomgrass, Bushy Beardgrass

Species:
Andropogon glomeratus (Walt.) BSP.

Description:
Perennial grass reaching 1.5 m tall with several tall, erect stems from a basal crown. Immature stems and leaves bluish-green, hence the common name, turning straw-brown colored upon maturity. Leaf sheaths flattened and keeled. Folded vernation. Ligule a short membrane usually longer than 1 mm. Flowers green to reddish-purple, becoming straw colored upon maturity widest at the top, once used to make brooms. Seeds with white silky hairs, paired. Flowers in summer. Differs from broomsedge (*Andropogon virginicus*) in that the seedheads are very dense and bushy in a cluster at the top of the stem. Found in wet areas of old fields, open pinelands, pastures, roadsides, and roadside ditches where tree canopies are absent or sparse.

Bushy Bluestem habit (dormant)

Propagation:
Seed and short rhizomes.

Distribution:
Massachusetts to Michigan, throughout the Atlantic coastal and southeastern states and Florida. Also in Ontario, the West Indies, Mexico, Central America, and Colombia. Naturalized in California, Hawaii, Japan, and Australia. Native to North America.

Bushy Bluestem habit

Control Strategies:
Adjust soil pH ≥5.5 and follow recommended fertility and mowing programs. Postemergence control for most grass weeds includes repeat applications of MSMA or DSMA, asulam, quinclorac, or metribuzin. Postemergence atrazine/simazine also provide suppression. Refer to the Appendix for additional control information. Check the herbicide label for specific application rates and turfgrass tolerance before use.

Bushy Bluestem seedhead

25

Gramineae = Poaceae (Grass Family)
Broomsedge

Synonyms:
Broomgrass, Broomstraw, Sagegrass; Broomsedge Bluestem

Species:
Andropogon virginicus L.

Description:
Clump-forming perennial with several tall stems from a
basal crown. Immature stems and leaves bluish-green, turning straw-brown colored upon maturity in fall, remaining
upright through winter into spring. Household brooms
were once made from these plants, hence the common
name. Leaf sheaths flattened and keeled. Folded vernation.
Ligule membranous sometimes with fringe of hairs on the
upper margin, usually less than 1 mm long. Flowers green
to reddish-purple, becoming straw colored in fall upon maturity. Seeds with white silky cotton-like hairs, paired.
Flowers in summer. Differs from bushy bluestem (*Andropogon glomeratus*) in that the seedheads extend along most
of the stem with scattered branching and flowers. Found in
low maintenance fields, forest openings, roadsides, and
pastures.

Propagation:
Wind-dispersed seed.

Broomsedge habit (dormant)

Broomsedge habit

Distribution:
Northeastern, southeastern, and middle Atlantic states, throughout Florida to Texas, Utah, and Nevada. Also in the West Indies and Central America. Native to North America.

Control Strategies:
Adjust soil pH to ≥5.5 and follow recommended fertility and mowing programs. Postemergence control for most grass weeds includes repeat applications of MSMA or DSMA, asulam, quinclorac, or metribuzin. Postemergence atrazine/simazine also provide suppression. Refer to the Appendix for additional control information. Check the herbicide label for specific application rates and turfgrass tolerance before use.

Broomsedge leaf (note: pubescence)

Gramineae = *Poaceae* (Grass Family)
Sweet Vernalgrass

Synonyms:
Annual Vernalgrass

Species:
Anthoxanthum odoratum L.

Description:
Tufted winter annual or cool-season perennial. Leaves smooth or hairy on both surfaces, pointed. Rolled vernation. Leaf sheath with thin marginal membrane. Visible membranous ligule at base of leaf blade, jagged. Seedheads "spike-like" panicle with awned spikelets. Pleasant, sweet aroma produced when crushed. Flowers spring into early summer. Found in lawns, roadsides, ditches, and other disturbed sites.

Sweet Vernalgrass habit with seedheads

Sweet Vernalgrass inflorescence

Sweet Vernalgrass membranous ligule

Propagation:
Seed.

Distribution:
Illinois, south throughout the southeastern United States, rare in peninsula Florida. Also in Arkansas, California, Oregon, Washington, and Hawaii. Also in Central and South America, Europe, Asia, and Australia. Native to Europe.

Control Strategies:
Postemergence control for most grass weeds includes repeat applications of MSMA or DSMA, fenoxaprop, fluazifop, sethoxydim, asulam, quinclorac, or metribuzin. Refer to the Appendix for additional control information. Check the herbicide label for specific application rates and turfgrass tolerance before use.

Sweet Vernalgrass habit

29

Gramineae = Poaceae (Grass Family)
Carpetgrass

Synonyms:
None reported.

Species:
Axonopus affinis Chase; [*Axonopus fissifolius* (Raddi) Kuhlm.]

Description:
Mat-forming perennial from somewhat flattened, smooth stolons. Leaf blade, smooth on both surfaces, tip rounded; few long hairs present on leaf sheath margin and at base of blade margin. Nodes densely hairy. Folded vernation. Ligule indistinct membrane with fringe of hairs on the upper part. Seedhead resembles crabgrass (*Digitaria*) spp., with two to five ascending spikes. Uppermost two branches usually paired. Fruits in midsummer. Most common on low, moist sites, frequently mixed into turf. Often seeded as a companion grass to centipedegrass (*Eremochloa ophiuroides*).

Propagation:
Seed and stolons.

Distribution:
Coastal plain of the Gulf states, north to North Carolina, and west to Arkansas and Oklahoma. Also in Central and South America, India, Australia, and southern Africa.

Control Strategies:
Postemergence control for most grass weeds includes repeat applications of MSMA or DSMA, fenoxaprop, fluazifop, sethoxydim, asulam, quinclorac, or metribuzin. Refer to the Appendix for additional control information. Check the herbicide label for specific application rates and turfgrass tolerance before use.

Carpetgrass leaf (note: blunt tip)

Carpetgrass habit

Carpetgrass seedhead

Gramineae = Poaceae (Grass Family)
Downy Brome

Synonyms:
Cheatgrass, cheat

Species:
Bromus tectorum L.

Description:
Erect winter annual 10 to 60 cm in height. Leaves lack auricles with a prominent jagged membranous ligule, 1 mm long, delicately fringed at the top. Rolled vernation. Leaf blade hairy on both sides with young leaves usually twisted. Sheaths are hairy with prominent pinkish veins. Flowers late spring through midsummer with characteristic drooping panicle seedheads that are sometimes purple. Spikelets flattened, 3–8 flowered with long (25 mm), purplish awns. Fruits spring into early summer. Often invades newly seeded areas. Found along roadsides, nurseries, waste areas, in old fields and disturbed open areas.

Propagation:
Seed.

Distribution:
Throughout most of the United States south into north Florida, Argentina, Japan, and Siberia. Native to Europe.

Control Strategies:
Preemergence control includes members of the dinitroaniline herbicide family and other preemergence products (e.g., benefin, bensulide, dithiopyr, napropamide, oryzalin, oxadiazon, pendimethalin, pronamide, and prodiamine). Postemergence control for most grass weeds includes repeat applications of MSMA or DSMA, fenoxaprop, fluazifop, sethoxydim, asulam, pronamide, quinclorac, or metribuzin. Refer to the Appendix for additional control information. Check the herbicide label for specific application rates and turfgrass tolerance before use.

Downy Brome habit

Downy Brome characteristic drooping inflorescence

Downy Brome stem (note: pubescence and prominent node)

Downy Brome membranous ligule

31

Gramineae = Poaceae (Grass Family)
Southern Sandbur

Synonyms:
Southern Sandspur

Species:
Cenchrus echinatus L.

Description:
Tufted summer annual, occasionally with some stems bending and rooting at the lower nodes. Stems frequently reddish at base. Leaf blade smooth or slightly sandpapery. Leaf sheath smooth. Folded vernation. Ligule a short fringe of hairs. Seedhead a spike of spiny burs. Spines on bur body flattened. Spines at base of bur a ring of rounded bristles. Fruits midsummer into early fall. Found in disturbed, open, sandy areas.

Propagation:
Seed.

Distribution:
Throughout the South from North Carolina west to New Mexico. Also in the West Indies, Mexico, Uruguay, South America, Africa, Oceania, India, and Hawaii.

Southern Sandbur habit

Control Strategies:
Follow recommended turfgrass fertility, watering, and mowing practices as this plant often invades poorly maintained sites in sandy soils. Preemergence control includes members of the dinitroaniline herbicide family and other preemergence products (e.g., benefin, bensulide, dithiopyr, napropamide, oryzalin, oxadiazon, pendimethalin, and prodiamine). Postemergence control for most grass weeds includes repeat applications of MSMA or DSMA, fenoxaprop, fluazifop, sethoxydim, asulam, quinclorac, or metribuzin. Refer to the Appendix for additional control information. Check the herbicide label for specific application rates and turfgrass tolerance before use.

Southern Sandbur inflorescence of spiny burs

Gramineae = Poaceae (Grass Family)
Field Sandbur

Synonyms:
Coast Sandspur, Field Sandspur

Species:
Cenchrus incertus M. A. Curtis; [*Cenchrus longispinus* (Hack.) Fern.; *Cenchrus pauciflorus* Benth.]

Description:
Yellow-green summer annual or short-lived perennial with erect or ascending stems. Leaf blades flat to slightly folded, sandpapery to the touch. Folded vernation. Ligule a narrow membrane fringed with short hairs. Seedheads in spikes of burs with flat spines. Burs finely hairy with one to three seeds. Fruits midsummer into early fall. Found in any open sandy site.

Propagation:
Seed.

Distribution:
Virginia along the coast to California, inland to Oklahoma and Arkansas. Also in the West Indies, Mexico to coastal Central and South America, South Africa, and the Philippines.

Control Strategies:
Follow recommended turfgrass fertility, watering, and mowing practices as this plant often invades poorly maintained sites in sandy soils. Preemergence control includes members of the dinitroaniline herbicide family and other preemergence products (e.g., benefin, bensulide, dithiopyr, napropamide, oryzalin, oxadiazon, pendimethalin, and prodiamine). Postemergence control for most grass weeds includes repeat applications of MSMA or DSMA, fenoxaprop, fluazifop, sethoxydim, asulam, quinclorac, or metribuzin. Refer to the Appendix for additional control information. Check the herbicide label for specific application rates and turfgrass tolerance before use.

Field Sandbur inflorescence of spiny burs

Field Sandbur habit

Gramineae = Poaceae (Grass Family)
Rock Fingergrass

Synonyms:
Pinewoods Fingergrass

Species:
Chloris petraea Sw.; [*Eustachys petraea* (Sw.) Desv.]

Description:
Summer annual or short-lived perennial with tufted or creeping flattened, smooth stems, rooting at nodes. Blades flat or sometimes folded, smooth. Folded vernation. Leaf sheaths smooth, keeled (flattened and joined along midrib). Ligule a minute fringe of hairs. Seedheads usually with two to eight or occasionally to ten spreading branches. Seeds dark to golden brown, on lower side of branch. Flowers in summer. Occurring in poor sandy or limestone soils in turf and in most open native and disturbed habitats.

Propagation:
Seed and stolons.

Distribution:
Coastal plain North Carolina into Florida, and west to Texas. Also in Central and South America and the West Indies.

Control Strategies:
Follow recommended turfgrass fertility, watering, and mowing practices as this plant often invades poorly maintained sites in sandy soils. Postemergence control for most grass weeds includes repeat applications of MSMA or DSMA, fenoxaprop, fluazifop, sethoxydim, asulam, quinclorac, or metribuzin. Refer to the Appendix for additional control information. Check the herbicide label for specific application rates and turfgrass tolerance before use.

Rock Fingergrass habit

Rock Fingergrass inflorescence, resembling fingers from a hand

Gramineae = *Poaceae* (Grass Family)
Common Bermudagrass

Synonyms:
Couchgrass, Wiregrass, Devils'-grass

Species:
Cynodon dactylon (L.) Pers.

Description:
Mat-forming perennial from stolons and rhizomes. Leaves smooth on both sides. Ligule a membrane fringed with hairs. Erect hairs similar to cat whiskers occur on the margins at the top of the sheath. Leaf color is gray-green to bluish-green turning straw-color with frost. Folded vernation. Seedhead consists of three to seven finger-like spikes 1 to 2 inches (2.5 to 5.0 cm) long radiating from a central point at the terminal end of the stems. Fruits summer into early fall. Many forms with widely varying vegetative characteristics are often planted for roadsides, pastures, fine turf, and soil conservation efforts. It has escaped into most dry to wet open habitats.

Propagation:
Seed, rhizomes, and stolons.

Distribution:
Throughout the southern and southwestern United States, north to southern New Jersey across through Kansas, Nevada, and Washington. Occurs throughout most tropical and subtropical regions of the world. Native of South Africa.

Control Strategies:
Avoid movement of contaminated soil. Fumigate infested soil before using or planting. Selective postemergence control includes repeat applications of clethodim, ethofumesate, fenoxaprop, fluazifop, or sethoxydim. Nonselective postemergence control includes repeat applications of glyphosate. Refer to the Appendix for additional control information. Check the herbicide label for specific application rates and turfgrass tolerance before use.

Common bermudagrass, right; Hybrid bermudagrass, left

Bermudagrass habit

Bermudagrass stolons (runners)

Bermudagrass inflorescence

Gramineae = *Poaceae* (Grass Family)
Orchardgrass

Synonyms:
None reported.

Species:
Dactylis glomerata L.

Description:
Tufted perennial. Stems bent at base. Leaf blade V-shaped (folded) in cross section near base, prominent midrib on underside, margins rough to the touch. Folded vernation. Visible sharp-pointed 5 to 7 mm long membranous ligule at base of blade, sometimes jagged across the top. Leaves bluish green. Seedhead a green panicle, densely clustered with fan-shaped spikelets. Flowers late spring into early summer. Found in open disturbed sites. Due to similar size, Orchardgrass seed often contaminate commercial tall fescue (*Festuca arundinaceae*) seed.

Propagation:
Seed.

Distribution:
An introduced cool-season forage grass found throughout most of North America, except peninsula of Florida. Also in Europe, Asia, Australia, South America, and Hawaii. Native to the Old World.

Control Strategies:
Postemergence control in bermudagrass (*Cynodon dactylon*) centipedegrass. zoysiagrass, and St. Augustinegrass is with pronamide. No selective postemergence control is available in most other turfgrasses. Spot treat with glyphosate. Refer to the Appendix for additional control information. Check the herbicide label for specific application rates and turfgrass tolerance before use.

Orchardgrass inflorescence

Orchardgrass habit

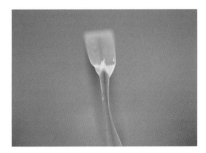

Orchardgrass membranous ligule

Gramineae = Poaceae (Grass Family)
Crowfootgrass

Synonyms:
Durban Crowfootgrass

Species:
Dactyloctenium aegyptium (L.) Willd. ex Asch. & Schweinf.

Description:
Yellow-green tufted summer annual with upwardly bent stems rooting at the lower nodes. Leaves with row of hairs extending outward from the margin along the lower portion of blade. Rolled vernation. Ligule a narrow fringed membrane. Seedhead spikelets arranged on two to five "fingers" radiating from a central point at tip of the stem. Outer tips of fingers extended resembling claws, giving seedhead a "crowfoot" appearance. Fruits midsummer until frost. Found in disturbed sites.

Propagation:
Seed.

Distribution:
Fairly common in poorly maintained sandy soils in the coastal plain and piedmont regions of the southern states, north to New York, and west to California. Also in the West Indies, Central and South America, Australia, Europe, Asia, tropical Africa, and Hawaii. Native to the Old World.

Crowfootgrass habit

Control Strategies:
Improve turf growing conditions including following recommended fertility, watering, and mowing practices. Preemergence control includes members of the dinitroaniline herbicide family and other preemergence products (e.g., benefin, bensulide, dithiopyr, napropamide, oryzalin, oxadiazon, pendimethalin, and prodiamine). Postemergence control for most grass weeds includes repeat applications of MSMA or DSMA, fenoxaprop, fluazifop, sethoxydim, or metribuzin. Refer to the Appendix for additional control information. Check the herbicide label for specific application rates and turfgrass tolerance before use.

Crowfootgrass inflorescence

Gramineae = Poaceae (Grass Family)
Tropical Crabgrass

Synonyms:
Asia Crabgrass

Species:
Digitaria bicornis (Lam.) Roem. & Schult.

Description:
Summer annual bending and rooting at lower nodes. Leaf sheaths and blades hairy. Rolled vernation. Blades usually over 2 inches (6 cm) long. Visible membranous ligule at base of leaf blade. Differs from large and southern crabgrass in that seedhead branches all join the stem at the same point whereas with large and southern crabgrass, seedhead branches arise from different points along the stalk. Fruits midsummer until frost. Occurs in open disturbed habitats, frequently in turf.

Propagation:
Seed.

Distribution:
The Gulf Coastal plain from Texas throughout Florida. Native to tropical America.

Control Strategies:
Preemergence control includes members of the dinitroaniline herbicide family and other preemergence products (e.g., benefin, bensulide, dithiopyr, napropamide, oryzalin, oxadiazon, pendimethalin, and prodiamine). Apply when soil temperatures at the 4-inch level remain above 50° F (10° C) for 24 consecutive hours. Postemergence control for most grass weeds includes repeat applications of MSMA or DSMA, fenoxaprop, fluazifop, sethoxydim, asulam, quinclorac, or metribuzin. Refer to the Appendix for additional control information. Check the herbicide label for specific application rates and turfgrass tolerance before use.

Tropical Crabgrass habit

Tropical Crabgrass seedhead (note: spikes join stem at same point)

Tropical Crabgrass leaf sheath (note: pubescence)

Gramineae = Poaceae (Grass Family)
Smooth Crabgrass

Synonyms:
Small Crabgrass

Species:
Digitaria ischaemum (Schreb. ex Schweig.) Schreb. ex Muhl.

Description:
Tufted or prostrate, spreading summer annual, rooting at the lower nodes. Leaves smooth on both surfaces, pointed. Rolled vernation. Leaf sheath smooth, few long hairs at collar, generally tinged with purple. Blades usually over 2-inches (5 cm) long. Tall, rounded membranous ligule at base of leaf blade. Seedhead with two to six "finger-like" spiked branches. Fruits midsummer until frost. Occurs in open disturbed sites, often in turf.

Propagation:
Seed.

Distribution:
Throughout the United States and in Europe.

Control Strategies:
Preemergence control includes members of the dinitroaniline herbicide family and other preemergence products (e.g., benefin, bensulide, dithiopyr, napropamide, oryzalin, oxadiazon, pendimethalin, and prodiamine). Apply when soil temperatures at the 4-inch level remain above 50° F (10°C) for 24 consecutive hours. Postemergence control for most grass weeds includes repeat applications of MSMA or DSMA, fenoxaprop, fluazifop, sethoxydim, asulam, quinclorac, atrazine, or metribuzin. Refer to the Appendix for additional control information. Check the herbicide label for specific application rates and turfgrass tolerance before use.

Smooth Crabgrass leaf sheath lacking pubescence

Smooth Crabgrass habit

Smooth Crabgrass membranous ligule

Gramineae = Poaceae (Grass Family)
India Crabgrass

Synonyms:
None reported.

Species:
Digitaria longiflora (Retz.) Pers.

Description:
Mat-forming summer annual or perennial, with creeping stolons. Flowering stems ascending. Rolled vernation. Leaves crowded on creeping stems, blades very short, usually about 1 inch (2 to 2.5 cm) long. Visible membranous ligule at base of leaf blade. Differs from blanket crabgrass (*Digitaria serotina*) in that the sheaths and blades are smooth. Fruits during warm months. Common in dry sandy, disturbed areas and turf.

Propagation:
Seed and stolons.

Distribution:
Panhandle and peninsula of Florida. Also in Hawaii, the West Indies, and Costa Rica. Native to the Old World Tropics.

Control Strategies:
Preemergence control includes members of the dinitroaniline herbicide family and other preemergence products (e.g., benefin, bensulide, dithiopyr, napropamide, oryzalin, oxadiazon, pendimethalin, and prodiamine). Apply when soil temperatures at the 4-inch level remain above 50° F (10° C) for 24 consecutive hours. Postemergence control for most grass weeds includes repeat applications of MSMA or DSMA, fenoxaprop, fluazifop, sethoxydim, asulam, quinclorac, or metribuzin. Refer to the Appendix for additional control information. Check the herbicide label for specific application rates and turfgrass tolerance before use.

India Crabgrass inflorescence

India Crabgrass leaves [note: sheaths and blades are smooth and leaf length is about 1-inch (2 to 2.5 cm)]

Gramineae = Poaceae (Grass Family)
Large Crabgrass and Southern Crabgrass

Synonyms:
Hairy Crabgrass

Species:
Large Crabgrass: *Digitaria sanguinalis* (L.) Scop.
Southern Crabgrass: *Digitaria ciliaris* (Retz.) Koel.

Description:
Tufted, or prostrate to spreading summer annuals with branched stems that root at the lower nodes. Leaf blade, longer than 2 inches (5 cm), usually hairy on both surfaces with tall visible toothed membranous ligule at base of leaf, pointed. Rolled vernation. Leaf sheath with dense hairs. Seedhead spikelets in two to nine finger-like branches. Fruits midsummer until frost. Southern crabgrass is distinguished from large crabgrass on the basis of the length of the second glume (a bract at the base of a spikelet). These species differ from tropical crabgrass (*Digitaria bicornis*) in that the seedhead branches arise from different points of attachment along the stalk compared to all joining the stem at one point for tropical crabgrass. Both species occur in various disturbed habitats, frequently in turf.

Large or Southern Crabgrass habit [note: leaf blades are longer than 2-inches (5 cm)]

Propagation:
Both species by seed.

Distribution:
Southern crabgrass occurs northward on the coastal plain occasionally to Connecticut, more common southward east of the Appalachian region, throughout Florida, extending west into Texas and north into Kansas and Nebraska. Also in the West Indies, Mexico, Central America, and South America. Large crabgrass is found throughout North America, except Florida, and the warm temperate regions of the world. Both species thought to be introduced from the Old World (Europe or Asia).

Seedhead which branches from different points along the stalk

Control Strategies:
Preemergence control includes members of the dinitroaniline herbicide family and other preemergence products (e.g., benefin, bensulide, dithiopyr, napropamide, oryzalin, oxadiazon, pendimethalin, and prodiamine). Apply when soil temperatures at the 4-inch level remain above 50° F (10° C) for 24 consecutive hours. Postemergence control for most grass weeds includes repeat applications of MSMA or DSMA, fenoxaprop, fluazifop, sethoxydim, asulam, atrazine, quinclorac, or metribuzin. Refer to the Appendix for additional control information. Check the herbicide label for specific application rates and turfgrass tolerance before use.

Hairy leaf sheath of Large or Southern Crabgrass

Gramineae = Poaceae (Grass Family)
Blanket Crabgrass

Synonyms:
Rabbit Crabgrass; Dwarf Crabgrass

Species:
Digitaria serotina (Walt.) Michx.

Description:
Mat-forming summer annual or short-term perennial in warmer climates with creeping stolons. Flowering stems ascending or erect. Leaves crowded on the creeping stems, blades very short, about 1 inch (2 to 2.5 cm) long. Visible membranous ligule at base of leaf blade. Rolled vernation. Fruits midsummer until frost. Differs from India crabgrass (*Digitaria longiflora*) in that the sheaths and blades are hairy. Found in pastures, moist disturbed areas, lawns, and low wet places.

Blanket Crabgrass leaves which are about 1-inch (2.5 cm) long

Propagation:
Seed and stolons.

Distribution:
Pennsylvania south throughout Florida, and west to Texas. Also found in Cuba.

Control Strategies:
Preemergence control includes members of the dinitroaniline herbicide family and other preemergence products (e.g., benefin, bensulide, dithiopyr, napropamide, oryzalin, oxadiazon, pendimethalin, and prodiamine). Apply when soil temperatures at the 4-inch level remain above 50° F (10° C) for 24 consecutive hours. Postemergence control for most grass weeds includes repeat applications of MSMA or DSMA, fenoxaprop, fluazifop, sethoxydim, asulam, quinclorac, or metribuzin. Refer to the Appendix for additional control information. Check the herbicide label for specific application rates and turfgrass tolerance before use.

Blanket Crabgrass habit

Blanket Crabgrass membranous ligule, and hairy sheath and leaves

Gramineae = Poaceae (Grass Family)
Junglerice

Synonyms:
Awnless Barnyardgrass

Species:
Echinochloa colona (L.) Link; [*Echinochloa colonum* (L.) Link]

Description:
Tufted summer annual up to 1 m tall with weak, erect or ascending smooth stems, often rooting at the nodes. Leaf blades smooth, occasionally with purple bands, ligule absent and no hairs at base of blade. Leaf sheaths smooth. Seedhead a panicle with appressed to spreading branches, green or purplish in color, spikelets awnless. Flowers throughout summer. Branches usually less than 1 inch (<2 cm) long. Seeds small, in four rows, covered with stiff short hairs. Fruits midsummer until frost. Found in ditches, moist disturbed areas and along roadsides. Separated from barnyardgrass [*Echinochloa crusgalli* (L.) Beauv.] by having sharp-pointed spikelet ends, while barnyardgrass spikelets end in a bristle.

Junglerice seedhead (note: purplish color)

Propagation:
Seed.

Distribution:
New Jersey, Virginia, Tennessee, Missouri, and Oklahoma south to Florida and west to Texas, California, and Oregon. Cosmopolitan in warm climates. Native to Africa and Asia.

Junglerice leaves and initial seedhead elongation

Control Strategies:
Preemergence control includes members of the dinitroaniline herbicide family and other preemergence products (e.g., benefin, bensulide, dithiopyr, napropamide, oryzalin, oxadiazon, pendimethalin, and prodiamine). Postemergence control for most grass weeds includes repeat applications of MSMA or DSMA, fenoxaprop, fluazifop, sethoxydim, asulam, quinclorac, or metribuzin. Refer to the Appendix for additional control information. Check the herbicide label for specific application rates and turfgrass tolerance before use.

Junglerice habit

Gramineae = Poaceae (Grass Family)
Barnyardgrass

Synonyms:
None reported.

Species:
Echinochloa crusgalli (L.) Beauv.

Description:
An upright to reclining coarse summer annual. One to many stems per plant. Sheaths smooth, flat, compressed, purple-tinged at base and blades often with roughened margins and thickened midrib, ligule absent. Rolled vernation. Seedhead upright or drooping panicle often with purple pigmentation. Spikelets ovoid, half as wide as long, and have an awn less than 1 cm long, or may be awnless. Stiff hairs on visible veins. Fruits midsummer until frost. Commonly found in moist to wet disturbed sites, marshes, and in wet turf.

Propagation:
Seed.

Distribution:
North to Nova Scotia, south throughout Florida and west to California. Native to the Old World.

Control Strategies:
Preemergence control includes members of the dinitroaniline herbicide family and other preemergence products (e.g., benefin, bensulide, dithiopyr, napropamide, oryzalin, oxadi-azon, pendimethalin, and prodiamine). Postemergence control for most grass weeds includes repeat applications of MSMA or DSMA, fenoxaprop, fluazifop, sethoxydim, asulam, quinclorac, or metribuzin. Refer to the Appendix for additional control information. Check the herbicide label for specific application rates and turfgrass tolerance before use.

Barnyardgrass seedhead with purple color

Barnyardgrass habit

Gramineae = Poaceae (Grass Family)
Goosegrass

Synonyms:
Crowfoot, Silver Crabgrass, Yardgrass, Indian Goosegrass

Species:
Eleusine indica (L.) Gaertn.

Description:
Tough, dark-green clumped summer annual, generally with a "whitish to silverish" coloration at the center of the plant. Stems often flattened. Leaf blade smooth on both surfaces, occasionally a few hairs near the base, folded vernation. Leaf sheaths with white margins. Visible, short-toothed, membranous ligule at base of leaf blade, divided at the center. Seedhead spikelets in two rows on two to thirteen fingers. Frequently a single finger below the terminal cluster of fingers. Fruits midsummer until frost. Tolerates close mowing, compacted, wet, or dry soils. Found in almost any cultivated or disturbed open habitat.

Propagation:
Seed.

Distribution:
Throughout the temperate and warm parts of the United States and throughout the warm temperate, subtropical, and tropical areas of the world. Native to the Old World.

Control Strategies:
Improve turf growing conditions including alleviating soil compaction and reducing excessive soil moisture. Preemergence control includes members of the dinitroaniline herbicide family and other preemergence products (e.g., benefin, bensulide, dithiopyr, napropamide, oryzalin, oxadiazon, pendimethalin, and prodiamine). Apply when soil temperatures at the 4-inch level remain above 60° F (15° C) for 24 consecutive hours. Postemergence control for most grass weeds includes repeat applications of MSMA or DSMA, diclofop, fenoxaprop, fluazifop, sethoxydim, metribuzin, and MSMA/DSMA plus metribuzin. Refer to the Appendix for additional control information. Check the herbicide label for specific application rates and turfgrass tolerance before use.

Goosegrass habit

Goosegrass seedhead

Membranous Goosegrass ligule

Seedling Goosegrass

Gramineae = Poaceae (Grass Family)
Gophertail Lovegrass

Synonyms:
none reported.

Species:
Eragrostis ciliaris (L.) R. Br.

Description:
Erect summer annual with smooth leaves. Leaf sheath with hairs on upper margins. Ligule a short fringe of hairs. Rolled vernation. Seedhead narrow, elongated, dense and fuzzy, resembling a gopher's tail. Individual flowers with long stiff hairs on the margins. Fruits midsummer until frost. Found in cultivated areas, roadsides, lawns, sod production, waste places, and pine woods.

Propagation:
Seed.

Distribution:
New Jersey south into Florida and west to Texas. Also in the West Indies, Mexico, Central America, South America, India, and Tropical Africa. Native to the Old World.

Control Strategies:
Preemergence control includes members of the dinitroaniline herbicide family and other preemergence products (e.g., benefin, bensulide, dithiopyr, napropamide, oryzalin, oxadiazon, pendimethalin, and prodiamine). Postemergence control for most grass weeds includes repeat applications of MSMA or DSMA, fenoxaprop, fluazifop, sethoxydim, asulam, quinclorac, or metribuzin. Simazine/atrazine also may help control. Refer to the Appendix for additional control information. Check the herbicide label for specific application rates and turfgrass tolerance before use.

Gophertail Lovegrass habit and inflorescence

Gramineae = Poaceae **(Grass Family)**
Tall Fescue

Synonyms:
None reported.

Species:
Festuca arundinacea Schreb.

Description:
Erect, tufted dark-green perennial that enlarges by tillering. Leaves alternate, long, flat, smooth, pointed, with strong, conspicuous parallel veins above and short (1 mm long), white membranous ligule. Blades coarse, thick with rough margins and glossy underside. Sheaths reddish-pink below ground. Stems hairless with swollen light-green nodes. Rolled vernation. Seedhead a loose or compressed terminal panicle; erect or nodding at tips. Fruits midspring into early summer. Rhizomatous cultivars are being developed. Used often for pastures, roadsides, turf, and soil stabilization. Occurs as an escape in open disturbed sites.

Tall Fescue collar region

Propagation:
Seed.

Distribution:
Throughout the eastern United States from Maine to central Florida and westward to Utah, Washington, and California. Introduced from Europe as a forage species.

Control Strategies:
Postemergence control includes atrazine/simazine, chlorsulfuron, and pronamide. Spot treat with glyphosate. Refer to the Appendix for additional control information. Check the herbicide label for specific application rates and turfgrass tolerance before use.

Tall Fescue inflorescence

Tall Fescue habit

Mature Tall Fescue inflorescence (note: brownish color and drooping appearance)

47

Gramineae = Poaceae (Grass Family)
Common Velvetgrass

Synonyms:
None reported.

Species:
Holcus lanatus L.

Description:
Grayish-green, velvety, tufted perennial that acts as a winter annual in warm climates, with closely clustered, erect stems. Stems and leaves velvety hairy and grayish in color. Leaves soft, flat, long and broad, pointed at the tip. Rolled vernation. Ligule a medium tall, notched or jagged membrane. Pale green to purple flower panicles dense, plume-like with ascending or spreading branches, borne at the ends of hairy stems. Fruits late spring through summer. Found in moist meadows, open fields, lawns, roadsides, and waste areas.

Common Velvetgrass seedheads and habit

Propagation:
Seed.

Distribution:
Throughout the USA except Florida, Texas, New Mexico, and Nevada. On the Pacific coast reaches south only into northern California. Also in British Columbia, Alberta, Ontario, Quebec, New Brunswick, and Nova Scotia. Native of Europe.

Membranous Common Velvetgrass ligule

Control Strategies:
Preemergence control includes members of the dinitroaniline herbicide family and other preemergence products (e.g., benefin, bensulide, dithiopyr, napropamide, oryzalin, oxadiazon, pendimethalin, and prodiamine). Postemergence control for most grass weeds includes repeat applications of MSMA or DSMA, fenoxaprop, fluazifop, sethoxydim, or metribuzin. Refer to the Appendix for additional control information. Check the herbicide label for specific application rates and turfgrass tolerance before use.

Pubescent Common Velvetgrass stem

Gramineae = Poaceae (Grass Family)
Little Barley

Synonyms:
None reported.

Species:
Hordeum pusillum Nutt.

Description:
Erect, tufted, or clumped, winter annual. Leaf blade smooth to hairy. Ligule membranous. Sheath smooth to hairy. Spikelets with long bristles formed in long, narrow foxtail-like seedheads. Fruits midspring through early summer. Found in open dry disturbed sites. Especially troublesome along roadsides and other low maintenance turf areas.

Propagation:
Seed.

Distribution:
Most of the United States, except for the northeastern and northernmost central states. Also in South America.

Control Strategies:
Preemergence control includes members of the dinitroaniline herbicide family and other preemergence products (e.g., benefin, bensulide, dithiopyr, napropamide, oryzalin, oxadiazon, pendimethalin, prodiamine, and pronamide). Postemergence control for most grass weeds includes repeat applications of MSMA or DSMA, fenoxaprop, fluazifop, sethoxydim, or metribuzin. Refer to the Appendix for additional control information. Check the herbicide label for specific application rates and turfgrass tolerance before use.

Little Barley habit

Little Barley seedheads

49

Gramineae = Poaceae (Grass Family)
Cogongrass

Synonyms:
Japgrass

Species:
Imperata cylindrica (L.) Beauv.; [*Imperata brasiliensis* Trin.]

Description:
Dense erect, spreading colony-forming, perennial grass from seed (rare) or scaly white rhizomes. Newly emerging shoots sharp and stiff to touch. Stems upright. Leaves very stiff or rigid, smooth except for tufts of hair on upper surface at base of blade. Base of blade often narrow and petiole-like. Midrib is not in the center of the leaf blade. Sheath smooth to hairy. Ligule a U-shaped fringed membrane. Seedhead a plume-like panicle. Spikelets numerous, each surrounded by long, silky hairs at base. Flowers in spring, except disturbed sites. Occurs mostly in open habitats, most frequently in cleared or excavated areas, pastures, and along roadsides.

Cogongrass habit

Propagation:
Mostly from sharp-tipped, white-scaly rhizomes, secondly by seed (rare).

Distribution:
Only in the Gulf Coast region of the southeast United States. Also in Mexico south into South America, tropical Africa, Europe, Australia, Asia, and Hawaii. Native to Southeast Asia and India.

Cogongrass habit close up

Control Strategies:
Avoid movement of contaminated soil. Fumigate contaminated soil before using or planting. Nonselective postemergence control includes repeat applications of glyphosate or imazapyr (Arsenal). Refer to the Appendix for additional control information. Check the herbicide label for specific application rates and turfgrass tolerance before use.

Cogongrass inflorescence

Gramineae = Poaceae (Grass Family)
Sprangletop

Synonyms:
None reported.

Species:
Leptochloa spp.

Description:
Tufted summer annuals or perennials with leafy stems. Leaf blades flat. Ligule papery, jagged membrane. Seedhead of many spreading branches with many spikelets, each with two to twelve flowers. Spikelets on the lower side of the branch. Flowers often with hairs on the nerves. Fruits during warm months. Occurs in disturbed and waste areas and low, moist to wet sites, ditches, and fields. Frequently in wet turf.

Propagation:
Seed.

Distribution:
New Hampshire to Indiana to North Dakota south into Florida, and west into Texas, Arizona, California, and Oregon. Also in Mexico, Central and South America, and the West Indies.

Control Strategies:
Preemergence control includes members of the dinitroaniline herbicide family and other preemergence products (e.g., benefin, bensulide, dithiopyr, metolachlor, napropamide, oryzalin, oxadiazon, pendimethalin, and prodiamine). Postemergence control for most grass weeds includes repeat applications of MSMA or DSMA, fenoxaprop, fluazifop, sethoxydim, or metribuzin. Refer to the Appendix for additional control information. Check the herbicide label for specific application rates and turfgrass tolerance before use.

Sprangletop plant

Sprangletop habit

Sprangletop inflorescence

51

Gramineae = Poaceae (Grass Family)
Annual Ryegrass

Synonyms:
Italian Ryegrass

Species:
Lolium multiflorum Lam.

Description:
Erect, tufted winter annual up to 1.3 m tall, often purplish at the base. Leaves long, narrow, with long clasping auricles usually present, ligule membranous and short. Rolled vernation. Blades have prominent veins above, smooth margins, characteristically glossy below. Seedhead a long, narrow, terminal spike with alternate spikelets consisting of 10 to 20 florets along the flowering stem and only 1 glume. Foliage turns characteristic straw-brown in summer. Fruits in spring. Perennial ryegrass (*Lolium perenne* L.) is similar except for being shorter (30 to 60 cm tall), folded vernation, spikelets with only 6 to 10 florets, awns usually absent or greatly reduced, auricles short and claw-like, and behaves as a perennial in cooler climates. Recent research indicates combining perennial and annual ryegrasses into *Lolium perenne* L. may be justified.

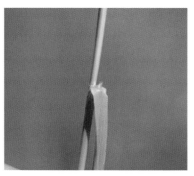

Annual Ryegrass membranous ligule

Annual Ryegrass seedhead (left) compared to perennial ryegrass (right). Note the presence of awns associated with annual ryegrass.

Purplish base of Annual Ryegrass shoots

Propagation:
Seed which have long awns.

Distribution:
Throughout the United States and temperate regions of the world as an escape from pastures, forage, grain, roadsides, turf, waste areas, and other cultivated crops. Introduced from Europe.

Control Strategies:
Preemergence control includes members of the dinitroaniline herbicide family and other preemergence products (e.g., benefin, bensulide, dithiopyr, napropamide, oryzalin, oxadiazon, pendimethalin, prodiamine, and pronamide). Postemergence control includes atrazine/simazine, metribuzin, metsulfuron, or pronamide. Refer to the Appendix for additional control information. Check the herbicide label for specific application rates and turfgrass tolerance before use.

Annual Ryegrass habit

Gramineae = *Poaceae* (Grass Family)
Annual Jewgrass

Synonyms:
Nepalese Browntop, Mary'sgrass

Species:
Microstegium vimineum (Trin.) A. Camus

Description:
Prostrate to somewhat erect, freely-branched summer annual, rooting at lower nodes. Leaf blade sparsely hairy on upper and lower surfaces (none basal), alternate, white midribs. Ligule membranous with hairs on the backside. Flowers terminal, thin, spike-like racemes; spikelets in one to three terminal upright fingers. Fruits in summer. Very shade tolerant. Usually found in shaded open areas including floodplains, stream banks, and damp turf.

Propagation:
Seed.

Distribution:
In the mountain and piedmont regions of the southern states, from Ohio and Virginia into Alabama. Native to Asia.

Control Strategies:
Preemergence control includes members of the dinitroaniline herbicide family and other preemergence products (e.g., benefin, bensulide, dithiopyr, napropamide, oryzalin, oxadiazon, pendimethalin, and prodiamine). Postemergence control includes repeat applications of fenoxaprop, fluazifop, sethoxydim, or metribuzin. Refer to the Appendix for additional control information. Check the herbicide label for specific application rates and turfgrass tolerance before use.

Annual Jewgrass leaves

Annual Jewgrass habit

Annual Jewgrass inflorescence

Gramineae = Poaceae (Grass Family)
Nimblewill

Synonyms:
None reported.

Species:
Muhlenbergia schreberi J. F. Gmel.

Description:
Delicate mat-forming blue-green perennial with a reclining growth habit, often rooting at nodes. Leaves very narrow, short, hairless, pointed, grayish green, alternate (none basal). Rolled vernation. Leaf collars hairy. Ligule a short (<0.5 mm), jagged membrane. Sheaths smooth. Seedhead a loose, spike-like narrow panicle with ascending branches. Fruits late summer into early fall. Thrives in moist, shady sites, roadsides, stream banks, forest openings. Turns brown in winter. Often confused with bermudagrass (*Cynodon dactylon*) but has membranous ligule compared to a hairy ligule for bermudagrass.

Propagation:
Seed and short, weak stolons.

Distribution:
The northeast, southeast and midwest United States. Also in Canada and Mexico. Native to North America.

Control Strategies:
No selective preemergence or postemergence control is available. Spot treat with glyphosate or glufosinate. Refer to the Appendix for additional control information. Check the herbicide label for specific application rates and turfgrass tolerance before use.

Nimblewill seedheads

Nimblewill habit (note: often found in shady conditions)

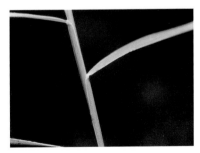

Smooth Nimblewill sheath

Gramineae = Poaceae (Grass Family)
Fall Panicum

Synonyms:
None reported.

Species:
Panicum dichotomiflorum Michx.

Description:
Sprawling to ascending bright-green summer annual that can be found at all seasons in subtropical conditions. Stems bent and branched outward. Leaf blade flat, smooth, occasionally hairy on the upper surface, with a distinct broad, light-green midrib. Dull appearance above, glossy beneath, pointed. Rolled vernation. Ligule a fringe of hairs. Panicle seedhead purplish colored at maturity, open and freely branched. Spikelets with prominent veins, purple tinged. Fruits in mid to late summer. Common during turfgrass establishment. Occurs most frequently in wet open habitats.

Fall Panicum habit

Propagation:
Seed.

Distribution:
Occurs from Maine, Michigan, and Minnesota, south into Florida and west to Texas, Arizona, California, and Hawaii. Also occurs in Europe.

Fall Panicum inflorescence with purplish color

Control Strategies:
Preemergence control includes members of the dinitroaniline herbicide family and other preemergence products (e.g., benefin, bensulide, dithiopyr, napropamide, oryzalin, oxadiazon, pendimethalin, and prodiamine). Postemergence control includes repeat applications of MSMA or DSMA, fenoxaprop, fluazifop, sethoxydim, asulam, or metribuzin. Refer to the Appendix for additional control information. Check the herbicide label for specific application rates and turfgrass tolerance before use.

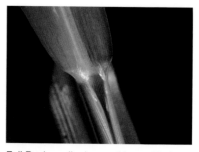

Fall Panicum ligule as a fringe of hairs at maturity

Gramineae = *Poaceae* (Grass Family)
Guineagrass

Synonyms:
None reported.

Species:
Panicum maximum Jacq.

Description:
Perennial or summer annual with densely tufted stems that can be found at all seasons in subtropical conditions. Stems sometimes bending and rooting at nodes, quite variable, smooth to hairy, branched or not branched. Leaf blades flat, large, usually smooth or occasionally hairy. Leaf sheaths usually hairy. Ligule membranous, with fringe of hairs on upper margin. Seedheads large, with spreading branches. Seedhead branches at lowest nodes usually whorled. Flowers somewhat blunt at tip. Fruits during warm weather. Seeds with fine wrinkles. Occurring in fields, wet prairies, roadsides, and most disturbed areas.

Propagation:
Seed and rarely by stolons.

Distribution:
Peninsula of Florida and southern Texas. Cosmopolitan in warm climates. Native to Africa.

Control Strategies:
Avoid movement of contaminated soil. Fumigate contaminated soil before using or planting. Postemergence nonselective control includes repeat applications of glyphosate or imazapyr (Arsenal). Maintain routine mowing schedule. Refer to the Appendix for additional control information. Check the herbicide label for specific application rates and turfgrass tolerance before use.

Guineagrass habit

Guineagrass seedhead

Whorled Guineagrass seedhead branches at lowest node

Gramineae = Poaceae (Grass Family)
Torpedograss

Synonyms:
None reported.

Species:
Panicum repens L.

Description:
Perennial with creeping, sharply pointed rhizomes. Stems stiff and erect. Leaves folded or flat and hairy on upper surface. Folded vernation. Small membranous ligule with fringe of hairs on upper margin. Seedheads with stiff, ascending or appressed branches. Spikelets almost white, on tiny stalks. Fruits during warm months.

Propagation:
Primarily by rhizomes and seed (rare).

Distribution:
Coastal region of the southeast United States from the Carolinas, through the Gulf states, west into Texas. Also in tropical Africa, tropical Asia, Europe, and Hawaii. Possibly native to the Old World.

Control Strategies:
Avoid movement of contaminated soil. Fumigate contaminated soil before using or planting. Selective postemergence control with repeat applications of quinclorac (Drive). Nonselective postemergence control includes repeat applications of glyphosate. Refer to the Appendix for additional control information. Check the herbicide label for specific application rates and turfgrass tolerance before use.

Torpedograss runner (stolon)

Torpedograss seedhead

Torpedograss habit

Torpedograss rhizomes

Gramineae = Poaceae (Grass Family)
Dallisgrass

Synonyms:
None reported.

Species:
Paspalum dilatatum Poir.

Description:
Coarse-textured, robust clumping perennial from short thick rhizomes. Leaf sheaths at base of plant sometimes rough hairy. Leaf blade smooth on both surfaces, with a few long hairs at leaf base and behind ligule at base of leaf blade. Leaf mid-vein prominent, edges rough. Rolled vernation. Ligule tall, membranous, either sharply or bluntly tipped. Spikelets hairy, arranged in four rows on three to seven alternate branches pointing upward on tall (up to 1.5 m) terminal stalks. Spikelets over 1.7 mm wide. Seed white, flat and somewhat round. Fruits in summer. Occurs in marshes and damp to wet disturbed habitats including pastures, lawns, golf courses, and other turf areas.

Dallisgrass habit

Propagation:
Seed and very short rhizomes.

Distribution:
Common throughout the southeastern states, north to New Jersey, west to Arizona, California, the Pacific Northwest and Hawaii. Also in the West Indies, Central and South America, and Europe. Native to South America, introduced as a forage crop.

Dallisgrass seedhead with alternate branches

Control Strategies:
Preemergence control with dithiopyr. Postemergence suppression with repeat applications every 5 days with MSMA/DSMA. Spot treat or rope-wick with glyphosate. Refer to the Appendix for additional control information. Check the herbicide label for specific application rates and turfgrass tolerance before use.

Membranous Dallisgrass ligule

Gramineae = Poaceae (Grass Family)
Knotgrass

Synonyms:
None reported.

Species:
Paspalum distichum L.

Description:
Erect dark-green perennial reclining at base forming matted patches from extensively creeping stolons with long internodes and smooth nodes. Leaf blade smooth except for long hairs on margin at base. Rolled vernation. Tall membranous ligule. Sheath smooth except for long hairs on margin at apex. Seedhead terminal with two V-shaped spike branches, sometimes a third below, having flowers and seeds on undersides. Spikelets elliptic, single, with scattered very small fine hairs. Fruits during warm months. Found in moist to wet turf, ditches, and open shallow swales and ponds in wet pinewoods.

Propagation:
Seed, stolons, and possibly rhizomes.

Distribution:
New Jersey west to Oklahoma and Texas and south into the West Indies, widespread in warm areas of the world.

Control Strategies:
Repeat applications every 5 days with MSMA/DSMA. Spot treat with glyphosate. Refer to the Appendix for additional control information. Check the herbicide label for specific application rates and turfgrass tolerance before use.

Knotgrass habit in bermudagrass

Membranous Knotgrass ligule

Knotgrass runners in finer-textured bermudagrass

Knotgrass V-shaped seedhead

Gramineae = Poaceae **(Grass Family)**
Field Paspalum

Synonyms:
None reported.

Species:
Paspalum laeve Michx.

Description:
Coarse, yellow-green tufted perennial from short, scaly rhizomes. Stems erect. Leaf sheaths and blades hairy to smooth, prominent midrib. Ligule membranous, medium tall, rounded, with notched edges. Rolled vernation. Seedhead with one to five ascending branches. Flowers and seeds on undersides of narrowly winged branches. Fruits during warm months. Seedhead with three to four branched spikes. Spikelets two-rowed, smooth, elliptic to round, with a single seed. Found in moist to wet turf, ditches, roadsides, low fields, and pinewoods, around ponds.

Propagation:
Seed and divisions of tufts.

Distribution:
Massachusetts south into Florida and west to Kansas and Texas. Native to North America.

Control Strategies:
Repeat applications every 5 days with MSMA/DSMA. Spot treat or rope-wick with glyphosate. Maintain routine mowing schedule. Refer to the Appendix for additional control information. Check the herbicide label for specific application rates and turfgrass tolerance before use.

Field Paspalum habit

Field Paspalum seedhead

61

Gramineae = Poaceae (Grass Family)
Bahiagrass

Synonyms:
Highwaygrass

Species:
Paspalum notatum Fluegge

Description:
Aggressive, mat-forming, warm-season perennial with shallow, often-exposed rhizomes. Leaves primarily basal, somewhat folded, smooth on both surfaces or often hairy only at the collar, pointed. Folded or rolled vernation. Ligule short, membranous. Seedheads spike-like racemes with usually two or occasionally three branches. Seedhead branches usually paired, V-shaped. Spikelets in two rows on lower sides with a single seed. Fruits late spring through late summer. Often planted for low maintenance turf along roadsides, canals, and for pastures. Found as an escape in many habitats adjacent to planted areas.

Propagation:
Seed and rhizomes.

Distribution:
Common primarily in the Gulf states, north to North Carolina and west to Texas. Also in the West Indies, Central America, and Hawaii. Native to South America.

Control Strategies:
Postemergence control with sethoxydim, metsulfuron twice yearly, or repeat applications every 5 days with MSMA/DSMA. Spot treat with glyphosate. Refer to the Appendix for additional control information. Check the herbicide label for specific application rates and turfgrass tolerance before use.

Purplish-colored Bahiagrass rhizome

Bahiagrass habit

V-shaped Bahiagrass seedhead

Gramineae = Poaceae (Grass Family)
Thin Paspalum

Synonyms:
Bull Paspalum

Species:
Paspalum setaceum Michx.

Description:
Perennial with stem leaning out from center as short rhizomes forming a large flat clump. Leaf sheaths hairy. Leaf blades flat, hairy to almost smooth, often with a fringe of stiff hairs (1 to 2 mm long) along margins. Ligule small, membranous with fringe of hairs on top. Seedhead branches one to six on slender stalks, spreading. Seeds small, in pairs on lower side of branch. Flowers during warm months. Common in sandy soils in most open habitats. Very common as a primary invader of disturbed areas.

Propagation:
Seed and fragmentation of larger clumps.

Distribution:
Throughout the Coastal plain from Long Island to Florida, west to New Mexico and Colorado, north through Nebraska and Ohio to Tennessee. Also in the West Indies, Panama and Mexico. Native to North America.

Control Strategies:
Repeat applications every 5 days with asulox or MSMA/DSMA. Spot treat with glyphosate. Refer to the Appendix for additional control information. Check the herbicide label for specific application rates and turfgrass tolerance before use.

Thin Paspalum seedhead (note: alternate branches and small seeds)

Thin Paspalum habit

Thin Paspalum leaf with hairy margin

Gramineae = Poaceae (Grass Family)
Vaseygrass

Synonyms:
None reported.

Species:
Paspalum urvillei Steud.

Description:
Tall (1 to 2 m), erect, clump forming perennial with densely tufted stems. Leaf sheaths usually rough hairy on lower portion of plant and smooth on upper stem. Leaf blades flat, smooth except for hairs at base of blade on upper surface; margins rough. Leaves mostly near base, alternate. Ligule membranous, pointed, tall. Seedheads with four to thirty spreading branches. Branches with paired, hairy spikelets, to 1.5 mm wide, in lines on the lower side. Fruits in warm months. Occurring along roadsides, in ditches, fields, pastures, disturbed areas, and pinelands usually where the soil is moist to wet.

Propagation:
Seed.

Distribution:
Virginia into Florida, west into Texas and southern California. Also throughout the warm and tropical areas of the world and Europe. Native to South America; introduced as a forage.

Control Strategies:
Maintain routine mowing schedule. Repeat applications every 5 days with MSMA/DSMA. Spot treat or rope-wick with glyphosate. Refer to the Appendix for additional control information. Check the herbicide label for specific application rates and turfgrass tolerance before use.

Vaseygrass habit

Vaseygrass leaf with wrinkled (wavy) margin

Vaseygrass seedhead

Membranous Vaseygrass ligule with hairy sheath

Gramineae = Poaceae (Grass Family)
Kikuyugrass

Synonyms:
None reported.

Species:
Pennisetum clandestinum Hochst. ex Chiov.

Description:
Spreading, prostrate, tough perennial with vigorous, thick, aggressively growing rhizomes and stolons. Not a profuse seed producer. Leaves 1 to 6 inches (2.5 to 15 cm) long, 0.125 to 0.5 inch (3 to 13 mm) in width. Leaf base with hairs on leaves and leaf sheath. Sheaths prominently veined. Folded vernation. Ligule hairy. Seedhead two to four spikelets with bristle-like awns. Fruits from midspring until frost. Forms a coarse-textured, medium green colored turf. Escaped from pastures and soil conservation efforts.

Propagation:
Primarily vegetatively from rhizomes and stolons, less so by seed.

Distribution:
In temperate coastal and near-coastal areas of California and Hawaii. Also in Australia, New Zealand, Central and South America, Africa, China, Indonesia, and Pacific Islands. Introduced from East Africa.

Control Strategies:
Avoid movement of contaminated soil. Fumigate contaminated soil before using or planting. Selective postemergence control with repeat applications of quinclorac, triclopyr, or triclopyr plus MSMA. Nonselective postemergence control includes repeat applications of glyphosate. Refer to the Appendix for additional control information. Check the herbicide label for specific application rates and turfgrass tolerance before use.

Kikuyugrass, left; Hybrid bermudagrass, right

Kikuyugrass runner (stolon)

Gramineae = Poaceae (Grass Family)
Annual Bluegrass

Synonyms:
None reported.

Species:
Poa annua L.

Description:
Small tufted to clumped yellow-green winter annual. Leaf blade smooth on both surfaces, with two distinct, clear lines, one on each side of the midrib. Folded vernation. Leaf tip keeled or boat-shaped. Ligule membranous, medium long, slightly pointed. Light green to whitish spikelets that lack cottony hairs, are arranged on branches, one to two per node, in dense to open flower clusters. Fruits throughout life cycle with majority of seedheads formed during spring. Reproduces by seed. Perennial biotypes [*P. annua* var. *reptans* (Hauskins) Timm.] occur in moist, closely mowed areas such as golf course greens. Compared to annual bluegrass, the perennial biotypes generally are darker colored, more prostrate growing, produce fewer seedheads, and often form patches from short stolons.

Propagation:
Both biotypes by seed plus short stolons for the perennial biotypes.

Annual Bluegrass seedhead

Annual Bluegrass habit

Short stolons associated with certain perennial *Poa annua* biotypes

Distribution:
Annual biotype is found throughout the world, especially in excessively wet, compacted soil. Perennial biotype is found from the transition zone north in the United States, usually on closely mowed golf greens, tees, and fairways under year-round high maintenance.

Control Strategies:
Control options/strategies change constantly. Check with your local state turfgrass specialist for the latest recommendations. Preemergence control includes members of the dinitroaniline herbicide family and other preemergence products (e.g., benefin, bensulide, dithiopyr, fenarimol, napropamide, oryzalin, oxadiazon, pendimethalin, and prodiamine). Apply in late summer when air temperatures reach 75°F (24° C) for several consecutive days. Early postemergence control includes atrazine/simazine/metribuzin, clethodim, diquat, ethofumesate, and pronamide. Selective suppression is provided by plant growth regulators such as paclobutrazol (Trimmit), flurprimidol (Cutless), and mefluidide (Embark). Refer to the Appendix for additional control information. Check the herbicide label for specific application rates and turfgrass tolerance before use.

Annual Bluegrass clump

Gramineae = Poaceae (Grass Family)
Knotroot Foxtail

Synonyms:
None reported.

Species:
Setaria parviflora (Poir.) Kerguelen; [*Setaria geniculata* (Poir.) Beauv.]

Description:
Spreading perennial from short knotty rhizomes. Leaves smooth, occasionally hairy at base of blade. Rolled vernation. Leaf sheath smooth. Ligule a fringe of hairs. Seedhead a dense spike resembling a fox's tail, yellow to purple. Spikelets surrounded by 4 to 12 bristles. Flowers midsummer until frost. Occurs in fresh and brackish marshes, open moist to wet woods, and open disturbed sites. Yellow foxtail [*Setaria glauca* (L.) Beauv. = *Setaria pumila* (Poir.) Roem. & Schult.] is similar but is an annual, lacks short rhizomes, has five or more bristles per spikelet and is native to Europe. Green foxtail [*Setaria viridis* (L.) Beauv.] is also similar, but lacks short rhizomes, has hairs at the top of the leaf sheath, and has zero to three bristles per spikelet. Both Yellow and Green Foxtail occur in open disturbed sites.

Knotroot Foxtail habit

Propagation:
Seed.

Distribution:
Throughout the United States. Also in the West Indies, Mexico, Central and South America, Hawaii, and Europe. Native to North America.

Knotroot Foxtail inflorescence

Control Strategies:
Preemergence control for plants from seed includes members of the dinitroaniline herbicide family and other preemergence products (e.g., benefin, bensulide, dithiopyr, napropamide, oryzalin, oxadiazon, pendimethalin, and prodiamine). Postemergence control for most grass weeds includes repeat applications of MSMA or DSMA, fenoxaprop, fluazifop, sethoxydim, asulam, quinclorac, or metribuzin. Refer to the Appendix for additional control information. Check the herbicide label for specific application rates and turfgrass tolerance before use.

Knotroot Foxtail hairy ligule

Gramineae = Poaceae (Grass Family)
Johnsongrass

Synonyms:
None reported.

Species:
Sorghum halepense (L.) Pers.

Description:
Coarse, erect, perennial from long, thick, scaly, sharp pointed rhizomes. Stems erect, forming dense stands to 6 feet (2 m) tall. Leaf blade margins rough, with prominent white midrib and hairs at base of upper surface, pointed, alternate. Prominent membranous ligule at base of leaf blade, top notched and with hairs. Vernation rolled. Large, open panicle seedhead often purple in color. Seeds hairy. Fruits midsummer until frost. Does not persist under close, frequent mowing. Found in disturbed sites, frequently in cultivated fields, roadsides, and pastures.

Johnsongrass habit

Propagation:
Seed and rhizomes.

Distribution:
Massachusetts to Iowa, south into Florida, and west into Texas, Arizona, and California. Also in the West Indies, Mexico, Central and South America, Hawaii, Europe, Africa, India, and Australia. Native from southern Eurasia east to India. Introduced as a forage into the warmer regions of the world.

Control Strategies:
Avoid movement of contaminated soil. Fumigate contaminated soil before using or planting. Maintain a routine mowing schedule. Selective seedling postemergence control with repeat applications of MSMA or DSMA, fenoxaprop, fluazifop, sethoxydim, or asulam. Nonselective postemergence control includes repeat applications or ropewicking with glyphosate. Refer to the Appendix for additional control information. Check the herbicide label for specific application rates and turfgrass tolerance before use.

Purplish-colored Johnsongrass seedhead

Johnsongrass rhizome

Gramineae = Poaceae (Grass Family)
Coral Dropseed

Synonyms:
None reported.

Species:
Sporobolus domingensis (Trin.) Kunth

Description:
Tufted, erect perennial. Leaf blade sandpapery on the upper surface. Leaf sheath often with hairs along upper margins. Ligule short, membranous with fringe of hairs. Seedhead branches ascending to appressed. Flowers, gray to purplish. Seedheads narrow, densely flowered. Fruits during warm months. Found in disturbed areas, ditches, sandy turf, beaches, and hammocks.

Propagation:
Seed.

Distribution:
Southern peninsula of Florida and the West Indies.

Control Strategies:
Preemergence control includes members of the dinitroaniline herbicide family and other preemergence products (e.g., benefin, bensulide, dithiopyr, napropamide, oryzalin, oxadiazon, pendimethalin, and prodiamine). Atrazine/simazine may provide selective postemergence control. Nonselective control by spot spraying or rope-wicking with glyphosate. Refer to the Appendix for additional control information. Check the herbicide label for specific application rates and turfgrass tolerance before use.

Coral Dropseed habit

Coral Dropseed inflorescence

Gramineae = Poaceae (Grass Family)
Smutgrass

Synonyms:
None reported.

Species:
Sporobolus indicus (L.) R. Br.; [*Sporobolus poiretii* (Roem. & Schult.) Hitchc.]

Description:
Tufted perennial with erect stems and possible short rhizomes. Leaf blades flat to usually folded at base of plant becoming rounded toward tip. Venation rolled. Ligule membranous with fringe of hairs on upper margin. Spike-like panicle seedhead very narrow or with spreading branches. Seeds infected with a black fungus (smut) or unaffected and brown. Fruits during warm months. Occurs in turf, pastures, and roadsides.

Smutgrass clump

Propagation:
Seed.

Distribution:
Throughout the southeast United States, from Virginia into Florida and Texas, inland to Oklahoma and Missouri. Also in the West Indies, Central and South America, Japan, and the Philippines. Native to Tropical America.

Smutgrass clump habit

Control Strategies:
Preemergence control for plants from seed includes members of the dinitroaniline herbicide family and other preemergence products (e.g., benefin, bensulide, dithiopyr, napropamide, oryzalin, oxadiazon, pendimethalin, and prodiamine). Some postemergence seedling control with atrazine/simazine alone or with MSMA/DSMA. Nonselective control by spot spraying with glyphosate. Refer to the Appendix for additional control information. Check the herbicide label for specific application rates and turfgrass tolerance before use.

Smutgrass seedheads infected with dark-colored smut fungus

Gramineae = Poaceae (Grass Family)
Broadleaf Panicum

Synonyms:
Tropic Panicum, Dominican Panicum, Dominican Signal-grass, Broadleaf Signalgrass

Species:
Urochloa adspersa (Trin.) R. D. Webster [*Panicum adspersum* Trin.; *Brachiaria adspersa* (Trin.) Parodi]

Description:
Summer annual grass to 1.2 m tall which sometimes bends and roots at the lower nodes. Stems leafy, erect to ascending. Leaf blades broad (6 to 20 cm wide, to 21 cm long), flat, often covered with fine hairs. Leaf sheaths entirely hairy or hairy in lines along the margins. Ligule hairy, small. Seedheads with ascending branched branches. Flowers purple to greenish-yellow, with obscure rectangular lines. Fruits during warm months. Found in disturbed and open areas, turf, roadsides, cultivated fields, beaches and banks, hillsides, vacant lots.

Propagation:
Seed.

Broadleaf Panicum habit

Distribution:
Only in peninsula of Florida from Volusia County southward. Also in the West Indies. Has been found on ballast in Philadelphia, PA; Camden, NJ; and Mobile, AL.

Control Strategies:
Preemergence control includes members of the dinitroaniline herbicide family and other preemergence products (e.g., benefin, bensulide, dithiopyr, metolachlor, napropamide, oryzalin, oxadiazon, pendimethalin, and prodiamine). Postemergence control includes repeat applications of MSMA or DSMA, fenoxaprop, fluazifop, sethoxydim, asulam, or metribuzin. Refer to the Appendix for additional control information. Check the herbicide label for specific application rates and turfgrass tolerance before use.

Broadleaf Panicum seedhead

Broadleaf Panicum leaf sheath with hairy margin

Gramineae = Poaceae (Grass Family)
Alexandergrass

Synonyms:
Creeping Signalgrass; Plantain Signalgrass

Species:
Urochloa plantaginea (Link) R. D. Webster; [*Brachiaria plantaginea* (Link) A. S. Hitchc.]

Description:
Yellow-green summer annual with prostrate, creeping smooth stems, rooting at nodes. Leaf blades usually smooth, flat, wide, and pointed. Folded vernation. Leaf sheath often with hairs on margin. Ligule a small hairy ring. Seedheads are alternating branches of three to ten spikes spreading outward like "signal flags" with seeds on underside. Fruits in midsummer. Occurring in turf and disturbed habitats. Often confused with crabgrass (*Digitaria* spp.) and broadleaf signalgrass (*Urochloa platyphylla*).

Alexandergrass habit

Propagation:
Seed.

Distribution:
Peninsula of Florida, Georgia, and isolated places in New Jersey, Pennsylvania, and Hawaii. Also in Mexico, Central America, and South America. Native to tropical America.

Control Strategies:
Postemergence control for most grass weeds includes repeat applications of MSMA or DSMA, fenoxaprop, fluazifop, sethoxydim, asulam, quinclorac, or metribuzin. Refer to the Appendix for additional control information. Check the herbicide label for specific application rates and turfgrass tolerance before use.

Alexandergrass inflorescence

Alexandergrass habit with creeping stem

Alexandergrass creeping stem

Gramineae = *Poaceae* (Grass Family)
Broadleaf Signalgrass

Synonyms:
None reported.

Species:
Urochloa platyphylla (Munro ex C. Wright) R. D. Webster
[*Brachiaria platyphylla* (Munro ex C. Wright) Nash]

Description:
Spreading, highly-branched summer annual rooting at lower nodes. Leaf blade short and wide, smooth on both surfaces, often partly folded or creased near the tip. Ligule a narrow membrane fringed with a ring of short hairs. Spikelets on underside of the two to six ascending branches. Angle of branches resembles a "signal flag." Fruits in midsummer. May be common during turfgrass establishment. Also found in cleared and otherwise disturbed areas, cultivated fields.

Propagation:
Seed.

Distribution:
Throughout the Southeast from North Carolina into Florida and west to Oklahoma and Texas.

Control Strategies:
Preemergence control includes member of the dinitroaniline herbicide family such as prodiamine and pendimethalin. Postemergence control for most grass weeds includes repeat applications of MSMA or DSMA, fenoxaprop, fluazifop, sethoxydim, asulam, quinclorac, or metribuzin. Refer to the Appendix for additional control information. Check the herbicide label for specific application rates and turfgrass tolerance before use.

Broadleaf Signalgrass habit

Gramineae = Poaceae (Grass Family)
Smallflowered Alexandergrass

Synonyms:
Tropical Signalgrass

Species:
Urochloa subquadripara (Trin.) R. D. Webster [*Brachiaria subquadripara* (Trin.) A. S. Hitchc.; *Brachiaria extensa* Chase]

Description:
Herbaceous perennial grass from stolons to 45 cm tall. Stems usually trailing and creeping, rooting at the nodes (joints). Leaf blades flat, 8 to 12 mm wide and up to 19 cm long. Leaf blade and sheath hairy. Ligule a short fringe of hairs. Flowering branches ascending, to 18 inches (45 cm) tall. Seedheads with two to seven branches or "fingers." Seeds located under and appressed to the branch. Angle of branches resembling a "signal flag." Fruits during warm months. Found in lawns, roadsides, athletic fields, pastures, vacant lots, ditches, hammocks, shell middens, cultivated fields, disturbed areas, and Coastal Plains hammocks.

Propagation:
Seed and stolons.

Distribution:
Throughout peninsula of Florida and Coastal Plains into South Carolina and Texas. Introduced into Africa, Mexico, Costa Rica, and the West Indies. Native to India, Burma, Malaysia, Java, some Pacific Islands, and Australia.

Control Strategies:
Preemergence control includes members of the dinitroaniline herbicide family and other preemergence products (e.g., benefin, bensulide, dithiopyr, metolachlor, napropamide, oryzalin, oxadiazon, pendimethalin, and prodiamine). Postemergence control for most grass weeds includes repeat applications of MSMA or DSMA, fenoxaprop, fluazifop, sethoxydim, asulam, quinclorac, or metribuzin. Refer to the Appendix for additional control information. Check the herbicide label for specific application rates and turfgrass tolerance before use.

Smallflowered Alexandergrass habit

Smallflowered Alexandergrass inflorescence

75

Iridaceae (Iris Family)
Annual Blue-eyed-grass

Synonyms:
None reported.

Species:
Sisyrinchium rosulatum Bickn.

Description:
Winter annual with usually zigzag stems. Leaves flat, light green, all clustered at the base. Flowers pale purple to white with a rose-purple eye ring. Flowers midspring through early summer. Found on moist sites in lawns, roadsides, golf courses, and pastures.

Propagation:
Seed.

Distribution:
North Carolina, south into central peninsula Florida and west to Texas and Arkansas. Native to South America.

Control Strategies:
Postemergence control includes repeat applications of imazaquin, metsulfuron, atrazine/simazine, or metribuzin. Refer to the Appendix for additional control information. Check the herbicide label for specific application rates and turfgrass tolerance before use.

Annual Blue-eyed-grass fruit

Annual Blue-eyed-grass habit

Annual Blue-eyed-grass flower

Juncaceae (Rush Family)
Toad Rush

Synonyms:
None reported.

Species:
Juncus bufonius L.

Description:
Tufted, branched, annual grass-like plant with round, smooth, hairless stems. Leaves hairless, usually flattened on the upper surface and rounded below, short, and few in number. Leaf sheaths gradually tapered at the top, lacking flanges. Upper stems are often almost leafless, with a few ascending branches. Flowers borne singly and are remote along the upper part of the branches. Fruits midsummer through early fall. Found in moist, open areas such as road-sides, lawns, low fields and ditches, often in saline habitats in coastal areas.

Propagation:
Seed.

Distribution:
Alaska and Canada south throughout most of the USA into north Florida. Nearly throughout the temperate regions of the world.

Control Strategies:
Control soil moisture, as excessive amount encourages most *Juncus* species. Preemergence control with either meto-lachlor, atrazine/simazine, or oxadiazon. Postemergence control with repeat applications of atrazine/simazine, benta-zon, halosulfuron, imazaquin alone or with MSMA/DSMA. Refer to the Appendix for additional control information. Check the herbicide label for specific application rates and turfgrass tolerance before use.

Toad Rush habit

Toad Rush flower heads

Juncaceae (Rush Family)
Slender Rush

Synonyms:
Path Rush, Poverty Rush

Species:
Juncus tenuis Willd.

Description:
Perennial with tufted, round stems. Leaf blades flat, basal, shorter than stem. Leaf sheaths with conspicuous papery margins. Seedhead branches ascending, flowers separated. Leaves at top of stem longer than seedhead. Fruits in summer. Found on moist roadsides, compacted soils, and shaded areas.

Propagation:
Seed.

Distribution:
Throughout the United States and worldwide.

Control Strategies:
Control soil moisture, as excessive amount encourages most *Juncus* species. Alleviate compacted soil. Preemergence control with either metolachlor, atrazine/simazine, or oxadiazon. Postemergence control is attempted with repeat applications of atrazine/simazine, bentazon, halosulfuron, imazaquin alone or with MSMA/DSMA. Nonselective control by spot spraying with glyphosate. Refer to the Appendix for additional control information. Check the herbicide label for specific application rates and turfgrass tolerance before use.

Slender Rush inflorescence stalks

Slender Rush clumping habit

Slender Rush inflorescence

Liliaceae = Amaryllidaceae (Amaryllis or Lily Family)
Wild Garlic

Synonyms:
Field Garlic

Species:
Allium vineale L.

Description:
Cool-season perennial with slender, hollow cylindrical leaves. Leaves occur on the flowering stem up to half the height of the plant. Underground white bulb bears offset bulblets that are flattened on one side and enclosed by a papery-like membrane. Flowers, greenish-white, small, on short stems above aerial bulbils; produced late spring through early summer. Plant with distinctive garlic odor when crushed. Occurs in lawns, fields, and pastures. Wild onion (*Allium canadense* L.) is often found on same sites as wild garlic. Wild onion can be distinguished from wild garlic by presence of a fibrous coat on the central bulb, no offset bulblets, and leaves that are flat, not hollow, and arise near the base of a solid flowering stem. Wild Onion occurs in open disturbed sites.

Wild Garlic habit

Propagation:
Seed, aerial bulbils, and underground bulblets.

Distribution:
Throughout most of the eastern and southern United States, west to Missouri and Arkansas. Also in Canada, North Africa, and Europe. Native to Europe.

Wild Garlic bulbs

Control Strategies:
Postemergence applications of 2,4-D, 2,4-D-containing herbicides, metsulfuron or imazaquin. Apply 2,4-D in late fall and again in late winter. Apply imazaquin to labeled warm-season turfgrasses in late fall after turfgrasses become dormant. Repeat this sequence for at least two years. Avoid moving or using soil contaminated with tubers. Refer to the Appendix for additional control information. Check the herbicide label for specific application rates and turfgrass tolerance before use.

Wild Garlic bulblet

79

Liliaceae = *Amaryllidaceae* (Amaryllis or Lily Family)
Star-of-Bethlehem

Synonyms:
None reported.

Species:
Ornithogalum umbellatum L.

Description:
Cool-season perennial from a central bulb. Leaves narrow, linear, with a conspicuous pale-green to white channeled midrib. Flowers, white, petals six, with a characteristic green stripe on underside. Flowers in spring. Occurs in fields, woods, and roadsides.

Propagation:
Seed and underground bulbs.

Distribution:
Primarily in the piedmont regions of the southern United States. Also in Canada, western Asia, North Africa, Europe, and Hawaii. Native to Europe.

Control Strategies:
Postemergence applications of 2,4-D or 2,4-D-containing herbicides. Apply 2,4-D in late fall and again in late winter. Repeat this sequence for at least two years. Avoid moving or using soil contaminated with tubers. Refer to the Appendix for additional control information. Check the herbicide label for specific application rates and turfgrass tolerance before use.

Star-of-Bethlehem flowers

Star-of-Bethlehem habit

BROADLEAF PLANTS

Aizoaceae (Carpetweed Family)
Carpetweed

Synonyms:
Indian Chickweed, Green Carpetweed

Species:
Mollugo verticillata L.

Description:
Prostrate summer annual with numerous smooth, branched stems. Leaves light green in color, smooth, spoon-shaped, and arranged in whorls of five to six at each node. Flowers white, tiny, arranged in clusters of two to five on slender stalks from leaf axils, petals five. Flowers midsummer through early fall. Usually a problem only in thin turf or during turfgrass establishment. Occurs in open disturbed sites.

Propagation:
Tiny, reddish seed.

Distribution:
Throughout most of the United States. Also in Canada, through Mexico into Central and South America, Africa, and Asia. Native to tropical America.

Carpetweed habit

Control Strategies:
Preemergence control includes members of the dinitroaniline herbicide family and other preemergence products (e.g., dithiopyr, isoxaben, metolachlor, oxadiazon, pendimethalin, and prodiamine). Postemergence control involves repeat applications of two- or three-way mixtures of 2,4-D, dicamba, MCPP, or MCPA. Other options include atrazine/simazine, metribuzin, triclopyr alone or combined with clopyralid (Confront) or 2,4-D, atrazine plus bentazon (Prompt), imazaquin, and metsulfuron. Refer to the Appendix for additional control information. Check the herbicide label for specific application rates and turfgrass tolerance before use.

Carpetweed stem with whorled leaves

Carpetweed leaves

83

Amaranthaceae (Amaranth Family)
Marcela

Synonyms:
Yellow Joyweed

Species:
Alternanthera flavescens HBK.; [*Alternanthera ramosissima* (Mart.) Chod.; *Achyranthes ramosissima* (Mart.) Standl.]

Description:
Much branched, spreading, hairy perennial often sprawling over low vegetation. Leaves elliptic, thin, sharp-pointed, opposite, with short petioles. Flowers in papery, white, round to oblong heads on long stalks. Flowers in warm months. Found in sandy, open, disturbed areas and woods.

Propagation:
Seed.

Distribution:
Southern peninsula of Florida. Also in the West Indies, Mexico, Central America, and South America.

Control Strategies:
Repeat applications of two- or three-way mixtures of 2,4-D, dicamba, MCPP, or MCPA. Other options include atrazine/simazine, metribuzin, triclopyr alone or combined with clopyralid or 2,4-D, atrazine plus bentazon, imazaquin, and metsulfuron. Refer to the Appendix for additional control information. Check the herbicide label for specific application rates and turfgrass tolerance before use.

Marcela habit

Marcela flower

Amaranthaceae (Amaranth Family)
Smooth Chaff-flower

Synonyms:
Chaff-flower, Whitlow-wort, Smooth Joyweed

Species:
Alternanthera paronychioides St. Hil.

Description:
Creeping perennial, usually with hairy stems. Leaves opposite, elliptic to spatulate, pointed to round tip. Flowers in white, papery, round to oblong sessile heads in leaf axils. Found in open, sandy, disturbed areas and sandy lawns. Flowers in warm months.

Propagation:
Seed and stem fragments.

Distribution:
North Carolina south into Florida and west into Texas. Also in the West Indies, Mexico, Central America, and South America. Native to tropical America.

Control Strategies:
Repeat applications of two- or three-way mixtures of 2,4-D, dicamba, MCPP, or MCPA. Other options include atrazine/simazine, metribuzin, triclopyr alone or combined with clopyralid or 2,4-D, atrazine plus bentazon, imazaquin, and metsulfuron. Refer to the Appendix for additional control information. Check the herbicide label for specific application rates and turfgrass tolerance before use.

Smooth Chaff-flower habit

Smooth Chaff-flower flowers

Amaranthaceae (Amaranth Family)
Khakiweed

Synonyms:
None reported.

Species:
Alternanthera pungens HBK.

Description:
Prostrate warm-season annual or perennial from a thick tap root. Stems hairy. Leaves opposite, broadest at the rounded tip, tapering to the petiole. Leaf margins smooth. Flowers white, in stiff-bracted, almost spiny, heads. Heads sessile, solitary or two or three clustered at the nodes. Flowers summer through early fall. Found in turf, pastures, and along roadsides in sandy soils.

Propagation:
Seed.

Distribution:
Florida, Georgia, Alabama, and Texas. Also in Cuba, Jamaica, eastern Mexico, Java, India, Kenya, South Africa, and Australia. Native to South America.

Control Strategies:
Repeat applications of two- or three-way mixtures of 2,4-D, dicamba, MCPP, or MCPA. Other options include atrazine/simazine, metribuzin, triclopyr alone or combined with clopyralid or 2,4-D, atrazine plus bentazon, imazaquin, and metsulfuron. Refer to the Appendix for additional control information. Check the herbicide label for specific application rates and turfgrass tolerance before use.

Khakiweed habit

Khakiweed leaves and hairy stems

Amaranthaceae (Amaranth Family)
Smooth Pigweed

Synonyms:
Common Pigweed, Slim Amaranth

Species:
Amaranthus hybridus L.

Description:
Tall warm-season annual with erect, smooth to hairy stems. Petioles long. Leaf blades oval with a sharp tip. Male and female flowers mixed in clusters in leaf axils and in large terminal panicles. Flowers in summer. Found in cultivated fields, moist areas, roadsides, newly established turf, and disturbed habitats.

Propagation:
Seed.

Distribution:
Massachusetts, Michigan to Iowa, south to Florida, west to Arizona and California. Also in Ontario, Quebec, the West Indies, Mexico, Central America, South America, Europe, Africa, Asia, and Australia. Native to the southwestern United States and tropical America.

Control Strategies:
Maintain a regular mowing schedule. Preemergence control includes dithiopyr, oxadiazon, and oryzalin. Repeat applications of 2,4-D or two- or three-way mixtures of 2,4-D, dicamba, MCPP, or MCPA. Other options include atrazine/simazine, metribuzin, triclopyr alone or combined with clopyralid or 2,4-D, atrazine plus bentazon, metsulfuron and chlorsulfuron. Refer to the Appendix for additional control information. Check the herbicide label for specific application rates and turfgrass tolerance before use.

Smooth Pigweed leaves

Smooth Pigweed habit

Smooth Pigweed inflorescence

87

Amaranthaceae (Amaranth Family)
Livid Amaranth

Synonyms:
Purple Amaranth

Species:
Amaranthus lividus L.; [*Amaranthus blitum* L.]

Description:
Warm season annual with prostrate, ascending or erect, smooth stems. Leaves with long petioles. Leaf blades usually oval, sometimes slightly broader above the middle. Leaf tips, at least some, with a notch. Flowers green, in dense clusters in leaf axils or at tips of stems. Male and female flowers separate but mixed in the clusters. Flowers summer through early fall. Found in lawns, pastures, gardens, and row crops.

Propagation:
Seed.

Distribution:
Massachusetts south into Florida. Also in Ontario, Quebec, the West Indies, South America, Europe, Africa, Middle East to Asia, and Hawaii. Native to the Mediterranean region.

Control Strategies:
Maintain a regular mowing schedule. Repeat applications of 2,4-D or two- or three-way mixtures of 2,4-D, dicamba, MCPP, or MCPA. Other options include atrazine/simazine, metribuzin, triclopyr alone or combined with clopyralid or 2,4-D, atrazine plus bentazon, imazaquin, and metsulfuron. Refer to the Appendix for additional control information. Check the herbicide label for specific application rates and turfgrass tolerance before use.

Livid Amaranth habit

Livid Amaranth inflorescence

Amaranthaceae (Amaranth Family)
Slender Amaranth

Synonyms:
None reported.

Species:
Amaranthus viridus L.; [*Amaranthus gracilis* Desf.]

Description:
Prostrate to erect warm-season annual with broadly egg-shaped, simple, alternate leaves. Seedheads terminal and axillary, spike-like. Flowers summer through early fall. Usually a problem only during turfgrass establishment. Found in disturbed sites.

Propagation:
Tiny, dark brown to black seeds.

Distribution:
North Carolina south into Florida, and west into Arizona. Also in the West Indies, Central and South America, tropical Africa, Asia, Europe, and Hawaii. Native to tropical America.

Control Strategies:
Maintain a regular mowing schedule. Repeat applications of 2,4-D or two- or three-way mixtures of 2,4-D, dicamba, MCPP, or MCPA. Other options include atrazine/simazine, metribuzin, triclopyr alone or combined with clopyralid or 2,4-D, atrazine plus bentazon, imazaquin, and metsulfuron. Refer to the Appendix for additional control information. Check the herbicide label for specific application rates and turfgrass tolerance before use.

Slender Amaranth habit

Slender Amaranth inflorescence

Cactaceae (Cactus Family)
Spreading Prickly-pear

Synonyms:
Prickly-pear Cactus

Species:
Opuntia humifusa (Raf.) Raf.

Description:
Pod-like flat, thick, succulent-leaved, low-growing perennial. Leaves with sharp spines, hence the name. Spines brown, gray, or white. Flowers yellow. Flowers in summer. Fruit large berry, rounded and tapering at base; spiny, purplish-red when ripe. Found in low maintenance turfgrass areas, especially in sandy soils or dry rocky sites. Common in most open sandy habitats, recovers rapidly after burning.

Propagation:
Seed and fragmentation of pads (leaves).

Distribution:
Massachusetts, Minnesota, Wisconsin, Kansas, South Dakota, and Montana south into Florida and west to Texas. Also in southern Ontario and Mexico. Native to North America.

Control Strategies:
Improve turf growing conditions and maintain a regular mowing schedule. Postemergence selective control options include triclopyr alone or combined with clopyralid or 2,4-D. Manual removal is often necessary. Refer to the Appendix for additional control information. Check the herbicide label for specific application rates and turfgrass tolerance before use.

Spreading Prickly-pear habit

Spreading Prickly-pear leaves with spines

90

Campanulaceae (Bellflower or Bluebell Family)
Florida Bellflower

Synonyms:
None reported.

Species:
Campanula floridana S. Wats. ex A. Gray

Description:
Perennial with sprawling to nearly erect stems, often rooting at the nodes. Leaves elliptic to linear. Flowers purple, stalked, petals five, tapering to a long, sharp point. Flowers in warm months. Found in moist lawns, roadsides, marshes, and swamps.

Propagation:
Seed.

Distribution:
Panhandle and peninsula of Florida.

Control Strategies:
Repeat applications of two- or three-way mixtures of 2,4-D, dicamba, MCPP, or MCPA. Other suggested options include atrazine/simazine, metribuzin, triclopyr alone or combined with clopyralid or 2,4-D, atrazine plus bentazon, imazaquin, and metsulfuron. Refer to the Appendix for additional control information. Check the herbicide label for specific application rates and turfgrass tolerance before use.

Florida Bellflower habit with elliptically-shaped leaves

Florida Bellflower flower

Campanulaceae (Bellflower or Bluebell Family)
Common Venus'-looking-glass

Synonyms:
None reported.

Species:
Triodanis perfoliata (L.) Nieuwl.

Description:
Winter annual or perennial with weak or prostrate stems.
Stems usually freely branched at base. Leaves alternate,
ovate to heart-shaped and clasp the stem. Leaf margins with
fine teeth. Bluish-violet tubular flowers with five petals are
borne in the leaf axils. Flowers spring through early summer. Found in disturbed sites, lawns, and roadsides.

Propagation:
Seed.

Distribution:
The continental United States except for the Rocky Mountains. Also in the Canadian provinces of British Columbia,
Alberta, Ontario, and Quebec, south to Mexico, Central
and South America.

Control Strategies:
Repeat applications of two- or three-way mixtures of 2,4-D,
dicamba, MCPP, or MCPA. Other suggested options include atrazine/simazine, metribuzin, triclopyr alone or combined with clopyralid or 2,4-D, atrazine plus bentazon,
imazaquin, and metsulfuron. Refer to the Appendix for additional control information. Check the herbicide label for
specific application rates and turfgrass tolerance before use.

Clasping leaves of Common Venus'-
looking-glass

Common Venus'-looking-glass habit

Common Venus'-looking-glass flower

Caryophyllaceae (Pink Family)
Sticky Chickweed

Synonyms:
Sticky Cerastium

Species:
Cerastium glomeratum Thuill.

Description:
Mat-forming, branched winter annual. Leaves opposite, densely hairy, oval to elliptic in shape. Stems slender, covered with dense hairs. Flowers white, arranged in clusters at ends of stems, five slightly notched petals. Flowers in spring. Mouse-ear chickweed [*Cerastium vulgatum* L.= *Cerastium fontanum* Baumg. subsp. *vulgare* (Hartman) Greuter & Burdet], a perennial that often roots at the lower nodes, is similar in appearance. Both species occur in turf and other open disturbed areas.

Propagation:
Seed.

Distribution:
Common in the southeastern states, west to Texas, California, and Alaska. Also in Asia, Europe, and the Canadian Yukon. Native to Europe.

Control Strategies:
Preemergence options include isoxaben, pendimethalin, and prodiamine. Repeat applications of two- or three-way mixtures of 2,4-D, dicamba, MCPP, or MCPA. Other options include atrazine/simazine, metribuzin, triclopyr alone or combined with clopyralid or 2,4-D, atrazine plus bentazon, imazaquin, and metsulfuron. Refer to the Appendix for additional control information. Check the herbicide label for specific application rates and turfgrass tolerance before use.

Hairy stem of Sticky Chickweed

Sticky Chickweed habit

Sticky Chickweed flower

Caryophyllaceae (Pink Family)
Heartleaf Drymary

Synonyms:
West Indian Chickweed

Species:
Drymaria cordata (L.) Willd. ex Roem. & Schult.

Description:
Weak-stemmed, spreading warm-season annual. Leaves opposite, kidney-shaped, bright green. Flowers greenish, small, in long, wide, spreading clusters with thin, easily broken branches. Flowers and fruits stick to clothing and/or hair. Flowers in warm months. Occurs in moist to wet woods and all disturbed sites.

Propagation:
Seed and stem fragments.

Distribution:
Louisiana to Florida. Also in the West Indies, Mexico, Central and South America, Tropical Africa, Tropical Asia, and Hawaii.

Control Strategies:
Repeat applications of two- or three-way mixtures of 2,4-D, dicamba, MCPP, or MCPA. Other suggested options include atrazine/simazine, metribuzin, triclopyr alone or combined with clopyralid or 2,4-D, atrazine plus bentazon, imazaquin, and metsulfuron. Refer to the Appendix for additional control information. Check the herbicide label for specific application rates and turfgrass tolerance before use.

Heartleaf Drymary habit

Heartleaf Drymary leaves

Caryophyllaceae (Pink Family)
Birdseye Pearlwort

Synonyms:
Trailing Pearlwort

Species:
Sagina procumbens L.

Description:
Small, spreading, tufted perennial with smooth, hairless stems. Plant persists only as a winter annual in southern USA. Prostrate to ascending, branched stems bear oppositely arranged, grass-like very narrow leaves, tipped with a sharp point. Creeping branched stems form mats. Leafless flower stalks found in the leaf axils near the ends of the stems. Flowers tiny, inconspicuous with four small, white petals and four longer sepals. Flowers late spring until frost. Found in fields, lawns, roadsides, and waste areas.

Propagation:
Seeds and branches rooting at the nodes.

Distribution:
East of the Mississippi River from Massachusetts to Illinois south to central Florida west to New Mexico and east Kansas. Also in Alaska, British Columbia, Europe, Alberta, Ontario, Quebec, New Brunswick, and Nova Scotia.

Control Strategies:
Repeat applications of two- or three-way mixtures of 2,4-D, dicamba, MCPP, or MCPA. Other suggested options include atrazine/simazine, metribuzin, triclopyr alone or combined with clopyralid or 2,4-D, atrazine plus bentazon, imazaquin, and metsulfuron. Refer to the Appendix for additional control information. Check the herbicide label for specific application rates and turfgrass tolerance before use.

Young Birdseye Pearlwort plant

Birdseye Pearlwort habit

Birdseye Pearlwort flower

95

Caryophyllaceae (Pink Family)
Knawel

Synonyms:
German Knotweed

Species:
Scleranthus annuus L.

Description:
Freely-branched winter annual or summer annual in temperate regions with a prostrate habit. Leaves opposite, very narrow, grass-like appearance, linear in shape, sharply pointed and generally bent downward. Small green flowers, that lack petals, found in clusters in the leaf axils. As a winter annual, flowers spring into early summer. Occurs in disturbed sites.

Propagation:
Seed.

Distribution:
The eastern half of the United States, north to Canada, west to California and Pacific Coast, and Europe.

Control Strategies:
Repeat applications of two- or three-way mixtures of 2,4-D, dicamba, MCPP, or MCPA. Other suggested options include atrazine/simazine, metribuzin, triclopyr alone or combined with clopyralid or 2,4-D, bentazon, atrazine plus bentazon, imazaquin, and metsulfuron. Refer to the Appendix for additional control information. Check the herbicide label for specific application rates and turfgrass tolerance before use.

Knawel habit

Young Knawel leaves

Caryophyllaceae (Pink Family)
Common Chickweed

Synonyms:
None reported.

Species:
Stellaria media (L.) Vill.

Description:
Mat-forming winter annual or short-lived perennial in temperate regions with numerous branched stems. Leaves opposite, smooth, egg or oval to broadly elliptic in shape. Upper leaves without petiole; lower leaves with sparsely hairy long petiole. Stems with vertical lines of hairs. Flowers in small clusters at ends of stems, white, with five deeply notched petals. Flowers early spring into early summer. Occurs in turf and wooded habitats. Mouse-ear chickweed [*Cerastium vulgatum* L. = *Cerastium fontanum* Baumg. subsp. *vulgare* (Hartman) Greuter & Burdet] is similar but is a perennial, roots at nodes, and leaves are oblong, gray-green, and prominently hairy, resembling the fur on the ears of mice. Occurs in lawns and other disturbed areas.

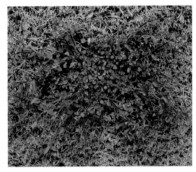

Common Chickweed habit

Propagation:
Seed.

Distribution:
Throughout North America except for the Rocky Mountains. Also in Mexico, Central and South America, Hawaii, Asia, Africa, and Europe. Native to Eurasia.

Common Chickweed stem and leaves

Control Strategies:
Preemergence control includes benefin, benefin plus trifluralin, dithiopyr, isoxaben, pendimethalin, prodiamine, and pronamide. Postemergence control with repeat applications of two- or three-way mixtures of 2,4-D, dicamba, MCPP, or MCPA. Other options include atrazine/simazine, metribuzin, triclopyr alone or combined with clopyralid or 2,4-D, atrazine plus bentazon, imazaquin, and metsulfuron. Refer to the Appendix for additional control information. Check the herbicide label for specific application rates and turfgrass tolerance before use.

Common Chickweed flower

Compositae = Asteraceae (Aster or Sunflower Family)
Common Yarrow

Synonyms:
None reported.

Species:
Achillea millefolium L.

Description:
Fragrant mat-forming perennial herb with prostrate stems (in mowed conditions) that vary from slightly to densely hairy. Leaves alternate, finely divided into feather-like divisions. Flowers in heads arranged in flat-topped clusters at tips of branched stems. Ray flowers white and disk flowers yellow. Flowers in summer. Mostly in open disturbed sites such as old fields.

Propagation:
Rhizomes and seed.

Distribution:
Canada south to central Florida, west to Mississippi. Also in the West Indies.

Control Strategies:
Repeat applications of two- or three-way mixtures of 2,4-D, dicamba, MCPP, or MCPA. Other suggested options include atrazine/simazine, metribuzin, triclopyr alone or combined with clopyralid or 2,4-D, atrazine plus bentazon, imazaquin, and metsulfuron. Refer to the Appendix for additional control information. Check the herbicide label for specific application rates and turfgrass tolerance before use.

Feather-like leaf of Common Yarrow

Common Yarrow habit

Common Yarrow flower

Compositae = Asteraceae (Aster or Sunflower Family)
Common Ragweed

Synonyms:
None reported.

Species:
Ambrosia artemisiifolia L.

Description:
Erect (1 to 3 m tall), taprooted summer annual with branched stems forming a bushy rounded top. Leaves hairy, deeply twice dissected; opposite basally, alternate upward. Foliage fragrant when crushed. Male and female flowers separate, green. Flowers spike-like racemes, erect to drooping, flowering late summer until frost. Pollen is common cause of hay fever. Giant ragweed (*A. trifida* L.) is similar except larger (1 to 6 m tall), leaves opposite and 3 to 5 lobed instead of alternate and deeply twice dissected with common ragweed. In fields, pastures, roadsides, and waste places.

Propagation:
Seed.

Distribution:
The northwestern and southeastern United States. Also in Canada, Central and South America, the West Indies, South Pacific, and Australia. Native to the United States.

Control Strategies:
Maintain a regular mowing schedule. Preemergence control with isoxaben. Postemergence control with repeat applications of two- or three-way mixtures of 2,4-D, dicamba, MCPP, or MCPA. Other options include atrazine/simazine, metribuzin, triclopyr alone or combined with clopyralid or 2,4-D, bentazon, atrazine plus bentazon, imazaquin, and metsulfuron. Refer to the Appendix for additional control information. Check the herbicide label for specific application rates and turfgrass tolerance before use.

Common Ragweed inflorescence

Common Ragweed habit

Twice dissected Common
Ragweed leaves

Compositae = Asteraceae (Aster or Sunflower Family)
Mugwort

Synonyms:
None reported.

Species:
Artemisia vulgaris L.

Description:
Creeping perennial from long rhizomes. Stems hairy, round in cross section. Leaves alternate, dissected, each segment linear to elliptic in shape. Upper leaf surface dark green, smooth to slightly hairy; lower leaf surface whitish to grayish, densely woolly. Flowers midsummer into early fall. Vegetatively resembles and has same characteristic odor of the garden chrysanthemum. Found in disturbed areas, flower beds, ornamentals, lawns, and waste areas.

Propagation:
Rhizomes, not believed to produce viable seed.

Distribution:
Eastern half of the United States, west to Texas. Occurs in the West Indies, Canada, Europe, Asia, and Hawaii. Native to Europe.

Control Strategies:
Repeat applications of dicamba or two- or three-way mixtures of 2,4-D, dicamba, MCPP, or MCPA. Other suggested options include atrazine/simazine, metribuzin, triclopyr alone or combined with clopyralid or 2,4-D, atrazine plus bentazon, and metsulfuron. Refer to the Appendix for additional control information. Check the herbicide label for specific application rates and turfgrass tolerance before use.

Mugwort habit

Mugwort leaves (note: underneath leaf surface whitish- to grayish-colored, right)

Compositae = Asteraceae (Aster or Sunflower Family)
Bushy Aster

Synonyms:
Rice Button Aster

Species:
Aster dumosus L.

Description:
Low to tall bushy perennial with extensive rhizomes. First leaves are elongate, spatulate in shape, broad at the tip with scattered teeth. Mature leaves are narrow, elongated and have smooth margins. Flowering occurs mostly in fall with limited production in spring. Flowers on long spreading stalks (peduncles), blue, but not seen under frequent mowing. Flowers late summer through midfall. Found in open sunny and shady habitats in moist soils, common along roadsides.

Propagation:
Seed and rhizomes.

Distribution:
Michigan and Massachusetts to south Florida, west to Louisiana and Arkansas. Native to North America.

Control Strategies:
Repeat applications of two- or three-way mixtures of 2,4-D, dicamba, MCPP, or MCPA. Other suggested options include atrazine/simazine, metribuzin, triclopyr alone or combined with clopyralid or 2,4-D, atrazine plus bentazon, imazaquin, and metsulfuron. Refer to the Appendix for additional control information. Check the herbicide label for specific application rates and turfgrass tolerance before use.

Bushy Aster habit

Bushy Aster flower

Bushy Aster habit with flowers

Bushy Aster leaves

101

Compositae = Asteraceae (Aster or Sunflower Family)
English Daisy

Synonyms:
European Daisy, Lawn Daisy

Species:
Bellis perennis L.

Description:
Prostrate, spreading perennial with short stems, forming extensive patches from rhizomes. Stems and leaves hairy and leaves form dense cluster at base of plant. Leaves simple. Leaf blade elliptic to spatula-like in shape, tapering at the base to a long petiole, margins have rounded teeth. A single daisy-like flower borne at the end of an almost bare, erect flower stalk. Outside (ray) petals white to pinkish-white in color and strap-shaped. Center (disk) flowers bright yellow. Flower stalk longer than the leaves. Flowers early spring through early summer, sometimes in midfall. Escaped from flower gardens. Occurs in lawns.

English Daisy habit with flowers

Propagation:
Seed and rhizomes.

Distribution:
Northern states east of the Mississippi River south into the mountains of North Carolina and in the states of the Northern Plains, Pacific Northwest, and western California. Also in Alaska, British Columbia, Alberta, Ontario, Quebec, New Brunswick, and Nova Scotia. Native of northern Europe.

English Daisy habit

Control Strategies:
Repeat applications of two- or three-way mixtures of 2,4-D, dicamba, MCPP, or MCPA. Other suggested options include atrazine/simazine, metribuzin, triclopyr alone or combined with clopyralid or 2,4-D, atrazine plus bentazon, and metsulfuron. Refer to the Appendix for additional control information. Check the herbicide label for specific application rates and turfgrass tolerance before use.

English Daisy flower

Compositae = Asteraceae (Aster or Sunflower Family)
Hairy Beggarticks

Synonyms:
Common Beggarticks, Romerillo, Spanish Needles

Species:
Bidens alba (L.) DC.

Description:
Warm-season annual or short-lived perennial with smooth, erect to spreading stems often rooting at lower nodes. First true leaves on seedlings simple and long-stalked. Other leaves opposite, stalked, with three to nine leaflets. Leaflets with teeth on margins. Flowers with white rays, and yellow centers, in stalked heads. Flowers in warm months until frost. Fruits 0.4 inch (1 cm) long with two or three barbed awns at the top. Found in virtually all disturbed areas including poorly maintained turf.

Propagation:
Seed attaching to fur or clothing.

Distribution:
North Carolina to south Florida and west to California. Also in the West Indies, Mexico, Central America, South America, Asia, Africa, and Europe.

Hairy Beggarticks leaves with toothed margins

Control Strategies:
Maintain a regular mowing schedule. Repeat applications of two- or three-way mixtures of 2,4-D, dicamba, MCPP, or MCPA. Other suggested options include atrazine/simazine, metribuzin, triclopyr alone or combined with clopyralid or 2,4-D, atrazine plus bentazon, and metsulfuron. Refer to the Appendix for additional control information. Check the herbicide label for specific application rates and turfgrass tolerance before use.

Hairy Beggarticks flower

Hairy Beggarticks habit

Hairy Beggarticks fruit

Compositae = Asteraceae (Aster or Sunflower Family)
Sprawling Horseweed

Synonyms:
Straggler Daisy

Species:
Calyptocarpus vialis Less.

Description:
Spreading hairy warm-season annual or short-lived peren-nial rooting at the nodes. Leaves oval, toothed, the petiole-like bases shorter than the blade. Flowers yellow, inconspic-uous, in heads on elongated stalks. Seed with roughened surface and two smooth awns at the tip. Flowers in warm months. Found in lawns and sandy open, disturbed areas, such as pastures, roadsides, and waste areas.

Propagation:
Seed.

Distribution:
Florida and west into Texas. Also in the West Indies, Mex-ico, Central America, and Java. Native to tropical America.

Control Strategies:
Maintain a regular mowing schedule. Repeat applications of two- or three-way mixtures of 2,4-D, dicamba, MCPP, or MCPA. Other suggested options include atrazine/simazine, metribuzin, triclopyr alone or combined with clopyralid or 2,4-D, atrazine plus bentazon, and metsulfuron. Refer to the Appendix for additional control information. Check the herbicide label for specific application rates and turfgrass tolerance before use.

Sprawling Horseweed flower and toothed margin leaves

Sprawling Horseweed habit

Compositae = Asteraceae (Aster or Sunflower Family)
Musk Thistle

Synonyms:
Nodding Thistle

Species:
Carduus nutans L.

Description:
Winter annual or biennial with erect, robust stems from a fleshy taproot. Leaves alternate, smooth, dark green with a light green midrib and a whitish margin. Leaves deeply dissected, each lobe having one to five spines at the tip. Flowers with spine-tipped bracts, deep pink to purple, rarely white, and arranged in nodding heads. Flowers midspring into early summer. Plant produces musk scent, hence, the common name. Occurs along roadsides and in other disturbed habitats.

Propagation:
Seed.

Distribution:
North Carolina to Louisiana excluding Florida. Also in India and Africa. Native to Eurasia.

Control Strategies:
Maintain a regular mowing schedule. Repeat applications of two- or three-way mixtures of 2,4-D, dicamba, MCPP, or MCPA. Other options include atrazine/simazine, metribuzin, triclopyr alone or combined with clopyralid or 2,4-D, bentazon, atrazine plus bentazon, and metsulfuron. Refer to the Appendix for additional control information. Check the herbicide label for specific application rates and turfgrass tolerance before use.

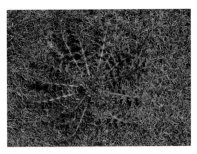

Musk Thistle habit

Musk Thistle seeds, left; flower, right

Spines on Musk Thistle leaves

Compositae = Asteraceae (Aster or Sunflower Family)
Chicory

Synonyms:
None reported.

Species:
Cichorium intybus L.

Description:
Freely-branched taprooted perennial, initially from a rosette. Leaves coarsely toothed, upper surface "rough" to the touch. Basal leaves usually absent at flowering. Stem leaves alternate, clasping and hairy. Stems smooth, with a "milky" juice. Flowers bright blue. Flowers late spring through summer. Found in open disturbed sites such as roadsides, pastures, and waste areas.

Propagation:
Seed.

Distribution:
Scattered throughout the United States, rare in Florida. Native to North Africa, Europe, and Western Asia.

Control Strategies:
Maintain a regular mowing schedule. Repeat applications of two- or three-way mixtures of 2,4-D, dicamba, MCPP, or MCPA. Other suggested options include atrazine/simazine, metribuzin, triclopyr alone or combined with clopyralid or 2,4-D, atrazine plus bentazon, and metsulfuron. Refer to the Appendix for additional control information. Check the herbicide label for specific application rates and turfgrass tolerance before use.

Chicory clasping stem leaves

Chicory habit

Chicory flower

Compositae = Asteraceae (Aster or Sunflower Family)
Yellow Thistle

Synonyms:
Horrible Thistle

Species:
Cirsium horridulum Michx.; [*Carduus spinosissimus* Walt.]

Description:
Erect, stout, pithy, spiny winter annual or infrequent biennial. Leaves with shallow, spiny lobes. Flowers purple, occasionally yellow, in large terminal, spiny head. Seeds with tuft of soft, white hairs at the tip. Flowers spring into early summer. Found in open, sandy areas including roadsides, pastures, and waste areas.

Propagation:
Seed.

Distribution:
Maine and Pennsylvania, south into Florida and west to Texas. Also in the West Indies, Mexico, and Central America. Native to North America.

Control Strategies:
Maintain a regular mowing schedule. Repeat applications of dicamba or two- or three-way mixtures of 2,4-D, dicamba, MCPP, or MCPA. Other suggested options include atrazine/simazine, metribuzin, triclopyr alone or combined with clopyralid or 2,4-D, atrazine plus bentazon, and metsulfuron. Refer to the Appendix for additional control information. Check the herbicide label for specific application rates and turfgrass tolerance before use.

Yellow Thistle habit

Yellow Thistle spiny flowers

Yellow Thistle spiny leaves

Yellow Thistle flowering stem

107

Compositae = Asteraceae (Aster or Sunflower Family)
Horseweed

Synonyms:
Marestail, Canadian Horseweed

Species:
Conyza canadensis (L.) Cronq.; [*Erigeron canadensis* L.]

Description:
Tall-growing (up to 2 m) summer or winter annual with bristly hairy stems. Seedling leaves form a basal rosette. Leaves alternate, spiraling, lack petioles, linear to oblanceolate. Leaf margins often toothed; lower margins with long hairs, ray petals white or lavender, center disks yellow. Flowers in numerous, small heads on branches in the upper portion of the plant. Flowers midsummer until frost. Found in open sandy disturbed habitats.

Propagation:
Wind-dispersed seed.

Distribution:
Throughout the United States. Also in Quebec, Ontario, Mexico, Central and South America, and Europe. Native to Europe.

Control Strategies:
Maintain a regular mowing schedule. Preemergence control options include isoxaben and oryzalin. Postemergence control involves repeat applications of two- or three-way mixtures of 2,4-D, dicamba, MCPP, or MCPA. Other options include atrazine/simazine, metribuzin, triclopyr alone or combined with clopyralid or 2,4-D, and atrazine plus bentazon. Refer to the Appendix for additional control information. Check the herbicide label for specific application rates and turfgrass tolerance before use.

Hairy Horseweed stem

Horseweed habit

Horseweed inflorescence

Compositae = Asteraceae (Aster or Sunflower Family)
Eclipta

Synonyms:
False Daisy, Yerba-de-tago

Species:
Eclipta prostrata (L.) L.; [*Eclipta alba* (L.) Hassk.]

Description:
Warm-season annual with prostrate to erect stems, rooting at the nodes. Leaves opposite, narrow, rough hairy with either smooth or toothed margins. Stem thick, succulent, rooting at lower nodes. Flowers white, with many small rays in long-stalked heads. Flowers midsummer until frost. Found in moist, open, disturbed areas.

Propagation:
Seed.

Distribution:
Massachusetts, New York, Wisconsin, Iowa, Indiana, Illinois, and Nebraska, south into Florida and west to Texas, Arizona, California, and Hawaii. Also in Ontario, Mexico, the West Indies, Central America, South America, tropical Africa, and tropical Asia.

Control Strategies:
Repeat applications of two- or three-way mixtures of 2,4-D, dicamba, MCPP, or MCPA. Other suggested options include atrazine/simazine, metribuzin, and triclopyr alone or combined with clopyralid or 2,4-D, atrazine plus bentazon, metsulfuron, and quinclorac. Refer to the Appendix for additional control information. Check the herbicide label for specific application rates and turfgrass tolerance before use.

Eclipta flower

Eclipta habit

Compositae = Asteraceae (Aster or Sunflower Family)
Cupid's-shaving-brush

Synonyms:
Tassel-flower, Florida Tassel-flower

Species:
Emilia fosbergii Nicols.; [*Emilia coccinea* of authors; *Emilia sonchifolia* of Britt. & Millsp.]

Description:
Introduced warm-season annual from a taproot with branched erect stems up to 0.5 m tall. Stems smooth near the top, hairy at the base. All leaves with toothed margins, alternate but mostly basal. Leaves at base with broad tip and winged petiole. Leaves at top with no petiole and clasp the stem. Flowers crimson or bright scarlet, in heads on long stalks, urn-shaped. Flowers in warm weather. Seeds are five angled with short, thick hairs on the angles. Found in open weedy areas, vacant lots, roadsides, lawns, and other moist disturbed areas.

Propagation:
Seed.

Distribution:
Florida. Also in the West Indies, Mexico, Central America south into Brazil, western Pacific Islands, Java, and Tropical Africa. A pantropical weed native to the Old World.

Control Strategies:
Repeat applications of two- or three-way mixtures of 2,4-D, dicamba, MCPP, or MCPA. Other suggested options include atrazine/simazine, metribuzin, and triclopyr alone or combined with clopyralid or 2,4-D, atrazine plus bentazon, imazaquin, and metsulfuron. Refer to the Appendix for additional control information. Check the herbicide label for specific application rates and turfgrass tolerance before use.

Cupid's-shaving-brush flowering stem

Cupid's-shaving-brush habit

Cupid's-shaving-brush flower

Compositae = Asteraceae (Aster or Sunflower Family)
American Burnweed

Synonyms:
Fireweed

Species:
Erechtites hieraciifolia (L.) Raf. ex DC.

Description:
Robust summer annual with solid, erect, smooth to hairy stems to 2.5 m tall. Has both short fat taproots and also often with many adventitious prop roots. Leaves alternate, spiraling, elliptic to lance-shaped with narrow, sharp-pointed bases on lower part of stem and clasping bases on upper part of stem. Leaf margins lobed or unlobed, unevenly toothed (serrate); midrib white. Flowers white to pinkish, in elongate heads. Flowers late-spring through fall, petals barely visible, cream to pinkish. Seeds with many white hairs at the top. May produce a rank odor when cut or crushed. Found in almost any disturbed area and frequently in pastures and roadsides.

Propagation:
Wind-dispersed seed.

Distribution:
Maine, Minnesota, and South Dakota south throughout the eastern, central, and southern states, and Oregon and Hawaii. Also in Newfoundland, Quebec, the West Indies, Mexico south through Central America, South America, and Asia. Native to North America.

Control Strategies:
Maintain a regular mowing schedule. Repeat applications of two- or three-way mixtures of 2,4-D, dicamba, MCPP, or MCPA. Other suggested options include atrazine/simazine and triclopyr alone or combined with clopyralid or 2,4-D. Additional options include atrazine plus bentazon, and metsulfuron. Refer to the Appendix for additional control information. Check the herbicide label for specific application rates and turfgrass tolerance before use.

American Burnweed habit

American Burnweed inflorescence

Unevenly toothed American Burnweed leaf

111

Compositae = Asteraceae (Aster or Sunflower Family)
Southern Fleabane

Synonyms:
Oakleaf Fleabane

Species:
Erigeron quercifolius Lam.

Description:
Short-lived perennial from rhizomes. Stems hairy, one to several from a basal rosette. Basal leaves hairy, broader at the tip, usually with several rounded lobes. Stem leaves few and clasping. Flowers white, in numerous heads. Flowers spring into early summer. Seeds tiny, with many hairs at top. Found in moist turf areas, pinelands, and open woods.

Propagation:
Seed.

Distribution:
Virginia south throughout Florida and west to Louisiana. Also in the West Indies.

Control Strategies:
Maintain a regular mowing schedule. Preemergence control with isoxaben. Postemergence control with repeat applications of two- or three-way mixtures of 2,4-D, dicamba, MCPP, or MCPA. Other options include atrazine/simazine and triclopyr alone or combined with clopyralid or 2,4-D. Additional options include atrazine plus bentazon, imazaquin, and metsulfuron. Refer to the Appendix for additional control information. Check the herbicide label for specific application rates and turfgrass tolerance before use.

Southern Fleabane flower

Southern Fleabane habit

Lobed lower Southern Fleabane leaves

Compositae = Asteraceae (Aster or Sunflower Family)
Rough Fleabane

Synonyms:
Daisy Fleabane, White-tops, Prairie Fleabane

Species:
Erigeron strigosus Muhl. ex. Willd.

Description:
Erect summer annual or biennial with sparse stem leaves and few hairs. Leaves elliptic, alternate. Basal leaves a rosette, with a few teeth or entire, usually absent at flowering. Stem leaves usually entire or rarely toothed. Flowers at terminal heads on slender stalks, heads few; ray petals white with yellow disks. Flowers summer until frost. Found in pastures, roadsides, old fields, and other open disturbed areas.

Propagation:
Wind-dispersed seed.

Distribution:
Throughout the United States except for Arizona. Also in Canada. Native to North America.

Control Strategies:
Maintain a regular mowing schedule. Repeat applications of two- or three-way mixtures of 2,4-D, dicamba, MCPP, or MCPA. Other suggested options include atrazine/simazine and triclopyr alone or combined with clopyralid or 2,4-D. Additional options include atrazine plus bentazon, and metsulfuron. Refer to the Appendix for additional control information. Check the herbicide label for specific application rates and turfgrass tolerance before use.

Rough Fleabane flowers

Rough Fleabane flower clusters

113

Compositae = Asteraceae (Aster or Sunflower Family)
Dogfennel

Synonyms:
Summer Cedar

Species:
Eupatorium capillifolium (Lam.) Small

Description:
Tall-growing (up to 2 m), erect, short-lived perennial with one to several densely, hairy stems from a woody crown. Leaves deeply cut into hair-like linear segments; feathery in appearance. Lower leaves opposite, upper leaves alternate. Leaves strongly aromatic when crushed. Flowers midsummer until frost, often nodding; greenish-white. Not tolerant to close, frequent mowing. Found in abandoned fields, waste areas, roadsides, nurseries, newly planted turf, and orchards.

Propagation:
Wind-dispersed seed and regrowth from woody base.

Distribution:
Massachusetts and New Jersey to south Florida, and west to Texas and Arkansas. Also in the West Indies and Guatemala. Native to North America.

Control Strategies:
Maintain a regular mowing schedule. Preemergence control of plants from seed with isoxaben. Postemergence control with repeat applications of two- or three-way mixtures of 2,4-D, dicamba, MCPP, or MCPA. Other suggested options include atrazine/simazine and triclopyr alone or combined with clopyralid or 2,4-D, atrazine plus bentazon, imazaquin, and metsulfuron. Refer to the Appendix for additional control information. Check the herbicide label for specific application rates and turfgrass tolerance before use.

Dogfennel habit

Young Dogfennel (note: hairy stem and feathery leaves)

Compositae = Asteraceae (Aster or Sunflower Family)
Facelis

Synonyms:
Annual Trampweed

Species:
Facelis retusa (Lam.) Sch.-Bip.

Description:
Winter annual with freely branched stems at base. Base of stems recline along ground. Stems covered with tufts of long, soft hairs. Leaves generally lack petioles and are crowded along length of stem. Leaves narrow in shape, lower surface covered with white tufts of long hairs and upper surface dull green. Leaf apex indented to rounded, usually with a tiny sharp point. Small white flowers are borne in multiflowered heads. Flowers in spring. Found in lawns, pastures, sandy fields, and waste areas.

Propagation:
Seed.

Distribution:
Tennessee and North Carolina south into north Florida and west to Texas and Oklahoma. Native of South America.

Control Strategies:
Improve turf growing conditions and maintain a regular mowing schedule. Repeat applications of two- or three-way mixtures of 2,4-D, dicamba, MCPP, or MCPA. Other suggested options include atrazine/simazine, metribuzin, triclopyr alone or combined with clopyralid or 2,4-D, atrazine plus bentazon, and metsulfuron. Refer to the Appendix for additional control information. Check the herbicide label for specific application rates and turfgrass tolerance before use.

Facelis plant

White, bristle-like Facelis inflorescence

Facelis habit

Alternate leaves of Facelis covered with gray, cobweb-like hair

Compositae = Asteraceae (Aster or Sunflower Family)
Yellowtop

Synonyms:
Narrowleaf Yellowtop

Species:
Flaveria linearis Lag.

Description:
Erect annual with smooth branched stems. Leaves opposite, narrow with usually smooth margins. Flowers yellow, very small, with only a few in each individual head. Heads in flat-topped clusters, showy. Flowers in warm months. Seeds tiny, usually lacking tiny papery scales at the top. Found in pastures, roadsides, open hammocks, pinewoods, and marshes.

Propagation:
Seed.

Distribution:
Central and southern peninsula of Florida. Also in the West Indies and Mexico.

Control Strategies:
Maintain a regular mowing schedule. Repeat applications of two- or three-way mixtures of 2,4-D, dicamba, MCPP, or MCPA. Other suggested options include atrazine/simazine and triclopyr alone or combined with clopyralid or 2,4-D. Refer to the Appendix for additional control information. Check the herbicide label for specific application rates and turfgrass tolerance before use.

Yellowtop flowers

Narrow Yellowtop leaves and stem

Compositae = Asteraceae (Aster or Sunflower Family)
Rosering Gaillardia

Synonyms:
Gaillardia, Blanket-flower, Bandana Daisy, Rose-ring Gaillardia, Indian Blanket, Fireweed

Species:
Gaillardia pulchella Foug.

Description:
Warm-season annual or short-lived, erect perennial from a
taproot. Leaves hairy. Leaves on the lower part of stem usually broader at the tip, stalkless or almost so, usually irregularly lobed and toothed. Leaves on the upper part of the
stem tending to be narrowly lance-shaped, stalkless, smooth
margins or with occasional, irregular teeth. Flowers dark
purple, dark purple with yellow tips, or yellow, on long
stalks, in heads. Fruit small, hairy, tipped with papery scales.
Flowers in summer. Found in sandy open areas such as roadsides and pastures, especially along the coastal beaches. Frequently planted as a wildflower along roadsides.

Propagation:
Seed.

Distribution:
North Carolina south throughout Florida, west to South
Dakota, Nebraska, Arizona, Colorado, and California. Also
in Mexico, Central America, and the West Indies.

Control Strategies:
Improve turf growing conditions. Repeat applications of
two- or three-way mixtures of 2,4-D, dicamba, MCPP, or
MCPA. Other suggested options include atrazine/simazine
and triclopyr alone or combined with clopyralid or 2,4-D.
Refer to the Appendix for additional control information.
Check the herbicide label for specific application rates and
turfgrass tolerance before use

Gaillardia habit and flower

Compositae = Asteraceae (Aster or Sunflower Family)
Wandering Cudweed

Synonyms:
Pennsylvania Everlasting

Species:
Gnaphalium pensylvanicum Willd.; [*Gnaphalium purpureum* L. var. *spathulatum* (Lam.) Ahles; *Gnaphalium spathulatum* Lam.; *Gamochaeta pensylvanica* (Willd.) Cabrera]

Description:
Summer or winter annual or biennial initially from a basal rosette of leaves. All stem leaves of similar size. Stem and all leaves covered by soft hairs. Leaf undersides densely white hairy. Upper leaf surface dull green. Flowers mostly purple to pink. Flowers either midspring into early summer or early fall. Occurs in sandy soils of disturbed areas.

Propagation:
Seed.

Distribution:
Pennsylvania, south into Florida, west to Texas, and in southern California. Also in the West Indies, Central and South America.

Control Strategies:
Improve turf growing conditions. Preemergence control with isoxaben. Postemergence control with repeat applications of two- or three-way mixtures of 2,4-D, dicamba, MCPP, or MCPA. Other suggested options include atrazine/simazine, metribuzin, triclopyr alone or combined with clopyralid or 2,4-D, atrazine plus bentazon, imazaquin, and metsulfuron. Refer to the Appendix for additional control information. Check the herbicide label for specific application rates and turfgrass tolerance before use.

Wandering Cudweed habit with whitish stems and leaves

Wandering Cudweed inflorescence

Compositae = Asteraceae (Aster or Sunflower Family)
Purple Cudweed

Synonyms:
Rabbit Tobacco, Spoonleaf Purple Everlasting

Species:
Gnaphalium purpureum L.; [*Gamochaeta purpurea* (L.) Cabrera]

Description:
Summer or winter annual or biennial developing a basal rosette of leaves. Stems highly branched from base of plant. Stem and underside of leaves with soft velvet-like hairs. Upper leaf surface dull green. Rosette and lower stem leaves spatula-shaped with blunt tips, upper leaves reduced in size. Flowers tannish-white in clusters at upper leaf axils. Bracts surrounding flower clusters pink or purple in color. Flowers either midspring into early summer or early fall. Occurs in dry, open, disturbed habitats.

Propagation:
Seed.

Distribution:
Throughout the continental United States except for North and South Dakota. Also in Saskatchewan, Manitoba, and Europe.

Control Strategies:
Improve turf growing conditions. Preemergence control with isoxaben. Postemergence control with repeat applications of two- or three-way mixtures of 2,4-D, dicamba, MCPP, or MCPA. Other suggested options include atrazine/simazine, metribuzin, triclopyr alone or combined with clopyralid or 2,4-D, atrazine plus bentazon, imazaquin, and metsulfuron. Refer to the Appendix for additional control information. Check the herbicide label for specific application rates and turfgrass tolerance before use.

Purple Cudweed inflorescence

Purple Cudweed habit

119

Compositae = Asteraceae (Aster or Sunflower Family)
Narrowleaf Cudweed

Synonyms:
Narrowleaf Purple Everlasting

Species:
Gnaphalium falcatum Lam.; [*Gnaphalium purpureum* L. var. *falcatum* (Lam.) Torr. & Gray; *Gamochaeta falcata* (Lam.) Cabrera]

Description:
Annual or biennial with basal rosette of leaves. Stems covered with dense, white hairs. Branches none to many. Leaves narrow, often broader toward the tip, densely white hairy on both surfaces. Flowers in brown to green heads. Heads usually dense in an elongate inflorescence. Flowers either mid-spring through early summer or in early fall. Found in disturbed areas, roadsides, fields and open woods, and pinelands.

Propagation:
Seed.

Distribution:
Virginia south to Florida and west to Texas. Also in Central and South America.

Control Strategies:
Improve turf growing conditions. Preemergence control with isoxaben. Postemergence control with repeat applications of two- or three-way mixtures of 2,4-D, dicamba, MCPP, or MCPA. Other suggested options include atrazine/simazine, metribuzin, triclopyr alone or combined with clopyralid or 2,4-D, atrazine plus bentazon, imazaquin, and metsulfuron. Refer to the Appendix for additional control information. Check the herbicide label for specific application rates and turfgrass tolerance before use.

Narrowleaf Cudweed with whitish stems and leaves

Narrowleaf Cudweed habit

Compositae = Asteraceae (Aster or Sunflower Family)
Shiny Cudweed

Synonyms:
American Everlasting

Species:
Gnaphalium americanum Mill.; [*Gnaphalium purpureum*
L. var. *americanum* (Mill.) Klatt; *Gnaphalium spicatum*
Lam.; *Gamochaeta americana* (Mill.) Weddell]

Description:
Erect summer or winter annual or biennial with a prominent
rosette of basal leaves. Leaves bright shiny green on upper
surface, densely white hairy beneath. Basal leaves very
broad. All stem leaves of similar size. Flower heads brown to
purple. Flowers either midspring through early summer or
early fall. Occurs in dry, open, sandy, disturbed areas.

Propagation:
Seed.

Distribution:
Southern Florida throughout the Southeast, north to New
York, west to Illinois, Missouri, Indiana, Kansas, and
Texas. Also in Oregon.

Control Strategies:
Improve turf growing conditions. Preemergence control
with isoxaben. Postemergence control with repeat applications of two- or three-way mixtures of 2,4-D, dicamba,
MCPP, or MCPA. Other suggested options include
atrazine/simazine, metribuzin, triclopyr alone or combined
with clopyralid or 2,4-D, atrazine plus bentazon, imazaquin, and metsulfuron. Refer to the Appendix for additional
control information. Check the herbicide label for specific
application rates and turfgrass tolerance before use.

Shiny Cudweed habit (note: whitish beneath leaf)

Compositae = Asteraceae (Aster or Sunflower Family)
Bitter Sneezeweed

Synonyms:
Bitterweed, Spanish Daisy

Species:
Helenium amarum (Raf.) H. Rock

Description:
Summer annual herb with upright growth habit and strong taproot. Stem purple, freely branched toward the middle; glandular (oily feel). Leaves numerous, small, thread-like, alternate, sticky. Basal stem leaves usually absent at flowering. Numerous flowers arranged in heads. Ray flowers yellow. Central disk dome-shaped and also yellow. Flowers in summer. Plant with pungent odor and bitter taste. Often found in poor turf-growing conditions in pastures, along roadsides, and waste areas. Occurs in prairies, open woods, fields, roadsides, and other open disturbed habitats.

Propagation:
Seed.

Distribution:
Throughout the continental United States, north to Massachusetts, west to Texas and California. Not found in the High Plains, Pacific Northwest, and Southwest states. Native to North America.

Control Strategies:
Improve turf growing conditions and maintain a regular mowing schedule. Repeat applications of two- or three-way mixtures of 2,4-D, dicamba, MCPP, or MCPA. Other suggested options include metsulfuron, atrazine/simazine and triclopyr alone or combined with clopyralid or 2,4-D. Refer to the Appendix for additional control information. Check the herbicide label for specific application rates and turfgrass tolerance before use.

Bitter Sneezeweed habit

Bitter Sneezeweed flower

Compositae = Asteraceae (Aster or Sunflower Family)
Yellow Hawkweed

Synonyms:
King Devil

Species:
Hieracium caespitosum Dumort.; [*Hieracium pratense* Tausch]

Description:
Perennial with leafy stolons and often elongated rhizomes. Leaves hairy on the upper surface and arise from a basal rosette. Leaves and stems exude a milky sap when broken. Flowering stalk is leafless and 4 to 18 inches tall. Several flowers arise from a single flowering stalk. Flowers in summer. Occurs in fields, pastures, roadsides, and dry woods. Yellow hawkweed has yellow flowers as opposed to orange hawkweed (*Hieracium aurantiacum* L.), which has orange to reddish-colored flowers and occurs similarly in fields and along roadsides.

Propagation:
Stolons, rhizomes, and seed.

Distribution:
Eastern North America from Quebec south to West Virginia, North Carolina, and Georgia. Native to Europe.

Control Strategies:
Improve turf growing conditions and maintain a regular mowing schedule. Repeat applications of two- or three-way mixtures of 2,4-D, dicamba, MCPP, or MCPA. Other suggested options include atrazine/simazine and triclopyr alone or combined with clopyralid or 2,4-D. Refer to the Appendix for additional control information. Check the herbicide label for specific application rates and turfgrass tolerance before use.

Yellow Hawkweed leaves with hairy margins

Yellow Hawkweed habit with a basal rosette of leaves

Yellow Hawkweed flower clusters

Compositae = Asteraceae (Aster or Sunflower Family)
Common Cat's-ear

Synonyms:
Cat's-ear Dandelion, Hairy Cat's-ear

Species:
Hypochoeris radicata L.

Description:
Perennial with densely hairy leaves arranged in a basal rosette. Leaf margins coarsely toothed; divisions or lobes with blunt to slightly pointed tips. Flower stalk with two to seven flowers, bright yellow, similar in appearance to dandelion flowers. Flowers primarily in late spring through early summer. Leaves and flower stalks exude a 'milky juice' when broken. Occurs in pastures, fields, and other disturbed sites.

Propagation:
Seed.

Distribution:
New Jersey south into panhandle Florida and west to Mississippi. Also in Ontario and North Africa. Native to Eurasia.

Control Strategies:
Improve turf growing conditions and maintain a regular mowing schedule. Repeat applications of 2,4-D, imazaquin or two- or three-way mixtures of 2,4-D, dicamba, MCPP, or MCPA. Apply in late fall and repeat in late winter. Repeat for two years. Refer to the Appendix for additional control information. Check the herbicide label for specific application rates and turfgrass tolerance before use.

Common Cat's-ear Dandelion habit

Basal leaf rosette of Common Cat's-ear Dandelion

Common Cat's-ear Dandelion flower

Compositae = Asteraceae (Aster or Sunflower Family)
Virginia Dwarf Dandelion

Synonyms:
Krigia Dandelion

Species:
Krigia virginica (L.) Willd.

Description:
Small, stemless perennial with a basal rosette of leaves. Leaf margins notched or lobed, tapered at base. Flowers yellow, in single heads at end of leafless stalk. Flowers primarily in late spring into early summer. Occurs in open woods and in most open disturbed areas.

Propagation:
Seed.

Distribution:
Throughout the continental United States except for the states in the High Plains, Pacific Northwest, Southwest, and California. Also found in Ontario.

Control Strategies:
Improve turf growing conditions and maintain a regular mowing schedule. Repeat applications of 2,4-D, imazaquin or two- or three-way mixtures of 2,4-D, dicamba, MCPP, or MCPA. Apply in late fall and repeat in late winter. Repeat for two years. Refer to the Appendix for additional control information. Check the herbicide label for specific application rates and turfgrass tolerance before use.

Virginia Dwarf Dandelion basal rosette of leaves

Virginia Dwarf Dandelion flower

Compositae = *Asteraceae* (Aster or Sunflower Family)
Tall Lettuce

Synonyms:
Wild Lettuce, Canada Lettuce

Species:
Lactuca canadensis L.

Description:
Tall (1 to 3 m), upright biennial with essentially no hairs; from a taproot. Leaves alternate, large, sessile or clasping, white midvein. Leaf margins entire or with small teeth and/or lobed. Flowers yellow-orange, turning purple with age, in heads at tips of stems. Forms a large taproot with a rosette of leaves in first year of growth. In the second year, a long, erect leafy stem which contains a bitter, sticky, milky juice is formed. Flowers orange-yellow, occurring from spring into early summer. Occurs in disturbed areas, road-sides, pastures, and open woods.

Propagation:
Wind- and animal-dispersed seed.

Tall Lettuce habit

Tall Lettuce leaf margin

Distribution:
Throughout the United States except for Arizona, New Mexico, and Wyoming. Also in Canada and the West Indies. Native to North America.

Control Strategies:
Improve turf growing conditions and maintain a regular mowing schedule. Preemergence control with isoxaben. Repeat applications of two- or three-way mixtures of 2,4-D, dicamba, MCPP, or MCPA. Other suggested options include triclopyr alone or combined with clopyralid or 2,4-D. Refer to the Appendix for additional control information. Check the herbicide label for specific application rates and turfgrass tolerance before use.

Tall Lettuce inflorescence (note: yellow flowers and whitish puffball seedheads)

Compositae = Asteraceae (Aster or Sunflower Family)
Stalked Chickenweed

Synonyms:
Sanddune Cinchweed

Species:
Pectis glaucescens (Cass.) D. J. Keil; [*Pectis leptocephala* (Cass.) Urban]

Description:
Annual or short-lived perennial with freely branched stems which lie near the ground, forming mats. Leaves opposite, narrow (<1 mm wide), 1 to 3 cm long with two rows of oil glands on lower surface. Flowers yellow, in long-stalked heads. Fruits with two to five very small scales at the top. Flowers in warm months. Found in disturbed areas, lawns, sandy pinelands, and beaches.

Propagation:
Seed.

Distribution:
Southern peninsula of Florida and the Keys. Also in the West Indies.

Control Strategies:
Improve turf growing conditions and maintain a regular mowing schedule. Repeat applications of two- or three-way mixtures of 2,4-D, dicamba, MCPP, or MCPA. Other suggested options include atrazine/simazine, metribuzin, triclopyr alone or combined with clopyralid or 2,4-D, atrazine plus bentazon, and metsulfuron. Refer to the Appendix for additional control information. Check the herbicide label for specific application rates and turfgrass tolerance before use.

Stalked Chickenweed bunch

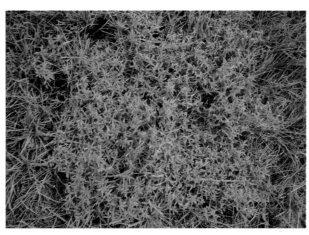

Stalked Chickenweed habit

Stalked Chickenweed flower

Compositae = Asteraceae (Aster or Sunflower Family)
Carolina False Dandelion

Synonyms:
Carolina Desert-Chicory

Species:
Pyrrhopappus carolinianus (Walt.) DC.

Description:
Winter annual or biennial with erect, branched flowering stems. Basal leaves a rosette, alternate on stems, sharply pointed, with entire to deeply-lobed margins. Basal leaves with petioles; stem leaves lack petioles. Bright yellow flowers, similar to dandelion, on ends of erect flowering stems. Seeds brown, with long stalk and a parachute of hairs at top, forming a "puff ball." Flowers late spring through summer (sporadically year-round). Occurs in dry, open, disturbed habitats.

Propagation:
Wind-dispersed seed.

Distribution:
Southern United States, west to Texas, north to Delaware, and inland to Kansas. Native to North America.

Control Strategies:
Improve turf growing conditions and maintain a regular mowing schedule. Repeat applications of 2,4-D, imazaquin or two- or three-way mixtures of 2,4-D, dicamba, MCPP, or MCPA. Apply in late fall and repeat in late winter. Two consecutive years of application may be required. Refer to the Appendix for additional control information. Check the herbicide label for specific application rates and turfgrass tolerance before use.

Basal leaves of Carolina False Dandelion

Carolina False Dandelion habit

Carolina False Dandelion flower

129

Compositae = Asteraceae (Aster or Sunflower Family)
Goldenrod

Synonyms:
None reported.

Species:
Solidago spp.

Description:
Tall (up to 2 m), erect to arching perennial herbs from root crowns or often with long, spreading rhizomes that form large colonies. Stems usually erect and unbranched below the inflorescence. Leaves alternate. Inflorescences branching, spreading, often arching; may be clusters, spike-like, or panicles with yellow ray and disk flowers. Flowers in small, dense, numerous terminal heads. Flowers midsummer until frost. Found in low, wet sites, frequently in low maintenance turf, nurseries, roadsides, fence rows, waste areas, and ditches. Over 150 species occur.

Propagation:
Seed and rhizomes.

Distribution:
Numerous goldenrod species occur through North America south into tropical America and the West Indies. Many are native to North America.

Giant Goldenrod (*Solidago gigantea*)

Hollow Goldenrod (*Solidago fistulosa*)

Old Field Goldenrod (*Solidago nemoralis*)

Goldenrod stem (*Solidago gigantea*)

Control Strategies:

Improve turf growing conditions and maintain a regular mowing schedule. Repeat applications of two- or three-way mixtures of 2,4-D, dicamba, MCPP, or MCPA. Other suggested options include atrazine/simazine and triclopyr alone or combined with clopyralid or 2,4-D. Refer to the Appendix for additional control information. Check the herbicide label for specific application rates and turfgrass tolerance before use.

Goldenrod flower (*Solidago nemoralis*)

Compositae = *Asteraceae* (Aster or Sunflower Family)
Lawn Burweed

Synonyms:
Spurweed, Field Burweed

Species:
Soliva sessilis Ruiz & Pavon [*Soliva pterosperma* (Juss.) Less.]

Description:
Low-growing, freely branched winter annual. Leaves opposite, sparsely hairy and twice divided into narrow segments or lobes. Flowers small and inconspicuous. Flowers in spring. Fruits clustered in leaf axils and having sharp spines that can cause injury. Occurs in most turf.

Propagation:
Seed.

Distribution:
Generally found in the Coastal Plain and Piedmont regions of most southern states, North Carolina south into Florida, and west to Texas. Also in South America and Europe. Native to South America.

Control Strategies:
Preemergence control with isoxaben, atrazine/simazine, and napropamide. Postemergence control with repeat applications of two- or three-way mixtures of 2,4-D, dicamba, MCPP, or MCPA. Other options include atrazine/simazine, metribuzin, triclopyr alone or combined with clopyralid or 2,4-D, and metsulfuron. Refer to the Appendix for additional control information. Check the herbicide label for specific application rates and turfgrass tolerance before use.

Divided Lawn Burweed leaves

Lawn Burweed habit

Spines in leaf axils of Lawn Burweed

Compositae = Asteraceae (Aster or Sunflower Family)
Spiny Sowthistle

Synonyms:
None reported.

Species:
Sonchus asper (L.) Hill

Description:
Upright winter annual. Leaves basal and alternate on stems, deeply lobed with spiny margins, less so up the stem. Leaf base with rounded lobes and clasps the stem. Stems hollow, smooth on the lower portion but with stalked, glandular hairs on the upper portion. Yellow flowers in clusters at top of plant. Leaves and stems exude a "milky" juice when broken. Flowers mid- to late-spring. Annual sowthistle (*Sonchus oleraceus* L.) is similar but with sharply-pointed, clasping lobes at leaf base. Both species found in open, disturbed habitats, including turf, roadsides, and cultivated fields.

Propagation:
Wind-dispersed seed.

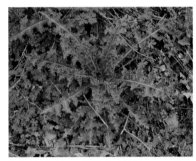

Spiny Sowthistle habit

Distribution:
Throughout the United States, north into Alaska and the Yukon. Also in the West Indies, South America, Eurasia, Africa, and Hawaii. Native to Europe.

Control Strategies:
Maintain a regular mowing schedule. Preemergence control with isoxaben and oxadiazon. Postemergence control with repeat applications of two- or three-way mixtures of 2,4-D, dicamba, MCPP, or MCPA. Other suggested options include atrazine/simazine, metribuzin, triclopyr alone or combined with clopyralid or 2,4-D, atrazine plus bentazon, imazaquin, and metsulfuron. Refer to the Appendix for additional control information. Check the herbicide label for specific application rates and turfgrass tolerance before use.

Spiny Sowthistle flower

Lobed Spiny Sowthistle leaves with spiny margins

133

Compositae = Asteraceae (Aster or Sunflower Family)
Dandelion

Synonyms:
None reported.

Species:
Taraxacum officinale Weber ex F. H. Wigg.

Description:
Deeply taprooted, stemless perennial. Leaves in a basal rosette, slightly to deeply cut, with lobes that point back toward base. Single yellow flowers at end of each long, smooth, hollow stalk. Leaves and flower stalks exude a "milky" juice when broken. Flowers during warm weather. Seeds brown, long stalked with a parachute of hairs, head forming a "globe." Occurs commonly in turf and in other open disturbed habitats.

Propagation:
Seed and from fragments of broken taproots.

Distribution:
Throughout the United States, Alaska, and Hawaii. Also in the West Indies, Mexico, Central and South America, Africa, Europe, and Asia.

Control Strategies:
Improve turf growing conditions and maintain a regular mowing schedule. Preemergence control with isoxaben. Postemergence control with repeat applications of 2,4-D, imazaquin or two- or three-way mixtures of 2,4-D, dicamba, MCPP, or MCPA. Apply in late fall and repeat in late winter. Two consecutive years of application may be required. Refer to the Appendix for additional control information. Check the herbicide label for specific application rates and turfgrass tolerance before use.

Dandelion flower

Dandelion habit with basal leaves

Dandelion "puff-ball" which contains seed

Compositae = Asteraceae (Aster or Sunflower Family)
Coat Buttons

Synonyms:
Mexican Daisy

Species:
Tridax procumbens L.

Description:
Hairy perennial from a taproot. Stems ascending or usually prostrate. Leaves opposite, hairy, with short petioles. Leaf margins irregular with large, rough teeth and small lobes. Flowers white or yellowish, in heads on long stalks at the tips of stems and branches. Flowers in warm weather. Seeds with many hairs at tip. Found in turf, open pinewoods, and disturbed areas.

Propagation:
Seed.

Distribution:
Central and southern peninsula of Florida and Hawaii. Also in the West Indies, Mexico, Central and South America, tropical Africa, tropical Asia, New Guinea, the Philippines, Taiwan, Australia, New Zealand, and Oceania. Native to tropical America.

Control Strategies:
Repeat applications of two- or three-way mixtures of 2,4-D, dicamba, MCPP, or MCPA. Other suggested options include atrazine/simazine, metribuzin, triclopyr alone or combined with clopyralid or 2,4-D, atrazine plus bentazon, imazaquin, and metsulfuron. Refer to the Appendix for additional control information. Check the herbicide label for specific application rates and turfgrass tolerance before use.

Coat Buttons habit (note: large teeth on leaf margins)

Coat Buttons flower

135

Compositae = Asteraceae (Aster or Sunflower Family)
Wedelia

Synonyms:
Creeping Oxeye

Species:
Wedelia trilobata (L.) Hitchc.

Description:
Creeping perennial, rooting at the nodes or sometimes with shallow rhizomes. Flowering branches erect, simple. Leaves opposite, three-nerved, lance-shaped to rhombic to oval, tapering at both ends, with very short petioles. Leaf margins with large teeth and often with a pair of lobes near the middle of the blade. Flowers yellow, in heads on long stalks from axils of leaves near the tip of the branch. Flowers in warm weather. Seeds bumpy and with a crown of scales at the tip. Found in disturbed areas, especially in lawns and gardens, occasionally in pinelands.

Propagation:
Seed and stem fragments.

Distribution:
Peninsula of Florida. Also in the West Indies, Central and South America, and Tropical Africa. Native to the West Indies.

Control Strategies:
Repeat applications of two- or three-way mixtures of 2,4-D, dicamba, MCPP, or MCPA. Other suggested options include atrazine/simazine, metribuzin, triclopyr alone or combined with clopyralid or 2,4-D, atrazine plus bentazon, imazaquin, and metsulfuron. Refer to the Appendix for additional control information. Check the herbicide label for specific application rates and turfgrass tolerance before use.

Wedelia habit (note: large teeth on leaf margins)

Wedelia flower

Compositae = Asteraceae (Aster or Sunflower Family)
Asiatic Hawksbeard

Synonyms:
Oriental False Hawksbeard

Species:
Youngia japonica (L.) DC.

Description:
Warm-season annual, from short taproot, often surviving winter. Leaves mostly basal, with lobes. Flowering stalks usually branched in the uppermost part of the plant. Flowers yellow to orange-yellow with five tiny teeth at end of outermost petals. Flowers in warm weather. Occurs commonly in nurseries, turf, and other open disturbed habitats.

Propagation:
Seed.

Distribution:
Pennsylvania south through Florida and west into Louisiana. Also in the West Indies. Native to Southeast Asia.

Control Strategies:
Repeat applications of two- or three-way mixtures of 2,4-D, dicamba, MCPP, or MCPA. Other suggested options include atrazine/simazine, metribuzin, triclopyr alone or combined with clopyralid or 2,4-D, atrazine plus bentazon, imazaquin, and metsulfuron. Refer to the Appendix for additional control information. Check the herbicide label for specific application rates and turfgrass tolerance before use.

Asiatic Hawksbeard basal rosette of leaves

Asiatic Hawksbeard flower

137

Convolvulaceae (Morningglory Family)
Carolina Dichondra

Synonyms:
Dichondra, Ponyfoot

Species:
Dichondra carolinensis Michx.

Description:
Creeping, prostrate perennial that roots at the nodes. Leaves alternate, sparsely-hairy, kidney-shaped to nearly round, resembling a pony's foot. Flowers inconspicuous, white. Flowers mainly in spring. Used in southern California as a lawn ground cover. Occurs in moist to wet woods, wet turf, and other moist to wet disturbed habitats.

Propagation:
Seed and stolons.

Distribution:
From Virginia to Texas. Also in the West Indies, Central and South America, Africa, Asia, Australia, and Hawaii.

Control Strategies:
Repeat applications of two- or three-way mixtures of 2,4-D, dicamba, MCPP, or MCPA. Other suggested options include atrazine/simazine, metribuzin, triclopyr alone or combined with clopyralid or 2,4-D, atrazine plus bentazon, imazaquin, and metsulfuron. Refer to the Appendix for additional control information. Check the herbicide label for specific application rates and turfgrass tolerance before use.

Dichondra habit (note: kidney-shaped to nearly round leaves)

Pony-foot-shaped leaves of Dichondra

Cruciferae = Brassicaceae (Mustard Family)
Shepherd's-purse

Synonyms:
None reported.

Species:
Capsella bursa-pastoris (L.) Medikus

Description:
Winter annual from a rosette of variously toothed or lobed leaves. Stem leaves few in number, arrow-shaped with the basal lobes extending past the stem. Flowers white, in clusters at end of stems; petals four, small. Flowers in spring. Fruit triangular or heart- to wedge-shaped, two-parted, flattened pod, resembling tiny purses. The inflorescence begins as a dense cluster of buds, gradually lengthening as the flowers die and capsules form. Occurs in most open disturbed habitats.

Propagation:
Seed.

Distribution:
Throughout North America except Arizona. Also in Hawaii, South America, Europe, North Africa, and Asia. Native to Europe.

Control Strategies:
Preemergence control with dithiopyr, isoxaben, pendimethalin, prodiamine, oryzalin, and oxadiazon. Postemergence, repeat applications of two- or three-way mixtures of 2,4-D, dicamba, MCPP, or MCPA. Other suggested postemergence options include atrazine/simazine, metribuzin, triclopyr alone or combined with clopyralid or 2,4-D, bentazon, atrazine plus bentazon, imazaquin, and metsulfuron. Refer to the Appendix for additional control information. Check the herbicide label for specific application rates and turfgrass tolerance before use.

Shepherd's-purse habit with lobed or toothed basal leaves

Shepherd's-purse inflorescence

Triangular or wedge-shaped Shepherd's-purse fruit

139

Cruciferae = *Brassicaceae* (Mustard Family)
Hairy Bittercress

Synonyms:
None reported.

Species:
Cardamine hirsuta L.

Description:
Winter annual from a basal rosette of dark green, dissected leaves. Leaf segments rounded to wedge-shaped, lower petioles hairy near the base. Flowers white, in dense clusters at end of stems, petals four. Flowers in late winter into spring. Fruit a flattened capsule, more than ten times longer than broad. Occurs in wet disturbed areas.

Propagation:
Seed.

Distribution:
Maine into Florida and west to Nebraska, Texas, and Washington. Also in Hawaii, Canada, Europe, Asia, North Africa, and Australia. Native to Eurasia.

Control Strategies:
Preemergence control with dithiopyr, isoxaben, oryzalin, and oxadiazon. Postemergence control with repeat applications of two- or three-way mixtures of 2,4-D, dicamba, MCPP, or MCPA in late fall or winter. Other options include atrazine/simazine, metribuzin, triclopyr alone or combined with clopyralid or 2,4-D, atrazine plus bentazon, imazaquin, and metsulfuron. Refer to the Appendix for additional control information. Check the herbicide label for specific application rates and turfgrass tolerance before use.

Hairy Bittercress habit with basal rosette of leaves

Narrow, elongated Hairy Bittercress fruit

Cruciferae = *Brassicaceae* (Mustard Family)
Swinecress

Synonyms:
Lesser Swinecress

Species:
Coronopus didymus (L.) Sm.

Description:
Freely-branched, prostrate winter annual. Leaves alternate, divided into numerous small segments. Stems usually partly angular or grooved. Tiny, white flowers arranged in clusters at ends of stems and leaf axils, petals four. Flowers in spring. Fruit with two inflated rounded sections. Foliage strongly pungent when crushed. Occurs in turf and fields.

Propagation:
Seed.

Distribution:
Throughout the eastern half of the United States as far west as Texas and California. Also in southern Canada, the West Indies, South America, Europe, and North Africa. Native to Europe.

Control Strategies:
Preemergence control with isoxaben and oxadiazon. Post-emergence control with repeat applications of two- or three-way mixtures of 2,4-D, dicamba, MCPP, or MCPA. Other options include atrazine/simazine, bentazon, metribuzin, triclopyr alone or combined with clopyralid or 2,4-D, atrazine plus bentazon, imazaquin, and metsulfuron. Refer to the Appendix for additional control information. Check the herbicide label for specific application rates and turfgrass tolerance before use.

Swinecress habit

Swinecress leaves

141

Cruciferae = Brassicaceae (Mustard Family)
Pinnate Tansymustard

Synonyms:
Western Tansymustard

Species:
Descurainia pinnata (Walt.) Britt.

Description:
Winter annual with one to several densely hairy stems. Basal leaves divided twice into small segments, densely hairy, resembling those of Tansy, hence the common name. Stem leaves divided once into small segments, densely hairy. Basal leaves wither as the flowering stem develops. Flowers bright yellow to almost white. Flowers in spring. Fruit long-stalked, club-shaped, elongated but short, several seeded. Seed dark red. Occurs in sandy soils in turf, fields, and disturbed areas.

Propagation:
Seed.

Distribution:
Virginia, south into Florida, west to Wyoming, Colorado, and California and inland up through Montana. Also in southern Canada.

Control Strategies:
Repeat applications of two- or three-way mixtures of 2,4-D, dicamba, MCPP, or MCPA. Other options include atrazine/simazine, bentazon, metribuzin, triclopyr alone or combined with clopyralid or 2,4-D, atrazine plus bentazon, imazaquin, and metsulfuron. Refer to the Appendix for additional control information. Check the herbicide label for specific application rates and turfgrass tolerance before use.

Pinnate Tansymustard basal leaves

Pinnate Tansymustard habit

Pinnate Tansymustard flowers

Cruciferae = *Brassicaceae* (Mustard Family)
Virginia Pepperweed

Synonyms:
None reported.

Species:
Lepidium virginicum L.

Description:
Winter, less so a summer annual from a rosette of leaves. Stems up to 2 feet tall, smooth, erect, and freely branched. Basal and stem leaves toothed, lobed, or deeply notched. Basal leaves lacking on mature plants. Stem leaves alternate, reduced in size, more toothed, and lobed toward the apex of the plant. Produces spike-like clusters of tiny white flowers at end of branches. Flowers in spring. Seedpod round, flat with notch at tip. Fruit with distinctive mustard or peppery taste. Occurs widely in open disturbed areas.

Propagation:
Seed.

Distribution:
Throughout the United States except for Arizona and New Mexico. Also in Saskatchewan and Manitoba. Native to North America.

Control Strategies:
Preemergence control with isoxaben. Postemergence control with repeat applications of two- or three-way mixtures of 2,4-D, dicamba, MCPP, or MCPA. Other options include atrazine/simazine, bentazon, metribuzin, triclopyr alone or combined with clopyralid or 2,4-D, atrazine plus bentazon, imazaquin, and metsulfuron. Refer to the Appendix for additional control information. Check the herbicide label for specific application rates and turfgrass tolerance before use.

Virginia Pepperweed fruiting stem

Virginia Pepperweed habit with basal rosette of leaves

143

Cruciferae = Brassicaceae (Mustard Family)
Sibara

Synonyms:
Virginia Winged Rockcress

Species:
Sibara virginica (L.) Rollins

Description:
Winter annual from a rosette of deeply dissected leaves. Leaves slightly hairy near base of plant. Leaf segments narrow, the terminal segment somewhat broader. Flowers white, with four small petals. Flowers in spring. Fruit stalked, long, very narrow, many-seeded, flat. Distinguished from hairy bittercress (*Cardamine hirsuta* L.) by larger fruit and narrow leaf segments. Occurs in woods, fields, roadsides, and disturbed habitats.

Propagation:
Seed.

Distribution:
West Virginia, south into northern Florida, west to Texas and California, and inland through Missouri into Kansas and Illinois. Also in Mexico.

Control Strategies:
Repeat applications of two- or three-way mixtures of 2,4-D, dicamba, MCPP, or MCPA. Other options include atrazine/simazine, bentazon, metribuzin, triclopyr alone or combined with clopyralid or 2,4-D, atrazine plus bentazon, imazaquin, and metsulfuron. Refer to the Appendix for additional control information. Check the herbicide label for specific application rates and turfgrass tolerance before use.

Sibara with deeply dissected leaves

Narrow, elongated, flat Sibara fruit

Euphorbiaceae (Spurge Family)
Roundleaf Spurge

Synonyms:
Heartleaf Sandmat

Species:
Chamaesyce cordifolia (Ell.) Small; [_Euphorbia cordifolia_ Ell.]

Description:
Mat-forming warm-season annual with much-branched, smooth stems not rooting at the nodes. Stems with "milky sap." Leaves opposite, round, or nearly so, with smooth margins and lopsided bases. Flowers mid- to late-summer. Capsule smooth, three-lobed and -seeded. Found in open sandy areas.

Propagation:
Seed.

Distribution:
North Carolina, south through Florida and west into Texas.

Control Strategies:
Check for and control parasitic nematodes, if present. Post-emergence herbicide control includes repeat applications of two- or three-way mixtures of 2,4-D, dicamba, MCPP, or MCPA. Other options include atrazine/simazine, metribuzin, triclopyr alone or combined with clopyralid or 2,4-D, atrazine plus bentazon, imazaquin, and metsulfuron. Refer to the Appendix for additional control information. Check the herbicide label for specific application rates and turfgrass tolerance before use.

Roundleaf Spurge leaves

Roundleaf Spurge habit

Smooth leaf margins of Roundleaf Spurge

145

Euphorbiaceae (Spurge Family)
Sand-dune Spurge

Synonyms:
Coastal Dune Sandmat

Species:
Chamaesyce cumulicola Small; [*Euphorbia cumulicola* Small]

Description:
Mat-forming warm-season annual or perennial with much-branched, smooth stems not rooting at the nodes. Stems with "milky sap." Leaves opposite, elliptic, with smooth margins and lopsided bases, nearly all the same size on a single plant. Flowers mid- through late-summer. Capsule smooth, three-lobed and -seeded. Found inland on dune-like sandhills and near the beach on dunes.

Propagation:
Seed.

Distribution:
Central and south peninsula and extreme western panhandle of Florida.

Control Strategies:
Check for and control parasitic nematodes, if present. Post-emergence herbicide control includes repeat applications of two- or three-way mixtures of 2,4-D, dicamba, MCPP, or MCPA. Other options include atrazine/simazine, metribuzin, triclopyr alone or combined with clopyralid or 2,4-D, atrazine plus bentazon, imazaquin, and metsulfuron. Refer to the Appendix for additional control information. Check the herbicide label for specific application rates and turfgrass tolerance before use.

Sand-dune Spurge habit

Elliptic-shaped, smoothed margin
Sand-dune Spurge leaves

Euphorbiaceae (Spurge Family)
Garden Spurge

Synonyms:
Pillpod Sandmat

Species:
Chamaesyce hirta (L.) Millsp.; [*Euphorbia hirta* L.]

Description:
Taprooted warm-season annual with erect to sprawling, very hairy, branched stems. Leaves opposite, with an unequal base, teeth on margins, hairy. Flowers tiny in clusters at stem tip and from bases of leaves, hairy. Flowers mid- through late-summer. Occurs in disturbed and waste areas.

Propagation:
Seed.

Distribution:
South Carolina south throughout Florida and west to Alabama. Also in the West Indies, Mexico, Central and South America.

Control Strategies:
Check for and control parasitic nematodes, if present. Pre-emergence control with isoxaben. Postemergence control with repeat applications of two- or three-way mixtures of 2,4-D, dicamba, MCPP, or MCPA. Other suggested options include atrazine/simazine, metribuzin, triclopyr alone or combined with clopyralid or 2,4-D, atrazine plus bentazon, imazaquin, and metsulfuron. Refer to the Appendix for additional control information. Check the herbicide label for specific application rates and turfgrass tolerance before use.

Garden Spurge habit

Pubescent Garden Spurge leaves with teeth on margins

Euphorbiaceae (Spurge Family)
Hyssop Spurge

Synonyms:
Hyssopleaf Sandmat

Species:
Chamaesyce hyssopifolia L. Small; [*Euphorbia hyssopifolia* L.]

Description:
Erect or ascending warm-season annual. Stems smooth, branched at upper nodes and with "milky sap." Leaves opposite, oblong to almost linear, with toothed margins and lopsided bases. Flowers mid- through late-summer. Capsules in clusters, smooth, three-lobed and three-seeded. Found in lawns and disturbed areas.

Propagation:
Seed.

Distribution:
South Carolina into Florida and west into Texas, New Mexico, and California. Also occurs in the West Indies, South America, and Java.

Control Strategies:
Check for and control parasitic nematodes, if present. Post-emergence herbicide control includes repeat applications of two- or three-way mixtures of 2,4-D, dicamba, MCPP, or MCPA. Other suggested options include atrazine/simazine, metribuzin, triclopyr alone or combined with clopyralid or 2,4-D, atrazine plus bentazon, imazaquin, and metsulfuron. Refer to the Appendix for additional control information. Check the herbicide label for specific application rates and turfgrass tolerance before use.

Hyssop Spurge habit

Oblong-shaped Hyssop Spurge leaves and toothed margins with lopsided bases

Euphorbiaceae (Spurge Family)
Spotted Spurge

Synonyms:
Prostrate Spurge, Spotted Sandmat

Species:
Chamaesyce maculata (L.) Small; [*Euphorbia maculata* L.]

Description:
Summer annual with freely branched prostrate, mat-forming stems that do not root at the nodes. Stems smooth or hairy, with "milky" sap. Leaves opposite, usually with a reddish spot, not symmetrical. Flowers mid- through late-summer. Occurring in moist open habitats and any disturbed area. Prostrate spurge [*Chamaesyce humistrata* (Engelm.) Small] is similar but roots at the nodes and occurs in wet open habitats..

Propagation:
Seed.

Distribution:
Eastern United States, west to North Dakota and Texas and into California and Oregon. Also in Canada, Mexico, Central America, South America, Japan, New Zealand, and Lebanon.

Control Strategies:
Check for and control parasitic nematodes, if present. Pre-emergence control with isoxaben, dithiopyr, and pendimethalin. Postemergence control with repeat applications of two- or three-way mixtures of 2,4-D, dicamba, MCPP, or MCPA. Other suggested options include atrazine/simazine, metribuzin, triclopyr alone or combined with clopyralid or 2,4-D, atrazine plus bentazon, imazaquin, and metsulfuron. Refer to the Appendix for additional control information. Check the herbicide label for specific application rates and turfgrass tolerance before use.

Spotted Spurge habit

Spotted Spurge leaves with reddish spot, toothed margins, and hairs

149

Euphorbiaceae (Spurge Family)
Niruri

Synonyms:
Gale-of-the-wind, Gripeweed, Leaf-flower, Little Mimosa, Cannonball Weed

Species:
Phyllanthus niruri L.

Description:
Small erect summer annual with angled or grooved stems. Leaves thin, smooth-margined, oblong, arranged in two rows on the branchlets. Flowers inconspicuous. Flowers in warm months. Fruit green, smooth, without a stalk, singly attached to underside of branch. Chamberbitter [*Phyllanthus urinaria* L.] is a similar species and also a summer annual but has fruit covered with small ridges resembling warts. Fruit open explosively. Occurs frequently in turf and nurseries and in other disturbed habitats.

Propagation:
Seed, often spread from containers and ornamental pots.

Distribution:
Alabama, Georgia, Florida, South Carolina, Texas, New Mexico, south into Argentina and is quickly spreading. Occurs throughout the tropics. Native to Asia.

Control Strategies:
Possible preemergence control with oxadiazon. Post-emergence control with repeat applications of two- or three-way mixtures of 2,4-D, dicamba, MCPP, or MCPA. Other suggested options include atrazine/simazine, metribuzin, triclopyr alone or combined with clopyralid or 2,4-D, atrazine plus bentazon, and metsulfuron. Refer to the Appendix for additional control information. Check the herbicide label for specific application rates and turfgrass tolerance before use.

Niruri habit

Chamberbitter with green, warty fruit connected directly on leaf axils

Euphorbiaceae (Spurge Family)
Longstalked Phyllanthus

Synonyms:
Mascarene Island Leaf-flower

Species:
Phyllanthus tenellus Roxb.

Description:
Erect perennial with smooth leaves and stems. Leaves thin, smooth margined, oval, arranged in two rows on the branchlets or singly in spirals on the main stem. Flowers inconspicuous. Flowers in warm months. Fruit green, smooth, round, on long stalks from the leaf axils, opens explosively. Occurs in open hammocks and in disturbed areas, a frequent nursery weed.

Propagation:
Seed, often spread from container ornamental pots.

Distribution:
Alabama, Georgia, South Carolina, and throughout Florida. Also in Australia and Hawaii. Native to Africa and the Mascarene Islands.

Control Strategies:
Possible preemergence control with oxadiazon. Postemergence control with repeat applications of two- or three-way mixtures of 2,4-D, dicamba, MCPP, or MCPA. Other suggested options include atrazine/simazine, metribuzin, triclopyr alone or combined with clopyralid or 2,4-D, atrazine plus bentazon, imazaquin, and metsulfuron. Refer to the Appendix for additional control information. Check the herbicide label for specific application rates and turfgrass tolerance before use.

Longstalked Phyllanthus habit

Longstalked Phyllanthus stem with fruit on long stalks from the leaf axils

151

Geraniaceae (Geranium Family)
Redstem Filaree

Synonyms:
Redstem Stork's-bill

Species:
Erodium cicutarium (L.) L'Her. ex Ait.

Description:
Prostrate to semierect winter annual or biennial with numerous branches that radiate from the basal rosette. Leaves
hairy, dissected into numerous segments, opposite on upper
portion of stem, alternate below. Flowers pinkish-purple, in
clusters of six to nine on long stalks. Flowers in spring.
Fruit a five-parted capsule that forms a characteristic
"stork's bill" up to 2 inches (5 cm) long. Occurs as a common weed in disturbed sites.

Propagation:
Seed.

Distribution:
In most of the United States, Alaska, and Hawaii, excluding
Florida. Also in Canada, Greenland, Mexico, Central and
South America, Europe, South Africa, and Australia. Native
to the Mediterranean region.

Control Strategies:
Preemergence control with isoxaben, oryzalin, and
pendimethalin. Postemergence control with repeat applications of two- or three-way mixtures of 2,4-D, dicamba,
MCPP, or MCPA. Other suggested options include
atrazine/simazine, metribuzin, triclopyr alone or combined
with clopyralid or 2,4-D, atrazine plus bentazon, imazaquin, and metsulfuron. Refer to the Appendix for additional
control information. Check the herbicide label for specific
application rates and turfgrass tolerance before use.

Redstem Filaree habit

Redstem Filaree flowers

Redstem Filaree fruit capsule,
resembling a "stork's bill"

Geraniaceae (Geranium Family)
Carolina Geranium

Synonyms:
Wild Geranium, Crane's-bill, Stork's-bill

Species:
Geranium carolinianum L.

Description:
Diffusely-branched semierect winter annual or biennial. Stems greenish-pink to red, densely hairy. Leaves with long petioles, hairy, dissected into variously divided segments, margins blunt toothed. Flowers pink to purplish with five petals. Flowers in spring. Fruit a five-parted capsule that forms a "stork's bill" up to 0.5 inch (1.2 cm) long. Occurs commonly in all open disturbed habitats with sandy soils, especially fields, lawns, roadsides, and pastures.

Propagation:
Seed.

Distribution:
Throughout the continental United States and Hawaii. Also in Canada, the West Indies, Mexico, Central and South America, and Australia.

Control Strategies:
Preemergence control with dithiopyr and isoxaben. Postemergence control with repeat applications of two- or three-way mixtures of 2,4-D, dicamba, MCPP, or MCPA. Other options include atrazine/simazine, metribuzin, and triclopyr alone or combined with clopyralid or 2,4-D, atrazine plus bentazon, imazaquin, and metsulfuron. Refer to the Appendix for additional control information. Check the herbicide label for specific application rates and turfgrass tolerance before use.

Carolina Geranium habit

Carolina Geranium flower and deeply dissected leaves

153

Labiatae = Lamiaceae (Mint Family)
Ground Ivy

Synonyms:
Creeping Charlie, Gill-Over-the-Ground, Run-Away-Robin, Field Balm

Species:
Glechoma hederacea L.

Description:
Prostrate, creeping perennial with four-sided (square), hairy stems. Leaves opposite, kidney-shaped to rounded, prominently veined and with scalloped margins. Readily roots at stem nodes. Emits mint-like odor when crushed. Flowers bluish to purplish with red speckles, arranged in groups of three to seven at stem ends or leaf axils. Flowers in spring. More common in shaded than full sunlight of disturbed areas. Henbit (*Lamium amplexicaule* L.) appears similar but lacks creeping stems and does not root at the nodes. Common mallow (*Malva neglecta* Wallr.) is also similar but has alternate leaves and round stems.

Propagation:
Seed and creeping stems.

Distribution:
In the eastern United States, extending south to the Piedmont region of the southern states; Georgia to Kansas, Oklahoma, Missouri, California, the Pacific Northwest, and Alaska. Also in Canada, Europe, and Asia. Native to Europe.

Ground Ivy habit with bluish flowers

Control Strategies:
Repeat applications of two- or three-way mixtures of 2,4-D, dicamba, MCPP, or MCPA. Other suggested options include atrazine/simazine, metribuzin, triclopyr alone or combined with clopyralid or 2,4-D. Refer to the Appendix for additional control information. Check the herbicide label for specific application rates and turfgrass tolerance before use.

Ground Ivy stems with opposite, kidney-shaped, scalloped-margined leaves

Labiatae = Lamiaceae (Mint Family)
Henbit

Synonyms:
Henbit Deadnettle

Species:
Lamium amplexicaule L.

Description:
Sparsely-hairy winter annual with greenish to purplish, tender, four-sided (square) stems. Similar in appearance to purple deadnettle (*Lamium purpureum* L.) but upper leaves lack petioles. Leaves opposite, broadly egg-shaped with bluntly toothed margins, and prominent veins on underside. Flowers reddish-purple with darker coloring in spots on lower petal, arranged in whorls. Flowers in spring. Found in open disturbed sites, often in fields and along roadsides.

Propagation:
Seed.

Distribution:
Throughout most of North America. Also in the West Indies, South America, Europe, Africa, Asia, and Australia. Native to Europe.

Control Strategies:
Preemergence control with atrazine/simazine, benefin, dithiopyr, isoxaben, oryzalin, pendimethalin, and prodiamine. Postemergence control with repeat applications of two- or three-way mixtures of 2,4-D, dicamba, MCPP, or MCPA. Other options include atrazine/simazine, metribuzin, triclopyr alone or combined with clopyralid or 2,4-D, and atrazine plus bentazon. Refer to the Appendix for additional control information. Check the herbicide label for specific application rates and turfgrass tolerance before use.

Henbit habit

Henbit with square stems and reddish-purple flowers

155

Labiatae = Lamiaceae (Mint Family)
Purple Deadnettle

Synonyms:
Red Deadnettle, Red Henbit

Species:
Lamium purpureum L.

Description:
Sparsely-hairy winter annual with greenish to purplish, tender, four-sided (square) stems. Leaves opposite, broadly egg-shaped with bluntly toothed margins. Lower leaves on long petioles, upper leaves on short petioles (as opposed to no petioles on upper leaves of henbit [*Lamium amplexicaule* L.]). Leaves often reddish or purplish tinged. Flowers reddish purple with darker coloring in spots on lower petal, arranged in whorls. Flowers in spring. Found in fields, gardens, turf, and other disturbed areas.

Purple Deadnettle with square stems

Propagation:
Seed.

Distribution:
In most of the United States except for the Rocky Mountains. Also in Canada, Greenland, Europe, and Asia. Native to Eurasia.

Reddish-purple tinged Purple
Deadnettle leaves

Control Strategies:
May respond similarly to preemergence herbicides for henbit. Postemergence control with repeat applications of two- or three-way mixtures of 2,4-D, dicamba, MCPP, or MCPA. Other options include atrazine/simazine, metribuzin, triclopyr alone or combined with clopyralid or 2,4-D, and atrazine plus bentazon. Refer to the Appendix for additional control information. Check the herbicide label for specific application rates and turfgrass tolerance before use.

Purple Deadnettle egg-shaped leaves
with bluntly toothed margins and
reddish-purple flowers

Labiatae = Lamiaceae (Mint Family)
Healall

Synonyms:
Carpenterweed, Common Selfheal

Species:
Prunella vulgaris L.

Description:
Perennial branched herb with upright to reclining growth habit. Numerous, opposite elliptic to lance-shaped leaves on square stems. Leaves and stems hairy. Lower leaves with long petioles, upper leaves sessile. Dense clusters of pale violet to purple trumpet-shaped flowers at the end of branches. Flowers in spring.

Propagation:
Seed and stolons.

Distribution:
Throughout the continental United States and Hawaii. Also in Canada, Central America, Europe, Asia, and Australia.

Control Strategies:
Repeat applications of two- or three-way mixtures of 2,4-D, dicamba, MCPP, or MCPA. Other suggested options include atrazine/simazine, metribuzin, triclopyr alone or combined with clopyralid or 2,4-D, atrazine plus bentazon, imazaquin, and metsulfuron. Refer to the Appendix for additional control information. Check the herbicide label for specific application rates and turfgrass tolerance before use.

Healall with square stems and lance-shaped leaves

157

Labiatae = *Lamiaceae* (Mint Family)
Florida Betony

Synonyms:
Rattlesnake Weed, Florida Hedgenettle, Hedgenettle

Species:
Stachys floridana Shuttlew.

Description:
Smooth or hairy, delicate, freely branched, upright perennial herb, from slender underground stems with segmented
white tubers resembling a "rattlesnake's rattle." Leaves opposite, long stalked, lance-shaped, with toothed margins,
usually with a nearly flat base. Stems square. Flowers white
to pink with purple spots, joined together except for the tips
which are two-lipped. The upper lip is hooded, the lower
lip is three-lobed. Flowers mainly in early spring. Turf,
roadsides, thickets, and shrub borders. Thought to be
moved with nursery stock and ornamental plants.

Propagation:
Primarily by tubers, secondarily by seed.

Distribution:
Native to Florida until it escaped in the 1940s or 1950s.
Now found from Virginia to Texas.

Control Strategies:
Fumigate contaminated soil. Repeat applications of two- or
three-way mixtures of 2,4-D, dicamba, MCPP, or MCPA.
Other suggested options include atrazine/simazine,
metribuzin, triclopyr alone or combined with clopyralid or
2,4-D, and atrazine plus bentazon. Refer to the Appendix
for additional control information. Check the herbicide
label for specific application rates and turfgrass tolerance
before use.

Florida Betony with square stems and
lance- (or shovel) shaped leaves

Florida Betony flowers

White, "rattlesnake's rattle"-shaped
Florida Betony tuber

Leguminosae = *Fabaceae* (Bean or Pea Family)
Alyce-clover

Synonyms:
Oneleaf-clover, White Moneywort

Species:
Alysicarpus vaginalis (L.) DC.

Description:
Perennial with trailing or ascending, smooth stems. Leaves single, round to narrow, with petioles. Lanceolate stipules at each node. Flowers purple, pink, or orange, in racemes. Flowers in warm months. Fruit a jointed pod (loment) which does not break apart when ripe. Found in most disturbed areas and low open woods.

Propagation:
Seed.

Distribution:
Throughout Florida into Georgia and west to Louisiana. Also in the West Indies, South America, tropical Africa, and tropical Asia.

Alyce-clover smooth stem

Control Strategies:
Repeat applications of two- or three-way mixtures of 2,4-D, dicamba, MCPP, or MCPA. Other options include atrazine/simazine, metribuzin, triclopyr alone or combined with clopyralid or 2,4-D, atrazine plus bentazon, imazaquin, and metsulfuron. Refer to the Appendix for additional control information. Check the herbicide label for specific application rates and turfgrass tolerance before use.

Jointed pod fruit of Alyce-clover

Alyce-clover habit

Alyce-clover leaves

159

Leguminosae = *Fabaceae* (Bean or Pea Family)
Creeping Beggarweed

Synonyms:
Zarzabacoa-comun

Species:
Desmodium canum (J. F. Gmel.) Schinz & Thellung;
[*Desmodium incanum* DC.]

Description:
Perennial from a large taproot with many, long, extensively branched runners which root at nodes. Leaves with three leaflets; leaflets quite variable as to size, elliptic, pointed at tip, rounded at base, hairy. Stems ascending to erect, hairy. Flowers pink to rose. Flowers in warm months. Fruit with six to eight rounded segments which are straight across the back while still hooked together. Segments break apart easily when ripe and attach to clothing or hair. Occurs in turf, open woods, and disturbed areas.

Propagation:
Seed, stolons, and broken taproots.

Distribution:
Throughout Florida and in southern Texas. Also in the West Indies, Mexico, Central and South America, Galapagos Islands, and Tropical Africa.

Control Strategies:
Repeat applications of two- or three-way mixtures of 2,4-D, dicamba, MCPP, or MCPA. Other suggested options include atrazine/simazine, metribuzin, triclopyr alone or combined with clopyralid or 2,4-D, atrazine plus bentazon, imazaquin, and metsulfuron. Refer to the Appendix for additional control information. Check the herbicide label for specific application rates and turfgrass tolerance before use.

Creeping Beggarweed leaves with three leaflets

Creeping Beggarweed habit

Creeping Beggarweed fruit leaflets

Leguminosae = Fabaceae (Bean or Pea Family)
Threeflower Beggarweed

Synonyms:
Sagotia Beggarweed, Threeflower Ticktrefoil

Species:
Desmodium triflorum (L.) DC.

Description:
Perennial with prostrate hairy stems that root at nodes. Leaves with three very small heart-shaped leaflets. Flowers blue or purplish-pink. Flowers in warm months. Fruits quite small, usually with two to four rounded segments which are straight across the back while still hooked together. Segments break apart easily when ripe and attach to clothing or hair. Occurs in turf and in open pinewoods.

Propagation:
Seed and stolons.

Distribution:
Peninsula and eastern panhandle of Florida. Also in the West Indies, Mexico, Central and South America, Asia, India, Sri Lanka, Burma, Thailand, Malaysia, Indo-China, Pacific Islands, Australia, and Africa. Native to the Old World.

Control Strategies:
Repeat applications of two- or three-way mixtures of 2,4-D, dicamba, MCPP, or MCPA. Other suggested options include atrazine/simazine, metribuzin, triclopyr alone or combined with clopyralid or 2,4-D, atrazine plus bentazon, imazaquin, and metsulfuron. Refer to the Appendix for additional control information. Check the herbicide label for specific application rates and turfgrass tolerance before use.

Threeflower Beggarweed leaves with three heart-shaped leaflets

Threeflower Beggarweed flower

161

Leguminosae = *Fabaceae* (Bean or Pea Family)
Creeping Indigo

Synonyms:
Trailing Indigo

Species:
Indigofera spicata Forsk.

Description:
Perennial with hairy creeping stems. Leaves with seven to nine leaflets, hairy. Numerous pink flowers on spikes from the bases of the leaves. Flowers in warm months. Fruits linear, pointed downward on the axis, tightly clustered. Occurs in almost all habitats except very dry sites; common in turf.

Propagation:
Seed.

Distribution:
Peninsula of Florida. Also in Madagascar, the Mascarene Islands, Yemen, India, Sri Lanka, and southeast Asia. Native to Africa.

Control Strategies:
Repeat applications of two- or three-way mixtures of 2,4-D, dicamba, MCPP, or MCPA. Other suggested options include atrazine/simazine, metribuzin, triclopyr alone or combined with clopyralid or 2,4-D, atrazine plus bentazon, imazaquin, and metsulfuron. Refer to the Appendix for additional control information. Check the herbicide label for specific application rates and turfgrass tolerance before use.

Creeping Indigo habit with pink flowers

Creeping Indigo linear-shaped fruit, pointed downward in a tight cluster

Leguminosae = *Fabaceae* (Bean or Pea Family)
Common Lespedeza

Synonyms:
Annual Lespedeza, Japanese-clover

Species:
Kummerowia striata (Thunb.) Schindler; [*Lespedeza striata* (Thunb.) Hook. & Arn.]

Description:
Wiry, prostrate, freely-branched summer annual. Leaves with three obovate to oblong, smooth leaflets. Leaflets with prominent midvein and many parallel veins that are nearly perpendicular to the midvein. Flowers late summer. Single flowers, pink to purple, in leaf axils. Found in dry soils of open woods and fields, frequently in turf and disturbed areas.

Propagation:
Seed.

Distribution:
Common in the southern United States, north to Pennsylvania, west to Texas, Kansas, and Missouri. Native to Asia.

Control Strategies:
Repeat applications of two- or three-way mixtures of 2,4-D, dicamba, MCPP, or MCPA. Other suggested options include atrazine/simazine, metribuzin, triclopyr alone or combined with clopyralid or 2,4-D, atrazine plus bentazon, imazaquin, and metsulfuron. Refer to the Appendix for additional control information. Check the herbicide label for specific application rates and turfgrass tolerance before use.

Common Lespedeza leaves with three oblong, smooth leaflets. Leaflets with prominent midvein and parallel veins.

Common Lespedeza flower

163

Leguminosae = *Fabaceae* (Bean or Pea Family)
Spotted Burclover

Synonyms:
Spotted Medick

Species:
Medicago arabica (L.) Huds.

Description:
Winter annual with smooth prostrate stems. Leaves alternate, each composed of three leaflets. Leaflets wedge-shaped, as long as broad, and toothed from mid-blade to tip. Leaflets with conspicuous reddish-purple spot in center. Stipules broad and coarsely toothed. Small, bright yellow flowers (two to five) borne in a cluster. Flowers mostly in spring. Seed pods spirally twisted and covered with spines. Found in fields, roadsides, and open disturbed areas.

Propagation:
Seed.

Distribution:
In the states of the Northwest, Southeast, Midwest, Pacific Northwest, and in California. Also in Canada, Central and South America, Europe, and Asia. Native to the Mediterranean region.

Control Strategies:
Repeat applications of two- or three-way mixtures of 2,4-D, dicamba, MCPP, or MCPA. Other suggested options include atrazine/simazine, metribuzin, triclopyr alone or combined with clopyralid or 2,4-D, atrazine plus bentazon, imazaquin, and metsulfuron. Refer to the Appendix for additional control information. Check the herbicide label for specific application rates and turfgrass tolerance before use.

Spotted Burclover leaves with three leaflets and yellow flower

Spotted Burclover habit with reddish-purple spotted leaves

Spirally twisted and spine-covered Spotted Burclover seed pods

Leguminosae = *Fabaceae* (Bean or Pea Family)
Black Medic

Synonyms:
Black Medick

Species:
Medicago lupulina L.

Description:
Dark green taprooted summer annual or less commonly a winter annual or biennial with a spreading, prostrate growth habit. Leaves alternate, composed of three leaflets on square stems. Leaflets wedge-shaped, as long as broad, toothed near tip, with a small spur at tip. Produces tight, compressed cluster of bright yellow flowers (10 to 50) at the leaf axils. At maturity, each flower forms a tightly coiled black seedpod. Flowers in summer. Occurs commonly in any open disturbed habitat, frequently in all turf.

Propagation:
Seed.

Distribution:
Throughout the continental United States and Hawaii. Also in Canada, the West Indies, Central and South America, Europe, Asia, and Australia. Native to Europe.

Control Strategies:
Repeat applications of two- or three-way mixtures of 2,4-D, dicamba, MCPP, or MCPA. Other suggested options include atrazine/simazine, metribuzin, triclopyr alone or combined with clopyralid or 2,4-D, atrazine plus bentazon, imazaquin, and metsulfuron. Refer to the Appendix for additional control information. Check the herbicide label for specific application rates and turfgrass tolerance before use.

Black Medic with leaves composed of three leaflets on square stems and yellow flowers

Black Medic coiled black seedpod

165

Leguminosae = *Fabaceae* (Bean or Pea Family)
Mimosa-vine

Synonyms:
Sensitive Vine, Powderpuff

Species:
Mimosa strigillosa Torr. & A. Gray

Description:
Perennial herb with prostrate, creeping stems. Stems with many stiff, somewhat appressed hairs. Leaves twice divided with four to six pairs of branches (pinnae) each with ten to fifteen pairs of leaflets. Flowers pink, in ball-shaped heads at the tip of long stalks. Flowers in warm months. Occurs in turf, along streams and in hammocks.

Propagation:
Seed and stem fragments.

Distribution:
Georgia and Florida west to Oklahoma and Texas. Also in Mexico and South America.

Control Strategies:
Repeat applications of two- or three-way mixtures of 2,4-D, dicamba, MCPP, or MCPA. Other suggested options include atrazine/simazine, metribuzin, triclopyr alone or combined with clopyralid or 2,4-D, atrazine plus bentazon, imazaquin, and metsulfuron. Refer to the Appendix for additional control information. Check the herbicide label for specific application rates and turfgrass tolerance before use.

Mimosa-vine with pinnately divided leaves

Ball-shaped Mimosa-vine flower

Leguminosae = Fabaceae (Bean or Pea Family)
Kudzu

Synonyms:
None reported.

Species:
Pueraria montana (Lour.) Merr. var. *lobata* (Willd.) Maesen & S. M. Almeida [*Pueraria lobata* (Willd.) Ohwi]

Description:
Aggressive robust perennial herbaceous twining vine that becomes woody with age, with large woody rootstock. Can climb to tree tops and form large blankets of draped vegetation. Vines can grow up to 12 inches (30 cm) daily. Compound leaves large with three ovate to suborbicular leaflets, alternate, leaflet margins entire to three-lobed with pointed tips, pubescent beneath. Flowers purple, occur in racemes, and emit "grape Kool-Aid odor." Flowers late summer until frost. Fruiting legume seedpods brown with long tan to bronze hairs. Very sensitive to frost, leaving tan or straw-colored vines. Intolerant of frequent mowing and cultivation. Found along roadsides, embankments, forests, utility rights-of-way, abandoned fields, fencerows, and waste areas.

Propagation:
Spreads prolifically by stolons and stem fragments, rarely by seed.

Distribution:
Introduced into Florida and the southeastern United States as a forage and for soil conservation from eastern Asia. Native to Asia. Occurs westward to Texas and Oklahoma, and north to Missouri, Illinois, Pennsylvania, and Massachusetts in disturbed sites.

Control Strategies:
Maintain regular mowing schedule. Repeat applications of triclopyr alone or combined with clopyralid, 2,4-D, or metsulfuron. Spot treat with glyphosate. Refer to the Appendix for additional control information. Check the herbicide label for specific application rates and turfgrass tolerance before use.

Kudzu habit

Kudzu vine

Kudzu compound leaf with 3 leaflets

Kudzu flowers in racemes

Leguminosae = Fabaceae (Bean or Pea Family)
Hemp Sesbania

Synonyms:
Danglepod

Species:
Sesbania exaltata (Raf.) Rydb. ex A. W. Hill; [*Sesbania exaltata* (Raf.) Cory = S. *macrocarpa* Muhl. ex. Nutt.; *Sesbania herbacea* (Mill.) McVaugh]

Description:
Tall summer annual herb to 10 feet (3 m) with smooth, waxy, upright stems. Leaves alternate, compound, to 1 foot (30 cm) long. Leaflets occur in even numbers 20 to 70 per leaf. Young leaves clustered at tip of main stem nearly hairless. Flowers yellow, often with purple or red spots. Flowers midsummer into early fall. Fruit (legume) a long narrow pod, becoming papery with age. Found along roadsides, in pastures, fields, and other moist disturbed areas. Toxic if ingested.

Propagation:
Seed.

Distribution:
Massachusetts south through Florida, and west to Texas, South Dakota, Arizona, and California. Also in northern Mexico.

Control Strategies:
Maintain a regular mowing schedule. Repeat applications of two- or three-way mixtures of 2,4-D, dicamba, MCPP, or MCPA. Other suggested options include atrazine/simazine, metribuzin, triclopyr alone or combined with clopyralid or 2,4-D, atrazine plus bentazon, metsulfuron, and quinclorac. Refer to the Appendix for additional control information. Check the herbicide label for specific application rates and turfgrass tolerance before use.

Hemp Sesbania habit with long, compound leaves

Leguminosae = *Fabaceae* (Bean or Pea Family)
Southern Pencil-flower

Synonyms:
Cheesy-toes

Species:
Stylosanthes hamata (L.) Taub.

Description:
Perennial from a deep tough rootstock, with many trailing prostrate stems. Leaves with three leaflets. Leaves narrowly elliptic, veiny. Stipules fused to the leaf stalk. Flowers yellow, in dense foliage at the tips of stems and branches. Flowers in warm months. Fruit a pod with two joints. Upper joint with a tip curved like a hook, and with a seed. Lower joint lacking a seed. Found in turf, open pinelands, open hammocks, and roadsides.

Propagation:
Seed.

Distribution:
Southern peninsula of Florida. Also in the West Indies, Mexico, Central America and South America.

Control Strategies:
Repeat applications of two- or three-way mixtures of 2,4-D, dicamba, MCPP, or MCPA. Other suggested options include atrazine/simazine, metribuzin, triclopyr alone or combined with clopyralid or 2,4-D, atrazine plus bentazon, imazaquin, and metsulfuron. Refer to the Appendix for additional control information. Check the herbicide label for specific application rates and turfgrass tolerance before use.

Southern Pencil-flower with elliptic-shaped leaves

169

Leguminosae = Fabaceae (Bean or Pea Family)
Rabbitfoot Clover

Synonyms:
None reported.

Species:
Trifolium arvense L.

Description:
Erect, branched winter annual with densely hairy leaves and stems. Leaves with three narrowly oblong leaflets, alternate. Leaf margins smooth with minute teeth-like projections at the tip. Flowers small, pale pink to pale purple, in grayish soft-silky cylinder-shaped heads resembling a rabbit's foot. Flowers spring into early summer. Occurs in sandy soils of roadsides and other disturbed areas.

Propagation:
Seed.

Distribution:
Throughout the southeastern United States to central peninsula of Florida, west to Louisiana and north to Missouri, especially in dry, sandy locations. Also in Ontario, Quebec, Australia, and Hawaii. Native to Eurasia and northern Africa.

Control Strategies:
Repeat applications of two- or three-way mixtures of 2,4-D, dicamba, MCPP, or MCPA. Other suggested options include atrazine/simazine, metribuzin, triclopyr alone or combined with clopyralid or 2,4-D, atrazine plus bentazon, imazaquin, and metsulfuron. Refer to the Appendix for additional control information. Check the herbicide label for specific application rates and turfgrass tolerance before use.

Rabbitfoot Clover leaves with three narrowly oblong leaflets

Rabbitfoot Clover flower in grayish-purple, soft-silky, cylinder-shaped heads resembling a rabbit's foot

Rabbitfoot Clover habit

Leguminosae = Fabaceae (Bean or Pea Family)
Large Hop Clover

Synonyms:
Field Clover, Pinnate Hop Clover

Species:
Trifolium campestre Schreb.

Description:
Winter annual with prostrate, hairy, branched stems. Leaves alternate, with three leaflets. Leaflets toothed from mid-blade to tip. Numerous bright yellow flowers (20-30) in loose clusters on long stalks attached at leaf axils. Larger leaves and flower heads than small hop clover (*Trifolium dubium* Sibth.). Distinguished from black medic (*Medicago lupulina* L.) by sessile (no stalk) attachment of central leaflet vs. petioled (stalked) attachment of black medic. Flowers midspring into early summer. Occurs along roadsides and other disturbed sites.

Propagation:
Seed.

Distribution:
Throughout the continental United States except for the Southwestern states. Also in Alaska, Canada, and Australia. Native to Eurasia.

Control Strategies:
Repeat applications of two- or three-way mixtures of 2,4-D, dicamba, MCPP, or MCPA. Other suggested options include atrazine/simazine, metribuzin, triclopyr alone or combined with clopyralid or 2,4-D, atrazine plus bentazon, imazaquin, metsulfuron, and quinclorac. Refer to the Appendix for additional control information. Check the herbicide label for specific application rates and turfgrass tolerance before use.

Large Hop Clover habit

Large Hop Clover leaves with three leaflets and yellow flowers

171

Leguminosae = *Fabaceae* (Bean or Pea Family)
Small Hop Clover

Synonyms:
Low Hop Clover, Suckling Clover, Little Hop Clover

Species:
Trifolium dubium Sibth.

Description:
Prostrate, freely-branched winter annual with hairy, reddish colored stems. Leaves with three leaflets, the terminal leaflet with a short stalk. Leaflets with prominent veins. Flowers, three to fifteen, bright yellow, in heads. Flowers midspring into early summer. Occurs in disturbed areas. Similar in appearance to large hop clover (*Trifolium campestre* Schreb.) but with smaller leaves and flower heads.

Propagation:
Seed.

Distribution:
Throughout the continental United States and Hawaii. Also in Canada, Europe, and Australia.

Control Strategies:
Repeat applications of two- or three-way mixtures of 2,4-D, dicamba, MCPP, or MCPA. Other suggested options include atrazine/simazine, metribuzin, triclopyr alone or combined with clopyralid or 2,4-D, atrazine plus bentazon, imazaquin, metsulfuron, and quinclorac. Refer to the Appendix for additional control information. Check the herbicide label for specific application rates and turfgrass tolerance before use.

Small Hop Clover habit

Leguminosae = Fabaceae (Bean or Pea Family)
White Clover

Synonyms:
Dutch Clover

Species:
Trifolium repens L.

Description:
Low-growing perennial with low creeping stems that root at the nodes. Stems smooth to sparsely covered with hairs. Leaves with three elliptic to oval shaped leaflets, often with a white, angled band partly encircling the base of each leaflet. Leaflets with small marginal teeth. Flowers white, often with pink tinge, arranged in aggregated, round heads. Flowers in spring and fall. Seed coats extremely hard. Often escapes from roadsides, pastures, and forage plantings. Occurs mostly in lawns, roadsides, and other turf.

Propagation:
Seed and possibly stolons.

Distribution:
Throughout the continental United States and Hawaii. Also in Canada, Mexico, the West Indies, Central and South America, Europe, Asia, and Australia. Native to Eurasia.

Control Strategies:
Repeat applications of two- or three-way mixtures of 2,4-D, dicamba, MCPP, or MCPA. Other options include atrazine/simazine, metribuzin, triclopyr alone or combined with clopyralid or 2,4-D, atrazine plus bentazon, imazaquin, metsulfuron, and quinclorac. Refer to the Appendix for additional control information. Check the herbicide label for specific application rates and turfgrass tolerance before use.

White Clover leaves with three leaflets and characteristic white-colored inner leaf "ring" or "band."

White Clover habit

White Clover flower arranged in round heads

173

Leguminosae = *Fabaceae* (Bean or Pea Family)
Sand Vetch

Synonyms:
Fourleaf Vetch

Species:
Vicia acutifolia Ell.

Description:
Perennial with leaning or climbing smooth stems. Leaves with two or four leaflets and a simple, unbranched tendril at the tip. Flowers blue to purplish, four to ten per spike. Flowers spring into summer. Spikes on stalks as long or longer than the leaves. Found in moist to wet disturbed areas usually in sandy soils.

Propagation:
Seed.

Distribution:
South Carolina south into Florida and west into Alabama. Also in the West Indies.

Control Strategies:
Repeat applications of two- or three-way mixtures of 2,4-D, dicamba, MCPP, or MCPA. Other options include atrazine/simazine, metribuzin, triclopyr alone or combined with clopyralid or 2,4-D, atrazine plus bentazon, imazaquin, and metsulfuron. Refer to the Appendix for additional control information. Check the herbicide label for specific application rates and turfgrass tolerance before use.

Sand Vetch flower

Elongated Sand Vetch leaves with tendril at the tip

Leguminosae = Fabaceae (Bean or Pea Family)
Narrowleaf Vetch

Synonyms:
Common Vetch

Species:
Vicia sativa L. subsp. *nigra* (L.) Ehrh.; [*Vicia angustifolia* L.]

Description:
Warm-or cool-season annual or short-lived nitrogen-fixing perennial from a taproot with reclining or climbing stems. Often forms dense entanglements in spring. Leaves alternate, compound with three to nine pairs of leaflets. Leaflet at the tip modified into a simple or branched tendril which enables plant to climb. Leaflets very narrowly elliptic to oval, usually longer than broad. Flowers blue, pale lavender, or purple, mostly in summer. Flowers in leaf axils, stalkless to long-stalked, one or two. Flowers spring into summer. Fruit a stalkless or short-stalked, flat pod brown turning black with six to twelve seeds. Found in turf, pastures, moist to wet woods, waste areas, and fields.

Propagation:
Seed.

Distribution:
Throughout the United States. Found worldwide in the temperate regions. Native from Europe into Russia.

Control Strategies:
Repeat applications of two- or three-way mixtures of 2,4-D, dicamba, MCPP, or MCPA. Other options include atrazine/simazine, metribuzin, triclopyr alone or combined with clopyralid or 2,4-D, atrazine plus bentazon, imazaquin, and metsulfuron. Refer to the Appendix for additional control information. Check the herbicide label for specific application rates and turfgrass tolerance before use.

Elliptic Narrowleaf Vetch leaves with tendril at the tip and flat seedpod

Narrowleaf Vetch flower

175

Loganiaceae = Spigeliaceae = Polypremum (Logania or Strychnine Family)
Rustweed

Synonyms:
Polypremen, Juniper-leaf, Goldweed

Species:
Polypremum procumbens L.

Description:
Annual or perennial herb with diffusely branched stems from a central crown usually forming low mats. Leaves opposite, linear, very narrow, green becoming rusty in color, hence the common name. Plants tend to be more slender in shade. Flowers near tip of branch among the leaves, tiny, white, four-lobed. Flowers in summer to fall. Fruit dry, heart-shaped. Occurs from wet bottomlands up into dry sandhills, in virtually all open habitats.

Propagation:
Seed.

Distribution:
Long Island south through Florida, and west to Texas, Missouri, and Colorado. Also in the West Indies, Mexico, Central and South America. Native to North America.

Control Strategies:
Repeat applications of two- or three-way mixtures of 2,4-D, dicamba, MCPP, or MCPA. Other suggested options include atrazine/simazine, metribuzin, and triclopyr alone or combined with clopyralid or 2,4-D, atrazine plus bentazon, imazaquin, and metsulfuron. Refer to the Appendix for additional control information. Check the herbicide label for specific application rates and turfgrass tolerance before use.

Characteristic orange or rustic color of Rustweed in late summer/early fall

Rustweed habit

Linear-shaped Rustweed leaves

Malvaceae (Mallow Family)
Common Mallow

Synonyms:
Cheeses, Amours, Low Mallow

Species:
Malva neglecta Wallr.

Description:
Annual or biennial, taprooted herbaceous plant. Stem prostrate, freely branched, and densely covered with hairs. Leaves alternate, with a very long petiole and round or heart-shaped blades. Leaf blades hairy, palmately veined with toothed or shallow-lobed margins. Flower-bearing stems upright, flowers borne in leaf axils. Flowers five-petaled and white to pale purple in color. Flowers late spring into early summer. The ring-shaped fruit is composed of 10 to 20 hairy segments. Found in pastures, roadsides, lawns, cultivated fields, and waste areas.

Propagation:
Seed.

Distribution:
Throughout the United States, except Florida, and Canada. Native of Eurasia and north Africa.

Control Strategies:
Repeat applications of two- or three-way mixtures of 2,4-D, dicamba, MCPP, or MCPA. Other suggested options include atrazine/simazine, metribuzin, triclopyr alone or combined with clopyralid or 2,4-D, atrazine plus bentazon, imazaquin, and metsulfuron. Refer to the Appendix for additional control information. Check the herbicide label for specific application rates and turfgrass tolerance before use.

Common Mallow flower and palmately veined leaves with toothed margins

Common Mallow habit with prostrate growing stems

177

Malvaceae (Mallow Family)
Bristly Mallow

Synonyms:
Carolina Bristle Mallow, Wheel Mallow

Species:
Modiola caroliniana (L.) G. Don

Description:
Creeping, prostrate perennial rooting at nodes. Leaves alternate, with six to seven lobes and irregular toothed margins. Flowers orange-red to deep purplish-pink, borne singly from stem nodes. Flowers spring into early summer. Fruit composed of a ring of 15 to 25 sections that radiate out from a central point of attachment. Occurs in disturbed habitats with moist to dry soils.

Propagation:
Seed.

Distribution:
The lower Piedmont and Coastal plain regions of the southern states, Virginia south into Florida, and west to Texas, California, and Hawaii. Also in the West Indies, Mexico, Central and South America, South Africa, and Australia.

Control Strategies:
Repeat applications of two- or three-way mixtures of 2,4-D, dicamba, MCPP, or MCPA. Other suggested options include atrazine/simazine, metribuzin, triclopyr alone or combined with clopyralid or 2,4-D, atrazine plus bentazon, imazaquin, and metsulfuron. Refer to the Appendix for additional control information. Check the herbicide label for specific application rates and turfgrass tolerance before use.

Bristly Mallow flower

Bristly Mallow habit and leaves with irregular toothed margins

Deeply lobed Bristly Mallow leaf

Malvaceae (Mallow Family)
Southern Sida

Synonyms:
Ironweed, Common Fanpetals, Common Wireweed

Species:
Sida acuta Burm. f.

Description:
Deep tap-rooted, tough, erect summer annual which may survive winter. Stems seldom- to much-branched, smooth to nearly so. Leaves alternate, broadly lanced-shaped, margins toothed from base to tip, green underneath. Flowers yellow, solitary from leaf bases. Flowers in summer. Fruit with two spines on top of each section. Occurs in pinelands, hammocks, and turf as well as other disturbed areas.

Propagation:
Seed.

Distribution:
South Carolina south throughout Florida and west into Mississippi. Also in Central America and Africa.

Control Strategies:
Maintain a regular mowing schedule. Repeat applications of two- or three-way mixtures of 2,4-D, dicamba, MCPP, or MCPA. Other suggested options include atrazine/simazine, metribuzin, triclopyr alone or combined with clopyralid or 2,4-D, atrazine plus bentazon, imazaquin, and metsulfuron. Refer to the Appendix for additional control information. Check the herbicide label for specific application rates and turfgrass tolerance before use.

Southern Sida habit with lance-shaped, toothed margin leaves

Southern Sida flower

179

Nyctaginaceae (Four-O'Clock Family)
Red Spiderling

Synonyms:
Wineflower

Species:
Boerhavia diffusa L.; [*Boerhavia coccinea* Mill.; *Boerhavia repens* L.]

Description:
Perennial from a taproot with few to many prostrate stems. Leaves opposite, stalked, irregularly rounded. Flowers reddish, in widely branched, sparse bunches at tips of stems, sticky. Flowers in warm months. Fruit very small, club-shaped, sticky. Occurs in disturbed sandy areas.

Propagation:
Seed and broken taproots.

Distribution:
North Carolina (rare), Florida, and from Texas to California. Also in Mexico, Central and South America, and the West Indies.

Control Strategies:
Repeat applications of two- or three-way mixtures of 2,4-D, dicamba, MCPP, or MCPA. Other suggested options include atrazine/simazine, metribuzin, triclopyr alone or combined with clopyralid or 2,4-D, atrazine plus bentazon, imazaquin, and metsulfuron. Refer to the Appendix for additional control information. Check the herbicide label for specific application rates and turfgrass tolerance before use.

Red Spiderling irregularly rounded leaves

Red Spiderling habit with prostrate growing stems

Red Spiderling small, reddish flowers

Onagraceae (Evening-primrose Family)
Cutleaf Evening-primrose

Synonyms:
None reported.

Species:
Oenothera laciniata Hill

Description:
Winter annual or biennial from a fibrous root system. Stems with a basal rosette of leaves, hairy, reclining, branched from base. Basal and stem leaves alternate, elliptic to lance-shaped, margins irregularly notched or lobed. Single five-petaled, yellow to reddish, tubular flowers borne in leaf axils. Flowers spring into summer from dusk until early morning. Fruit a cylindrical, four-ribbed seedpod. Both flowers and seedpods present at same time. Along road-sides, forest margins, low maintenance turf, abandoned fields.

Propagation:
Seed.

Cutleaf Evening-primrose habit with irregularly lobed leaves

Distribution:
The continental United States except for the Pacific North-west and Southwest. Also in Quebec, Ontario, Central and South America, and Europe. Native to North America.

Control Strategies:
Preemergence control with isoxaben, oxadiazon, and pendimethalin. Postemergence control with repeat applications of two- or three-way mixtures of 2,4-D, dicamba, MCPP, or MCPA. Other options include atrazine/simazine, metribuzin, triclopyr alone or combined with clopyralid or 2,4-D, atrazine plus bentazon, imazaquin, and metsulfuron. Refer to the Appendix for additional control information. Check the herbicide label for specific application rates and turfgrass tolerance before use.

Cutleaf Evening-primrose flower

Cutleaf Evening-primrose cylindrically-shaped, four-ribbed seedpod

181

Onagraceae (Evening-primrose Family)
Showy Evening-primrose

Synonyms:
White Evening-primrose

Species:
Oenothera speciosa Nutt.

Description:
Erect to spreading, usually-branched perennial from a creeping rootstock. Stems slender, greenish. Leaves alternate, elliptic to linear, with irregularly lobed margins. Flowers large, white to pink with four petals and yellow centers, without notched tips. Flowers spring into early summer from dusk until early morning. Fruit a capsule. Extremely drought resistant. Found in dry open disturbed habitats.

Propagation:
Seed.

Distribution:
Florida, west into Texas, and in Kansas, Illinois, Tennessee, and Virginia. Also in Mexico. Native to North America.

Control Strategies:
Repeat applications of two- or three-way mixtures of 2,4-D, dicamba, MCPP, or MCPA. Other suggested options include atrazine/simazine, metribuzin, triclopyr alone or combined with clopyralid or 2,4-D, atrazine plus bentazon, imazaquin, and metsulfuron. Refer to the Appendix for additional control information. Check the herbicide label for specific application rates and turfgrass tolerance before use.

Showy Evening-primrose habit

Showy Evening-primrose flower

182

Oxalidaceae (Woodsorrel Family)
Cuban Purple Woodsorrel

Synonyms:
Broadleaf Woodsorrel

Species:
Oxalis latifolia Kunth; [*Oxalis intermedia* A. Rich.]

Description:
Perennial from clustered bulbs. Leaves deeply three-parted with pronounced, blunt pointed corners, on very long petioles. Leaves folding at night. Flowers purple. Flowers during warm months. Found in shady turf, hammocks, and woods.

Propagation:
Seed and bulbs.

Distribution:
Throughout peninsula of Florida. Native to the West Indies.

Control Strategies:
Repeat applications of two- or three-way mixtures of 2,4-D, dicamba, MCPP, or MCPA. Other suggested options include atrazine/simazine, metribuzin, triclopyr alone or combined with clopyralid or 2,4-D, atrazine plus bentazon, imazaquin, and metsulfuron. Refer to the Appendix for additional control information. Check the herbicide label for specific application rates and turfgrass tolerance before use.

Three-parted Cuban Purple Woodsorrel leaves

Cuban Purple Woodsorrel flowers

183

Oxalidaceae (Woodsorrel Family)
Yellow Woodsorrel

Synonyms:
Oxalis

Species:
Oxalis stricta L.; [*Oxalis dillenii* Jacq.]

Description:
Upright, herbaceous perennial with slender rhizomes. Stems hairy, slender, much branched, often mat-forming, green to yellow-green. Leaves alternate, long petioled, divided into three partly-folded, deeply cut, heart-shaped lobes, margins hairy. Foliage with sour, acrid taste. Flowers bright yellow, with five petals, on stalks bent below the fruit and attached to a common point. Flowers mainly during spring and into early summer. Fruit a narrow "okra-like" capsule, five-angled, slender with point, green. Occurs in most native and disturbed habitats. Creeping woodsorrel, (*Oxalis corniculata* L.), has a more prostrate growth habit than yellow woodsorrel and creeping woodsorrel stolons readily root at the nodes. Leaves similar to yellow woodsorrel but may be green to reddish purplish. Florida yellow woodsorrel (*Oxalis florida* Salisb.) is similar in appearance to yellow woodsorrel, but has slender stems and a smooth to sparingly hairy, smaller capsule. Occurring in nurseries, greenhouses, gardens, and turf. Occurs in some native and nearly all disturbed habitats.

Yellow Woodsorrel with three deeply cut, heart-shaped leaves

Propagation:
All species reproduce by seed.

Distribution:
Most of the eastern and central United States. Also in Canada, Europe, Africa, Asia, Japan, and New Zealand. Native to North America.

Narrow "okra-like" Yellow Woodsorrel fruit

Control Strategies:
Repeat applications of two- or three-way mixtures of 2,4-D, dicamba, MCPP, or MCPA. Other suggested options include atrazine/simazine, metribuzin, triclopyr alone or combined with clopyralid or 2,4-D, atrazine plus bentazon, imazaquin, and metsulfuron. Refer to the Appendix for additional control information. Check the herbicide label for specific application rates and turfgrass tolerance before use.

Creeping Woodsorrel (*Oxalis corniculata*) habit and flower

Plantaginaceae (Plantain Family)
Bracted Plantain

Synonyms:
Largebract Plantain

Species:
Plantago aristata Michx.

Description:
Winter annual with basal leaves from a taproot. Leaves softly hairy to smooth, linear, with smooth margins. Flowers in dense spike on hairy, leafless stalk, "bottlebrush"-like. Numerous bracts, linear, extend outward from the flower spike. Flowers spring into early summer. Found in low maintenance turfgrasses and other sandy disturbed habitats.

Propagation:
Seed.

Distribution:
In most southern states, north to Michigan, west to Texas, California, the Pacific Northwest, and Hawaii. Also in Mexico. Native to North America.

Control Strategies:
Repeat applications of two- or three-way mixtures of 2,4-D, dicamba, MCPP, or MCPA. Other suggested options include atrazine/simazine, metribuzin, triclopyr alone or combined with clopyralid or 2,4-D. Refer to the Appendix for additional control information. Check the herbicide label for specific application rates and turfgrass tolerance before use.

Bracted Plantain habit (note: linear bracts extending from the flower spike)

185

Plantaginaceae (Plantain Family)
Buckhorn Plantain

Synonyms:
English Plantain, Narrowleaf Plantain

Species:
Plantago lanceolata L.

Description:
Perennial with a distinctive basal rosette of leaves and a slender, fibrous root system. Leaves narrowly elliptic to lance-shaped, often twisted or curled, with ribbed veins on lower leaf surface. Flowering is on an erect, leafless, hairy stalk terminated by dense, tapered, white to tannish flower spike. Flowers midspring into early summer. Found commonly in lawns and along roadsides and in moist disturbed areas.

Propagation:
Seed.

Distribution:
Throughout the continental United States. Also in Canada, the West Indies, Central and South America, Europe, and Asia. Native to Europe.

Control Strategies:
Repeat applications of two- or three-way mixtures of 2,4-D, dicamba, MCPP, or MCPA. Other suggested options include atrazine/simazine, metribuzin, triclopyr alone or combined with clopyralid or 2,4-D. Refer to the Appendix for additional control information. Check the herbicide label for specific application rates and turfgrass tolerance before use.

Buckhorn Plantain habit with long stalked flower spikes

Buckhorn Plantain basal rosette of leaves

Buckhorn Plantain flower spike

Plantaginaceae (Plantain Family)
Broadleaf Plantain

Synonyms:
Common Plantain

Species:
Plantago major L.

Description:
Perennial herb with a distinctive basal rosette of leaves, and slender, fibrous root system. Leaves broad, egg-shaped, with several main veins. Erect, leafless stems terminate in dense, flower spikes. Flowers midspring into early summer. Occurs in lawns and along roadsides and in other disturbed sites. Blackseed plantain (*Plantago rugellii* Dcne.) is similar except stems and petioles longer and leaves somewhat larger. Blackseed plantain occurs in lawns, gardens, and other disturbed areas.

Propagation:
Both species reproduce by seed.

Distribution:
In all of North America except the northeastern United States. Also in the West Indies, Central and South America, Europe, Asia, Australia, and Hawaii. Native to Eurasia.

Control Strategies:
Repeat applications of two- or three-way mixtures of 2,4-D, dicamba, MCPP, or MCPA. Other suggested options include atrazine/simazine, metribuzin, triclopyr alone or combined with clopyralid or 2,4-D. Refer to the Appendix for additional control information. Check the herbicide label for specific application rates and turfgrass tolerance before use.

Broadleaf Plantain habit

Broadleaf Plantain basal rosette of leaves

Broadleaf Plantain flower spikes

Plantaginaceae (Plantain Family)
Paleseed Plantain

Synonyms:
Southern Plantain, Virginia Plantain

Species:
Plantago virginica L.

Description:
Winter annual with basal leaves, from a taproot. Leaves densely-hairy, elliptic in shape with slightly toothed to nearly smooth leaf margins. Flowering stalk leafless, hollow, and terminates in a densely flowered spike without prominent linear bracts. Flowers mid to late spring. Occurs in dry sandy soil of disturbed areas.

Propagation:
Seed.

Distribution:
Rhode Island to Florida, and west to Texas, California, Oregon, and Hawaii. Also in Canada, Mexico, South America, the West Indies, and Japan. Native to North America.

Control Strategies:
Repeat applications of two- or three-way mixtures of 2,4-D, dicamba, MCPP, or MCPA. Other suggested options include atrazine/simazine, metribuzin, triclopyr alone or combined with clopyralid or 2,4-D. Refer to the Appendix for additional control information. Check the herbicide label for specific application rates and turfgrass tolerance before use.

Paleseed Plantain habit with densely-hairy, basal leaves

Paleseed Plantain flower spike

Polygonaceae (Smartweed or Buckwheat Family)
Prostrate Knotweed

Synonyms:
None reported.

Species:
Polygonum aviculare L.

Description:
Prostrate, mat-forming, blue-green colored summer annual. Leaves alternate, smooth, oblong to linear, short-petioled, joined to stem by a sheathing membrane (ocrea). Inconspicuous white flowers are formed in the leaf axils. Flowers from late spring until frost. Fruit dull brown, three-sided, which remain viable for years. Common on infertile and compacted soils of cultivated fields and disturbed areas. One of the first summer annuals to germinate in the spring.

Propagation:
Seed.

Distribution:
Throughout the United States. Also in Canada, Central and South America, Europe, Asia, Australia, and Hawaii. Native to Eurasia.

Control Strategies:
Repeat applications of dicamba or two- or three-way mixtures of 2,4-D, dicamba, MCPP, or MCPA. Other suggested options include atrazine/simazine, metribuzin, triclopyr alone or combined with clopyralid or 2,4-D. Refer to the Appendix for additional control information. Check the herbicide label for specific application rates and turfgrass tolerance before use.

Prostrate Knotweed oblong to linear-shaped leaves

Prostrate Knotweed mat-forming habit, blue-green color

Prostrate Knotweed leaves joined to stem by a sheathing membrane

189

Polygonaceae (Smartweed or Buckwheat Family)
Tufted Knotweed

Synonyms:
Smartweed, Oriental Lady's-thumb

Species:
Polygonum caespitosum Blume var. *longisetum* (De Bruyn)
A. N. Steward

Description:
Erect to sprawling summer annual with smooth round
stems and swollen nodes. Leaves alternate, smooth above,
sparsely hairy on veins, elliptic- to lanced-shaped, joined to
stem with a sheathing membrane (ocrea) tipped with long
hairs. Deep pink to nearly red flowers in spikes at tips of
stems. Flowers midsummer until frost. Occurs in moist disturbed habitats, frequently along borders.

Propagation:
Seed.

Distribution:
From Massachusetts to Illinois, south to north Florida and
Louisiana. Native to Asia.

Control Strategies:
Repeat applications of dicamba or two- or three-way mixtures of 2,4-D, dicamba, MCPP, or MCPA. Other suggested
options include atrazine/simazine, metribuzin, triclopyr
alone or combined with clopyralid or 2,4-D. Refer to the
Appendix for additional control information. Check the
herbicide label for specific application rates and turfgrass
tolerance before use.

Tufted Knotweed with elliptic- to
lanced-shaped leaves joined to stem by
a sheathing membrane tipped with long
hairs

Tufted Knotweed habit

Tufted Knotweed flowers in spikes at
stem tips

Polygonaceae (Smartweed or Buckwheat Family)
Red Sorrel

Synonyms:
Sheep Sorrel, Sour-grass, Indian Cane

Species:
Rumex acetosella L.

Description:
Perennial with smooth, erect, four-sided stems. Produces large yellow taproot and spreads from sprouts from numerous rhizomes and roots. Leaves mostly basal, distinctively arrow- or lance-shaped; sour tasting, eaten in salads. Flowers borne in clusters at end of stems. Flowers green to red at maturity. Flowers midspring through summer. Fruit three-sided with golden brown nutlets. Common in acid soils with low fertility of lawns and fields. Heartwing sorrel (*Rumex hastatulus* Baldw.), a winter annual, is similar, but lacks rhizomes and produces larger red masses of flowers and fruits at maturity. Occurs in old fields.

Propagation:
Rumex acetosella L.—seed and rhizomes.
Rumex hastatulus Baldw.—seed only.

Distribution:
Continental United States, except peninsula Florida, and in Alaska and Hawaii. Also in Central and South America, Australia, Indonesia, Iceland, Africa, and Asia. Native to Europe.

Control Strategies:
Adjust soil pH and follow recommended fertility programs. Preemergence control with isoxaben and pronamide. Postemergence control with repeat applications of two- or three-way mixtures of 2,4-D, dicamba, MCPP, or MCPA. Other options include atrazine/simazine, metribuzin, triclopyr alone or combined with clopyralid or 2,4-D, atrazine plus bentazon, imazaquin, and metsulfuron. Refer to the Appendix for additional control information. Check the herbicide label for specific application rates and turfgrass tolerance before use.

Red Sorrel habit with reddish flowers on stems

Arrow- or lance-shaped Red Sorrel basal leaves

191

Polygonaceae (Smartweed or Buckwheat Family)
Curly Dock

Synonyms:
Sour Dock

Species:
Rumex crispus L.

Description:
Taprooted perennial with mostly basal leaves up to 1 foot long in a rosette. Stem leaves alternate, with wavy to curled margins, tapered at the base. Leaf petiole joined to stem by a membranous sheath. Greenish flowers on long terminal spikes, up to 3 feet tall. Flowers midspring into summer. Three-angled fruit reddish-brown with three wing-like projections. Produces large, thick taproot. Broadleaf dock or Bitter dock (*Rumex obtusifolius* L.) is similar but has leaves that are wide and heart-shaped at the base and lack curly margins. Both occurring in roadsides, ditches, fields, and wet habitats.

Curly Dock basal leaves with curly or wavy margins

Propagation:
Seed.

Distribution:
Throughout the United States. Also in the West Indies, Mexico, and Central America, Europe, Asia, and Australia. Native to Europe.

Control Strategies:
Preemergence control with isoxaben. Postemergence control with repeat applications of two- or three-way mixtures of 2,4-D, dicamba, MCPP, or MCPA. Other options include atrazine/simazine, metribuzin, triclopyr alone or combined with clopyralid or 2,4-D. Refer to the Appendix for additional control information. Check the herbicide label for specific application rates and turfgrass tolerance before use.

Curly Dock flower inflorescence

Heart-shaped Broadleaf Dock (*Rumex obtusifolius*) leaves that lack wavy margins

Portulacaceae (Purslane Family)
Spring Beauty

Synonyms:
None reported.

Species:
Claytonia virginica L.; [*Claytonia media* (DC.) Small]

Description:
Small tufted delicate perennial herb originating from corms. Leaves opposite, fleshy, lance-shaped, or linear. Flowers borne at tops of erect stems up to 1 foot tall. Flowers pinkish or whitish striped with darker pink colors. Flowers with two sepals, five petals, five recurved stamens, and a three-lobed stigma. Sweetly scented. One of the earliest (March-April) blooming springtime flowers. Escaped native ornamental. Characteristic of rich woods, fields, and clearings.

Propagation:
Corms.

Distribution:
Mountain and Piedmont regions from Virginia to Georgia westward to Mississippi and Texas, northward to Nova Scotia to Minnesota.

Control Strategies:
Fumigate contaminated soil. Repeat applications of two- or three-way mixtures of 2,4-D, dicamba, MCPP, or MCPA. Other suggested options include atrazine/simazine, metribuzin, triclopyr alone or combined with clopyralid or 2,4-D, atrazine plus bentazon, imazaquin, and metsulfuron. Refer to the Appendix for additional control information. Check the herbicide label for specific application rates and turfgrass tolerance before use.

Spring Beauty habit

Spring Beauty flower

Portulacaceae (Purslane Family)
Broadleaf Pink Purslane

Synonyms:
Paraguayan Purslane

Species:
Portulaca amilis Speg.

Description:
Prostrate, mat-forming summer annual with fleshy, flat, thick leaves. Leaves broadly oblong and pointed at the tip. Brownish to white hairs in leaf axils. Pink to pink-purple showy flowers in terminal heads. Flowers midsummer into early fall. Occurs in open disturbed habitats.

Propagation:
Seed.

Distribution:
North Carolina south into and throughout Florida. Native to South America.

Control Strategies:
Preemergence control with atrazine/simazine, dithiopyr, isoxaben, oryzalin, oxadiazon, pendimethalin, and prodiamine. Postemergence control with repeat applications of dicamba alone or two- or three-way mixtures of 2,4-D, dicamba, MCPP, or MCPA. Other options include atrazine/simazine, bentazon, metribuzin, MSMA, triclopyr alone or combined with clopyralid or 2,4-D, and atrazine plus bentazon. Refer to the Appendix for additional control information. Check the herbicide label for specific application rates and turfgrass tolerance before use.

Broadleaf Pink Purslane habit with fleshy, thick leaves

Broadleaf Pink Purslane flower

Portulacaceae (Purslane Family)
Common Purslane

Synonyms:
Little Hogweed

Species:
Portulaca oleracea L.

Description:
Prostrate, succulent, mat-forming summer annual. Leaves alternate or nearly opposite, fleshy, somewhat spoon- or wedge-shaped, rounded at the tip, narrowed to the base (spatulate). Stems smooth, usually purplish-red. Flowers yellow, solitary in leaf axils or clustered on ends of stems. Flowers midsummer into early fall. Fruit a round capsule, splitting open around the middle. Common in nurseries, sod farms, thin or newly seeded turfgrass, and vegetable production.

Propagation:
Seed.

Distribution:
Throughout the United States, more common in northwest United States, less common in the Pacific Northwest. Also in Canada, the West Indies, Central and South America, Europe, Africa, Asia, Oceania, and Hawaii. Believed native of western Asia.

Control Strategies:
Preemergence control with atrazine/simazine, dithiopyr, isoxaben, oryzalin, oxadiazon, pendimethalin, and prodiamine. Postemergence control with repeat applications of dicamba alone or two- or three-way mixtures of 2,4-D, dicamba, MCPP, or MCPA. Other options include atrazine/simazine, bentazon, metribuzin, MSMA, triclopyr alone or combined with clopyralid or 2,4-D, and atrazine plus bentazon. Refer to the Appendix for additional control information. Check the herbicide label for specific application rates and turfgrass tolerance before use.

Common Purslane habit with fleshy, spoon-shaped leaves

Common Purslane flower

Ranunculaceae (Buttercup or Crowfoot Family)
Smallflower Buttercup

Synonyms:
Little Buttercup

Species:
Ranunculus abortivus L.

Description:
Winter annual with erect almost hairless stems and leaves. Basal leaves heart-shaped, long-petioled, margins toothed. Stem leaves on shorter petioles and divided into three-lobed segments. Yellow flowers singly on stem at leaf axils. Flowers in spring. Seeds in tight round cluster. Seed round, flattened, with a short beak that is slightly curved to straight. Occurs in dry to moist to wet woods, fields, and disturbed areas.

Propagation:
Seed.

Distribution:
Continental United States and Alaska, except for the Southwest states. Also throughout Canada.

Control Strategies:
Repeat applications of 2,4-D alone or two- or three-way mixtures of 2,4-D, dicamba, MCPP, or MCPA. Other suggested options include atrazine/simazine, metribuzin, triclopyr alone or combined with clopyralid or 2,4-D. Refer to the Appendix for additional control information. Check the herbicide label for specific application rates and turfgrass tolerance before use.

Smallflower Buttercup habit

Smallflower Buttercup flower

Ranunculaceae (Buttercup or Crowfoot Family)
Hairy Buttercup

Synonyms:
None reported.

Species:
Ranunculus sardous Crantz

Description:
Winter annual with erect, hairy stems and leaves. Basal leaves with long petioles. Leaves pinnately divided and lobed. Yellow flowers singly on stem at leaf axils. Flowers in spring. Seeds in round clusters. Seed flattened, with curved, hooked, or straight beak. Occurs in moist to wet disturbed sites.

Propagation:
Seed.

Distribution:
Continental United States except for the states in the High Plains and Southwest. Also in Europe where it is native.

Control Strategies:
Repeat applications of 2,4-D alone or two- or three-way mixtures of 2,4-D, dicamba, MCPP, or MCPA. Other suggested options include atrazine/simazine, metribuzin, triclopyr alone or combined with clopyralid or 2,4-D. Refer to the Appendix for additional control information. Check the herbicide label for specific application rates and turfgrass tolerance before use.

Hairy Buttercup habit

Hairy Buttercup flowers

Rosaceae (Rose Family)
Parsley-piert

Synonyms:
Slender Parsley-piert

Species:
Aphanes microcarpa (Boiss. & Reut.) Rothm.

Description:
Freely-branched, low-growing winter annual to 5 inches (13 cm) tall. Leaves alternate, three-lobed with each lobe again three- to four-lobed. Inconspicuous flowers in leaf axils. Flowers in spring. Found in lawns, fields, and pastures. Field Parsley-piert (*Aphanes arvensis* L. = *Alchemilla arvensis* (L.) Scop.) is similar except plants reach 1 foot (30 cm) and is reported only from Nova Scotia.

Propagation:
Seed.

Distribution:
Maryland through Tennessee into Georgia. Also in Europe, Asia, and Australia. Native to Europe.

Control Strategies:
Preemergence control with atrazine/simazine, bensulide, oxadiazon, and prodiamine. Postemergence control with repeat applications of two- or three-way mixtures of 2,4-D, dicamba, MCPP, or MCPA. Other suggested options include atrazine/simazine, metribuzin, triclopyr alone or combined with clopyralid or 2,4-D, atrazine plus bentazon, imazaquin, and metsulfuron. Refer to the Appendix for additional control information. Check the herbicide label for specific application rates and turfgrass tolerance before use.

Parsley-piert habit

Parsley-piert lobed, hairy leaves

Rosaceae (Rose Family)
Indian Mock-strawberry

Synonyms:
Wild Strawberry, Indian-strawberry

Species:
Duchesnea indica (Andr.) Focke

Description:
Low-growing perennial with long stolons. Leaves alternate, rosettes with three leaflets and toothed margins as opposed to the five leaflets found on Oldfield Cinquefoil (*Potentilla simplex* Michx.). Single flowers, on long petioles, five yellow petals. Flowers in spring. Fruit red, spongy, round, and "strawberry-like," not poisonous but not palatable. Common in moist, shaded, and open areas.

Propagation:
Seed and stolons.

Distribution:
Southeast United States, west to Oklahoma, Texas, California, and the Pacific Northwest, north into Pennsylvania and New York. Also in the West Indies, Central and South America, Asia, and Europe. Native to Asia.

Control Strategies:
Repeat applications of dicamba alone or two- or three-way mixtures of 2,4-D, dicamba, MCPP, or MCPA. Other suggested options include atrazine/simazine, metribuzin, triclopyr alone or combined with clopyralid or 2,4-D, and atrazine plus bentazon. Refer to the Appendix for additional control information. Check the herbicide label for specific application rates and turfgrass tolerance before use.

Indian Mock-strawberry flower

Indian Mock-strawberry habit with three leaflet, toothed margin leaves

Indian Mock-strawberry "strawberry-like" fruit

199

Rosaceae (Rose Family)
Oldfield Cinquefoil

Synonyms:
None reported.

Species:
Potentilla simplex Michx.

Description:
Low-growing perennial herb with long, wiry stolons. Dies back to ground in winter, new shoots and leaves appear in early spring. Leaves with long petioles. Leaves with five leaflets—as opposed to the three leaflets of Indian Mock-strawberry [*Duchesnea indica* (Andr.) Focke] and toothed margins, dark green above, whitish-green beneath. Flowers single on long petioles with five bright yellow petals. Flowers in spring. Found in dry woods and fields.

Propagation:
Seed and stolons.

Distribution:
Eastern United States north into Minnesota, extending south into Kansas, Oklahoma, Texas, and Piedmont region of Georgia. Also in southern Canada. Native to North America.

Control Strategies:
Repeat applications of two- or three-way mixtures of 2,4-D, dicamba, MCPP, or MCPA. Other suggested options include atrazine/simazine, metribuzin, triclopyr alone or combined with clopyralid or 2,4-D, atrazine plus bentazon, imazaquin, and metsulfuron. Refer to the Appendix for additional control information. Check the herbicide label for specific application rates and turfgrass tolerance before use.

Oldfield Cinquefoil leaves with toothed margins

Oldfield Cinquefoil leaves with five leaflets

Oldfield Cinquefoil flower

Rubiaceae (Madder Family)
Poorjoe

Synonyms:
Rough Buttonweed

Species:
Diodia teres Walt.

Description:
Freely-branched, spreading to semierect summer annual,
often in mats, from shallow roots with a slender taproot.
Stem often reddish-purplish with lines of hairs. Leaves opposite, linear, usually light green in color nearly round in cross
section. Leaf bases joined by membrane with several "hair-
like" projections. Flowers tubular, white to pinkish white, in
leaf axils. Flowers midsummer until frost. Common on dry
infertile soils of sandhills, dunes, and dry pinelands.

Propagation:
Seed.

Distribution:
Southeastern United States, north to Connecticut, Illinois,
and Montana, and west to Texas and Arizona. Also in
Mexico, the West Indies, Central America and South America. Native to North America.

Control Strategies:
Repeat applications of two- or three-way mixtures of 2,4-D,
dicamba, MCPP, or MCPA. Other suggested options include atrazine/simazine, metribuzin, triclopyr alone or combined with clopyralid or 2,4-D, atrazine plus bentazon,
imazaquin, and metsulfuron. Refer to the Appendix for additional control information. Check the herbicide label for
specific application rates and turfgrass tolerance before use.

Poorjoe habit with flower

Poorjoe linear leaves and reddish-purple stems

Poorjoe stem with lines of hairs

Rubiaceae (Madder Family)
Virginia Buttonweed

Synonyms:
None reported.

Species:
Diodia virginiana L.

Description:
Mat-forming spreading perennial herb with hairy branched stems. Leaves opposite, elliptic to lance-shaped, sessile, joined across stem by membrane. Membrane with a few "hair-like" projections. Leaves often yellow, mottled by a virus in late summer. White tubular flowers with four lobes at each leaf axil along the stem. Flower usually with only two sepals. Flowers in summer. Subterranean flowers also produced. Fruit green, elliptically shaped, hairy, ridged and at each leaf axil. Favors moist to wet sites of woods, marshes, and wet turf.

Virginia Buttonweed flowers at each leaf axil along stems

Propagation:
Seed, roots, and stem fragments.

Distribution:
New Jersey west to Missouri, south into the Gulf Coast states.

Control Strategies:
Preemergence applications of oxadiazon or simazine help to control plants from seed. Postemergence control with repeat applications of two- or three-way mixtures of 2,4-D, dicamba, MCPP, or MCPA. Other suggested options include triclopyr alone or combined with clopyralid or 2,4-D. Refer to the Appendix for additional control information. Check the herbicide label for specific application rates and turfgrass tolerance before use.

Virginia Buttonweed green fruit with hairy margin

Virginia Buttonweed habit

Virginia Buttonweed leaves mottled by a virus.

Rubiaceae (Madder Family)
Catchweed Bedstraw

Synonyms:
Spring Cleavers, Stickywilly

Species:
Galium aparine L.

Description:
Mat-forming winter annual with prostrate or trailing, angled stems. Stems square, with stiff bristles on edges that point toward the base, often pale green. Leaves whorled, six to eight at each node, with small bristles on the margins. Plant easily breaks apart and attaches to clothes, hair, etc. Flowers white, on long stems from the leaf axils. Flowers in spring. Fruit a clinging bristly two-sided capsule. Occurs in shaded woods, flower beds, and ornamental plantings.

Propagation:
Seed.

Distribution:
Throughout North America. Also in Europe, Asia, and Australia. Native to Europe.

Control Strategies:
Repeat applications of two- or three-way mixtures of 2,4-D, dicamba, MCPP, or MCPA. Other suggested options include atrazine/simazine, metribuzin, triclopyr alone or combined with clopyralid or 2,4-D, atrazine plus bentazon, imazaquin, and metsulfuron. Refer to the Appendix for additional control information. Check the herbicide label for specific application rates and turfgrass tolerance before use.

Catchweed Bedstraw with whorled leaves

Catchweed Bedstraw habit with small bristles on leaf margins

Catchweed Bedstraw fruit

203

Rubiaceae (Madder Family)
Marsh Bedstraw

Synonyms:
Stiff Marsh Bedstraw

Species:
Galium tinctorium L.

Description:
Perennial with spreading or reclining, branched stems. Stems angled, with downwardly pointing sandpapery hairs on the angles. Leaves whorled, four to six at each node, narrow, sometimes enlarged at the tip. Flowers white, small, usually three-lobed, in clusters of two or three at the tips of branches. Flowers spring into early summer. Fruit black, smooth, nearly round, and in pairs. Found in roadside ditches, marshes, swamps, and other moist sites.

Propagation:
Seed.

Distribution:
Nebraska into the central, eastern, and southern United States into Florida, and west to Texas and Arizona. Also in Newfoundland, Ontario, and Quebec.

Control Strategies:
Repeat applications of two- or three-way mixtures of 2,4-D, dicamba, MCPP, or MCPA. Other suggested options include atrazine/simazine, metribuzin, triclopyr alone or combined with clopyralid or 2,4-D, atrazine plus bentazon, imazaquin, and metsulfuron. Refer to the Appendix for additional control information. Check the herbicide label for specific application rates and turfgrass tolerance before use.

Marsh Bedstraw habit with branched stems

Marsh Bedstraw flowering stem

Rubiaceae (Madder Family)
Old World Diamond-flower

Synonyms:
Flat-top Mille Graines

Species:
Hedyotis corymbosa (L.) Lam.; [*Oldenlandia corymbosa* L.]

Description:
Smooth, spreading summer annual with branched stems. Leaves opposite, narrow. Flowers white, usually two or more on long stalks from the tip of a common long stalk. Flowers midsummer until frost. Found in all moist turf and in moist disturbed areas.

Propagation:
Seed.

Distribution:
South Carolina south throughout Florida and along the Gulf Coast into Texas. Widespread in the tropics throughout the world. Native to the Old World.

Control Strategies:
Repeat applications of two- or three-way mixtures of 2,4-D, dicamba, MCPP, or MCPA. Other suggested options include atrazine/simazine, metribuzin, triclopyr alone or combined with clopyralid or 2,4-D, atrazine plus bentazon, imazaquin, and metsulfuron. Refer to the Appendix for additional control information. Check the herbicide label for specific application rates and turfgrass tolerance before use.

Old World Diamond-flower habit

Small, whitish-colored flower of Old World Diamond-flower

Old World Diamond-flower fruit

Rubiaceae (Madder Family)
Brazil Pusley

Synonyms:
Tropical Mexican-clover

Species:
Richardia brasiliensis (Moq.) Gomez

Description:
Perennial with hairy, many-branched stems from a thickened woody rootstock. Leaves opposite, hairy, connected by a thin membrane with hair-like projections on top. Flowers white, in clusters. Flowers in warm months. Distinguished from Florida pusley (*Richardia scabra* L.) by presence of fruit with short stiff hairs and thickened rootstock. Found in lawns, roadsides, and disturbed areas. Appears to tolerate nematode-infested soil.

Propagation:
Seed and rootstock.

Distribution:
From Texas to Virginia along the Coastal plain. Also in Mexico, South Africa, Indonesia, and Hawaii. Native to South America.

Control Strategies:
Check and treat soil for nematodes, if present. Repeat applications of two- or three-way mixtures of 2,4-D, dicamba, MCPP, or MCPA. Other suggested options include atrazine/simazine, metribuzin, triclopyr alone or combined with clopyralid or 2,4-D, atrazine plus bentazon, imazaquin, and metsulfuron. Refer to the Appendix for additional control information. Check the herbicide label for specific application rates and turfgrass tolerance before use.

Brazil Pusley habit with opposite, hairy leaves

Brazil Pusley thickened woody rootstock

Brazil Pusley flower cluster

Rubiaceae (Madder Family)
Largeflower Pusley

Synonyms:
Large-flower Mexican-clover

Species:
Richardia grandiflora (Cham. & Schlecht.) Steud.

Description:
Creeping perennial, rooting at the nodes, with hairy, branching stems. Leaves opposite, hairy, narrowly elliptical, tapering sharply to points at both ends, with a petiole. Flowers white, blue, pink, or violet, about 0.8 inch (2 cm) long, clustered at tips of branches. Flowers during warm months. Found in disturbed sandy areas and turf.

Propagation:
Seed and stem fragments.

Distribution:
Central and southern peninsula of Florida. Native to South America.

Control Strategies:
Check and treat soil for nematodes, if present. Repeat applications of two- or three-way mixtures of 2,4-D, dicamba, MCPP, or MCPA. Other suggested options include atrazine/simazine, metribuzin, triclopyr alone or combined with clopyralid or 2,4-D, atrazine plus bentazon, imazaquin, and metsulfuron. Refer to the Appendix for additional control information. Check the herbicide label for specific application rates and turfgrass tolerance before use.

Largeflower Pusley habit

Largeflower Pusley flower cluster

207

Rubiaceae (Madder Family)
Florida Pusley

Synonyms:
Rough Mexican-clover

Species:
Richardia scabra L.

Description:
Prostrate and spreading summer annual with branched hairy stems. Leaves opposite, oval-shaped, and somewhat thickened. Tubular flowers, white, clustered at the ends of branches. Flowers in summer. Distinguished from Brazil pusley [(*Richardia brasiliensis* (Moq.) Gomez)] by presence of fruit with small bump-like projections and lack of thickened rootstock. Occurs in dry, open disturbed sites.

Propagation:
Seed.

Distribution:
Southeast, Northeast, and Midwest United States. Also in Mexico and Central and South America. Native to South America.

Control Strategies:
Check and treat soil for nematodes, if present. Preemergence control with atrazine/simazine, isoxaben, oryzalin, oxadiazon, pendimethalin, and prodiamine. Postemergence control with repeat applications of two- or three-way mixtures of 2,4-D, dicamba, MCPP, or MCPA. Other suggested options include atrazine/simazine, metribuzin, triclopyr alone or combined with clopyralid or 2,4-D, atrazine plus bentazon, imazaquin, and metsulfuron. Refer to the Appendix for additional control information. Check the herbicide label for specific application rates and turfgrass tolerance before use.

Florida Pusley habit with hairy stems

Florida Pusley flower cluster

Rubiaceae (Madder Family)
Field Madder

Synonyms:
Blue Field Madder

Species:
Sherardia arvensis L.

Description:
Low-growing, mat-forming winter annual with square stems. Leaves whorled, four to six per node, elliptic in shape with sharply-pointed tips. Flowers lavender to pink, in clusters at ends of stems. Flowers in spring. Occurs in cultivated and other disturbed sites.

Propagation:
Seed.

Distribution:
Mountains and Piedmont of the southern states, west into East Texas and Arkansas, north into southern Canada, California, and the Pacific Northwest. Also in the West Indies, Central America, Hawaii, Europe, and Australia. Native to the Old World.

Control Strategies:
Repeat applications of two- or three-way mixtures of 2,4-D, dicamba, MCPP, or MCPA. Other suggested options include atrazine/simazine, metribuzin, triclopyr alone or combined with clopyralid or 2,4-D, atrazine plus bentazon, imazaquin, and metsulfuron. Refer to the Appendix for additional control information. Check the herbicide label for specific application rates and turfgrass tolerance before use.

Field Madder whorled, elliptic-shaped leaves with sharply-pointed tips

Field Madder habit with square stems

Field Madder flower cluster at stem tips

Rubiaceae (Madder Family)
Bushy Buttonweed

Synonyms:
Woodland False Buttonweed

Species:
Spermacoce assurgens Ruiz & Pavon; [*Borreria laevis* (Lam.) Griseb. of authors]

Description:
Annual with much-branched stems. Leaves opposite, smooth, elliptic to oval, veiny, tapering to sharp tip and a sharp base, with a short petiole. Flowers white, in clusters at the upper nodes, longer than the four lobes of the calyx. Flowers in warm months. Fruit hairy. Found in disturbed areas, lawns, and moist open woods.

Propagation:
Seed.

Distribution:
Throughout Florida and into Louisiana. Also in the West Indies, Central and South America, Asia, Indonesia, the Philippines, New Guinea, and the South Pacific including Hawaii.

Control Strategies:
Repeat applications of two- or three-way mixtures of 2,4-D, dicamba, MCPP, or MCPA. Other suggested options include atrazine/simazine, metribuzin, triclopyr alone or combined with clopyralid or 2,4-D, atrazine plus bentazon, imazaquin, and metsulfuron. Refer to the Appendix for additional control information. Check the herbicide label for specific application rates and turfgrass tolerance before use.

Bushy Buttonweed habit

Bushy Buttonweed smooth, elliptic- to oval-shaped leaves and flower cluster at the upper nodes

Rubiaceae (Madder Family)
Whitehead Broom

Synonyms:
Shrubby False Buttonweed

Species:
Spermacoce verticillata L.; [*Borreria verticillata* (L.) Meyer]

Description:
Perennial with much-branched stems, rooting at the nodes. Leaves opposite, smooth, narrowly elliptic to elliptic, veiny, tapering to a sharp tip and a sharp base, with a short petiole. Flowers white, in clusters at the upper nodes, longer than the two lobes of the calyx. Flowers in warm months. Fruit smooth, or with a few hairs. Found in open or disturbed sandy areas, especially turf, also in pinelands.

Propagation:
Seed.

Distribution:
Southern peninsula of Florida. Also in the West Indies, Mexico, Central and South America, West Tropical Africa, and the South Pacific. Native to tropical America.

Control Strategies:
Repeat applications of two- or three-way mixtures of 2,4-D, dicamba, MCPP, or MCPA. Other options include atrazine/simazine, metribuzin, and triclopyr alone or combined with clopyralid or 2,4-D, atrazine plus bentazon, imazaquin, metsulfuron, and quinclorac. Refer to the Appendix for additional control information. Check the herbicide label for specific application rates and turfgrass tolerance before use.

Whitehead Broom with opposite, smooth, elliptically-shaped leaves

Whitehead Broom flower cluster at upper nodes

Scrophulariaceae (Figwort Family)
Oldfield Toadflax

Synonyms:
Canada Toadflax

Species:
Linaria canadensis (L.) Chaz. [*Nuttallanthus canadensis* (L.) D. A. Sutton]

Description:
Winter annual or biennial; when biennial, it often forms a dense basal cluster of prostrate stems. Leaves linear, those in the basal cluster opposite or whorled; those of the main erect stem usually alternate. Flowers blue to purple, with finger-like projection (spur). Flowers in spring. Occurring in pastures, old fields, and along roadsides.

Propagation:
Seed.

Distribution:
Throughout the United States. Also in southern Canada, Mexico, and South America. Native to Eurasia.

Control Strategies:
Maintain a regular mowing schedule. Repeat applications of two- or three-way mixtures of 2,4-D, dicamba, MCPP, or MCPA. Other suggested options include atrazine/simazine, metribuzin, triclopyr alone or combined with clopyralid or 2,4-D, atrazine plus bentazon, imazaquin, and metsulfuron. Refer to the Appendix for additional control information. Check the herbicide label for specific application rates and turfgrass tolerance before use.

Oldfield Toadflax habit

Oldfield Toadflax basal linear-shaped leaves

Oldfield Toadflax flowers on long, erect stems

Scrophulariaceae (Figwort Family)
Common Mullein

Synonyms:
None reported.

Species:
Verbascum thapsus L.

Description:
Densely-hairy or woolly biennial to 6 feet (2 m) tall. Basal leaves in a rosette with a stout stem elongating the second year. Stem leaves alternate, densely-hairy, elliptic in shape, without petioles and with a leaf base that is fused to and extends down the stem. Flowers yellow, densely-packed in a tall growing cylindrical spike. Only a few flowers open at any one time. Flowers summer until frost. Commonly found on roadsides and in waste places.

Propagation:
Seed.

Distribution:
Throughout the United States except for the upper Great Plains. Also in Canada, Europe, Asia, Australia, and Hawaii. Native to Europe.

Control Strategies:
Repeat applications of two- or three-way mixtures of 2,4-D, dicamba, MCPP, or MCPA. Other suggested options include atrazine/simazine, metribuzin, triclopyr alone or combined with clopyralid or 2,4-D, atrazine plus bentazon, imazaquin, and metsulfuron. Refer to the Appendix for additional control information. Check the herbicide label for specific application rates and turfgrass tolerance before use.

Common Mullein habit with flowers on tall, cylindrically-shaped spike

Common Mullein basal rosette of densely-hairy leaves

213

Scrophulariaceae (Figwort Family)
Corn Speedwell

Synonyms:
None reported.

Species:
Veronica arvensis L.

Description:
Low-growing, freely-branched winter annual. Lower leaves round- to egg-shaped, toothed on the margins, with prominent veins. Upper leaves linear in shape and smaller than lower leaves. Leaves and stems with fine hairs. Flowers light blue, nearly stalkless. Flowers in spring. Seed capsules heart-shaped with a line of hairs on the outer edge. Found in lawns, gardens, roadsides, and fields.

Propagation:
Seed.

Distribution:
Throughout most of the United States except for the Rocky Mountains. Also in Central and South America, South Africa, Australia, and Hawaii. Native to Europe and Asia.

Control Strategies:
Preemergence control options include atrazine/simazine, benefin, dithiopyr, isoxaben, napropamide, oxadiazon, pendimethalin. Postemergence control with repeat applications of two- or three-way mixtures of 2,4-D, dicamba, MCPP, or MCPA. Other suggested options include atrazine/simazine, metribuzin, triclopyr alone or combined with clopyralid or 2,4-D. Refer to the Appendix for additional control information. Check the herbicide label for specific application rates and turfgrass tolerance before use.

Corn Speedwell habit with egg-shaped, toothed margin leaves

Corn Speedwell heart-shaped seed capsules with a line of hairs on the outer margin

Scrophulariaceae (Figwort Family)
Slender Speedwell

Synonyms:
Creeping Speedwell

Species:
Veronica filiformis Sm.

Description:
Slender, trailing perennial with narrow rhizomes. Usually found in dense patches. Stems round, roots at the nodes. Leaves opposite, leaf blades round to heart-shaped and palmately veined. Leaf margins slightly toothed. Leaves borne on short petioles. Single deep blue to violet flower found on leafless flower stalk from the leaf axils. Flowers spring into early summer. Heart-shaped seed capsule produced from each flower. Found in lawns, gardens, roadsides, and waste areas.

Propagation:
Seed and rhizomes.

Distribution:
Northeastern states and the Pacific Northwest. Also in British Columbia, Alberta, Ontario, and Quebec. Native of Eurasia.

Control Strategies:
Preemergence control with isoxaben. Postemergence control with repeat applications of two- or three-way mixtures of 2,4-D, dicamba, MCPP, or MCPA. Other suggested options include atrazine/simazine, metribuzin, triclopyr alone or combined with clopyralid or 2,4-D, atrazine plus bentazon, imazaquin, metsulfuron, and quinclorac. Refer to the Appendix for additional control information. Check the herbicide label for specific application rates and turfgrass tolerance before use.

Slender Speedwell rhizomes and round to heart-shaped leaves on short petioles

Slender Speedwell habit with flowers

215

Scrophulariaceae (Figwort Family)
Ivyleaf Speedwell

Synonyms:
None reported.

Species:
Veronica hederaefolia L.

Description:
Prostrate or loosely ascending winter annual. Stems covered with spreading hairs, branched at base. Leaves mostly wider than long, ivy-like, usually three- to five-lobed and palmately veined, long-stalked, opposite at the base of the plant and alternate toward the tip. Flowers in the axils of leaves at branch tips, pale blue, short stalks elongating in fruit. Flowers in spring. Fruit slightly four-lobed, smooth. Found in disturbed soils in fields, grassy areas, and open woods.

Propagation:
Seed.

Distribution:
New York to Ontario and south to Kentucky, South Carolina, and Georgia. Native to Europe.

Control Strategies:
Preemergence control with isoxaben. Postemergence control with repeat applications of two- or three-way mixtures of 2,4-D, dicamba, MCPP, or MCPA. Other suggested options include atrazine/simazine, metribuzin, triclopyr alone or combined with clopyralid or 2,4-D, atrazine plus bentazon, imazaquin, metsulfuron, and quinclorac. Refer to the Appendix for additional control information. Check the herbicide label for specific application rates and turfgrass tolerance before use.

Prostrate-growing Ivyleaf Speedwell stem

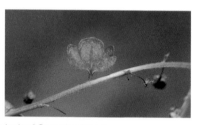

Ivyleaf Speedwell leaf

Ivyleaf Speedwell flowers at branch tips

Smooth, four-lobed Ivyleaf Speedwell fruit

Ivyleaf Speedwell habit

Scrophulariaceae (Figwort Family)
Common Speedwell

Synonyms:
Gipsyweed

Species:
Veronica officinalis L.

Description:
Creeping, prostrate herbaceous perennial which roots at the nodes. Stems and leaves hairy. Leaves opposite, with petioles. Leaves broadly elliptically-shaped with serrate (toothed) leaf margin. Upright leafless flower stalks found in leaf axils. Small dense clusters of pale blue flowers are borne in spike-like racemes. Flowers spring into early summer. Seed capsules heart-shaped. Found in fields, lawns, and roadsides, mostly in dry soils.

Propagation:
Seed and stem fragments.

Distribution:
States east of the Mississippi River and in the North Plains and Pacific Northwest states. Also in British Columbia, Alberta, Ontario, Quebec, New Brunswick, and Nova Scotia. Native of Europe.

Control Strategies:
Preemergence control with isoxaben. Postemergence control with repeat applications of two- or three-way mixtures of 2,4-D, dicamba, MCPP, or MCPA. Other suggested options include atrazine/simazine, metribuzin, triclopyr alone or combined with clopyralid or 2,4-D, atrazine plus bentazon, imazaquin, metsulfuron, and quinclorac. Refer to the Appendix for additional control information. Check the herbicide label for specific application rates and turfgrass tolerance before use.

Common Speedwell habit with hairy stems and broadly elliptically-shaped, toothed, hairy leaves

Common Speedwell flower clusters and broadly elliptically-shaped, toothed leaves

217

Scrophulariaceae (Figwort Family)
Purslane Speedwell

Synonyms:
Neckweed

Species:
Veronica peregrina L.

Description:
Low-growing, freely-branched winter annual with smooth to somewhat fleshy leaves and stems that often root at nodes. Leaves opposite, longer than broad, coarsely toothed on the margins. Flowers white, small, nearly stalkless, in the upper axils. Flowers in spring. Fruit a smooth heart-shaped capsule. Found in damp open soils, usually in low spots in fields, pastures, roadsides, turf, and banks along flowing water.

Propagation:
Seed.

Distribution:
Throughout North America. Also in the West Indies, Mexico, Central and South America, Europe, Asia, and Australia. Native of eastern North America.

Control Strategies:
Preemergence control with isoxaben. Postemergence control with repeat applications of two- or three-way mixtures of 2,4-D, dicamba, MCPP, or MCPA. Other suggested options include atrazine/simazine, metribuzin, triclopyr alone or combined with clopyralid or 2,4-D, atrazine plus bentazon, imazaquin, metsulfuron, and quinclorac. Refer to the Appendix for additional control information. Check the herbicide label for specific application rates and turfgrass tolerance before use.

Purslane Speedwell flower

Purslane Speedwell stem with fruit

Purslane Speedwell smooth, heart-shaped fruit

Purslane Speedwell smooth, longer than wide leaves

Solanaceae (Nightshade Family)
Horsenettle

Synonyms:
Carolina Horsenettle

Species:
Solanum carolinense L.

Description:
Erect to spreading spiny perennial from deep rooted rhizomes with taproots. Stems with few branches, scattered prickles, hairy. Leaves thick, alternate, folded at midrib, wavy-edged to coarsely lobed and with spines along midrib. Leaves with small star-shaped hairs with four to eight spreading rays. Flowers white to pale-violet, clustered. Flowers in summer. Fruit smooth, round, yellow "tomato-like" berry with many seeds. Found in open woods, gardens, pastures, and other disturbed habitats.

Propagation:
Seed and rhizomes.

Distribution:
Eastern half of the United States, west to Kansas, Texas, and California. Also in southern Canada and Mexico. Native to North America.

Control Strategies:
Maintain a routine mowing schedule. Repeat applications of 2,4-D, metsulfuron, or two- or three-way mixtures of 2,4-D, dicamba, MCPP, or MCPA. Other suggested options include triclopyr alone or combined with clopyralid or 2,4-D. Refer to the Appendix for additional control information. Check the herbicide label for specific application rates and turfgrass tolerance before use.

Horsenettle flowers

Horsenettle wavy-edged to coarsely-lobed leaves with spines along midrib

Horsenettle "'tomato-like" yellow fruit

219

Umbelliferae = Apiaceae (Carrot Family)
Asiatic Pennywort

Synonyms:
Centella, Coinwort, Spadeleaf

Species:
Centella asiatica (L.) Urban

Description:
Low-growing, spreading perennial from long rhizomes.
Leaves shovel-shaped with toothed, often dark red margins.
Leaves on slightly-hairy petioles and generally oriented in
an upright or vertical (as opposed to horizontal) fashion.
Flowers short-lived, white, in clusters on short stalks at the
leaf axils. Flowers in summer. Found on moist to wet, sandy
soils in most habitats.

Propagation:
Seed and rhizomes.

Distribution:
Delaware south to Florida, and west to Texas. Also in the
West Indies, Mexico, Central and South America, Asia,
Africa, Hawaii, Australia, and New Zealand.

Control Strategies:
Repeat applications of two- or three-way mixtures of 2,4-D,
dicamba, MCPP, or MCPA. Other suggested options include atrazine/simazine, metribuzin, triclopyr alone or combined with clopyralid or 2,4-D, atrazine plus bentazon,
imazaquin, and metsulfuron. Refer to the Appendix for additional control information. Check the herbicide label for
specific application rates and turfgrass tolerance before use.

Asiatic Pennywort habit

Asiatic Pennywort shovel- or spade-
shaped, toothed leaves with dark red
margins

Umbelliferae = Apiaceae (Carrot Family)
Wild Carrot

Synonyms:
Queen Anne's-lace

Species:
Daucus carota L.

Description:
Slender, branched biennial with a white fleshy taproot shaped like a carrot. First year, develops only a rosette of finely divided leaves. Mature plant with hollow stems and carrot-like odor. Leaves alternate, pinnately divided into small linear segments. Petiole sheath-like, clasping the stem. Flowers small, white, in dense, flat or concave clusters at ends of stems or branches. Center flower in cluster, maroon to black in color. Flowers late-spring through summer. Fruit bristled, in clusters. Occurs along roadsides and in fields and pastures.

Propagation:
Seed.

Distribution:
Southern Canada south into northern Florida and west to Texas, Oklahoma, Kansas, and California. Also in Mexico, Central and South America, Australia, Europe, Asia, and Hawaii. Native to Eurasia.

Control Strategies:
Maintain a routine mowing schedule. Repeat applications of two- or three-way mixtures of 2,4-D, dicamba, MCPP, or MCPA. Other suggested options include atrazine/simazine, metribuzin, triclopyr alone or combined with clopyralid or 2,4-D, atrazine plus bentazon, imazaquin, and metsulfuron. Refer to the Appendix for additional control information. Check the herbicide label for specific application rates and turfgrass tolerance before use.

Wild Carrot habit with flower clusters at ends of stems or branches

Wild Carrot finely divided leaves

Wild Carrot flower cluster

221

Umbelliferae = Apiaceae (Carrot Family)
Pennywort

Synonyms:
Dollarweed, Marsh Pennywort

Species:
Hydrocotyle spp.

Description:
Specific species include: Coastal Plain Pennywort [*Hydrocotyle bonariensis* Comm. ex Lam.]; Water or Many-flower Pennywort [*Hydrocotyle umbellata* L.]; and Whorled Pennywort [*Hydrocotyle verticillata* Thunb.]. All are perennials from rhizomes, occasionally with tubers. Erect long-stalked leaves with scalloped margins. Petiole in center of leaf, "umbrella-like." Flowers in elongated spikes or rounded umbels at top of long stalk. Flowers in summer. Fruit greenish, rounded and somewhat flattened. Found in moist to wet sites or anywhere moisture is in excess.

Propagation:
Seed, rhizomes, and tubers.

Distribution:
Maine south into Florida, and west to Minnesota and Texas, Utah, Arizona, and California. Also in Nova Scotia, British Columbia, the West Indies, Mexico, Central and South America, southern Europe, and tropical Africa

Control Strategies:
Repeat applications of two- or three-way mixtures of 2,4-D, dicamba, MCPP, or MCPA. Other suggested options include atrazine/simazine, metribuzin, triclopyr alone or combined with clopyralid or 2,4-D, atrazine plus bentazon, imazaquin, metsulfuron, and quinclorac. Refer to the Appendix for additional control information. Check the herbicide label for specific application rates and turfgrass tolerance before use.

Pennywort "umbrella-like" leaves with scalloped margins (*Hydrocotyle umbellata*)

Pennywort habit with flowers on elongated spikes (*Hydrocotyle umbellata*)

Pennywort, left; Dichondra, right.

Urticaceae (Nettle Family)
Florida Pellitory

Synonyms:
None reported.

Species:
Parietaria floridana Nutt.

Description:
Weakly erect to sprawling, annual or short-lived perennial herbs, usually not more than 20 cm long or tall. Stem round in cross section. Stem and leaves watery, fleshy, pale green. Leaves thin, oval with a short rounded tip, with three prominently raised veins underneath when fresh, and clearly raised dots on the surface when dry. Leaf margins entire but usually with a line of hairs. Petioles translucent, hairy. Flowers tiny, green, in the axils of leaves. Flowers in warm months. Occurs in moist woods and shady sites.

Propagation:
Seed.

Distribution:
New Hampshire south into Florida, and west to Texas and California. Also in Mexico, Central America, and Africa.

Control Strategies:
Repeat applications of two- or three-way mixtures of 2,4-D, dicamba, MCPP, or MCPA. Other suggested options include atrazine/simazine, metribuzin, triclopyr alone or combined with clopyralid or 2,4-D, atrazine plus bentazon, imazaquin, and metsulfuron. Refer to the Appendix for additional control information. Check the herbicide label for specific application rates and turfgrass tolerance before use.

Florida Pellitory habit

Florida Pellitory leaves

223

Verbenaceae (Verbena or Vervain Family)
Mat Lippia

Synonyms:
Matchweed, Match-head, Capeweed, Turkey-tangle

Species:
Phyla nodiflora (L.) Green; [*Lippia nodiflora* (L.) Michx.]

Description:
Mat-forming perennial with prostrate hairy stems. Stems freely branched, rooting at nodes. Leaves opposite with a few large teeth toward the tip. Flowers rose-purple or white, in a head at the tip of a long stalk, resembling the head of a match. Flowers in warm months. Occurring in low moist areas in open woods and turf, common along the coastal beaches and marshes, preferring open sandy areas often with limestone outcrops.

Propagation:
Seed and stolons.

Distribution:
Pennsylvania to Florida, Arkansas, Oklahoma, Texas, and in California. Also in Hawaii, Mexico, Central and South America, the West Indies, Japan, and India.

Control Strategies:
Repeat applications of two- or three-way mixtures of 2,4-D, dicamba, MCPP, or MCPA. Other suggested options include atrazine/simazine, metribuzin, triclopyr alone or combined with clopyralid or 2,4-D, atrazine plus bentazon, imazaquin, and metsulfuron. Refer to the Appendix for additional control information. Check the herbicide label for specific application rates and turfgrass tolerance before use.

Mat Lippia opposite leaves with large teeth toward the tip

Mat Lippia habit with prostrate-growing, hairy stems

Mat Lippia flowerhead resembling a "match-head"

Verbenaceae (Verbena or Vervain Family)
Stiff Verbena

Synonyms:
Tuber Vervain, Roadside Vervain, Rigid Vervain

Species:
Verbena rigida Spreng.

Description:
Perennial from tubers with erect or ascending four-angled, rigid stems. Leaves opposite, lance-shaped with flaring coarsely-toothed margins, prominently veined. Purple to violet flowers in clusters. Flowers in summer. Occurs in prairies and along roadsides. A related species, Moss Vervain [*Verbena tenuisecta* Briq., {*Glandularia pulchella* (Sweet) Troncosco}], has a prostrate growth habit, finely divided leaves and fibrous roots, occurring along roadsides and in fields.

Propagation:
Seed, tuberous roots, and rooted stems.

Distribution:
North Carolina south to the Florida panhandle and west to Texas; south into South America. Also introduced into the West Indies. Native to Brazil and Paraguay.

Control Strategies:
Repeat applications of two- or three-way mixtures of 2,4-D, dicamba, MCPP, or MCPA. Other suggested options include atrazine/simazine, metribuzin, triclopyr alone or combined with clopyralid or 2,4-D, atrazine plus bentazon, imazaquin, and metsulfuron. Refer to the Appendix for additional control information. Check the herbicide label for specific application rates and turfgrass tolerance before use.

Stiff Verbena square stems and lance-shaped, coarsely-toothed leaves

Moss Vervain (*Verbena tenuisecta*) habit

Stiff Verbena flower cluster

Violaceae (Violet Family)
Violet

Synonyms:
None reported.

Species:
Viola spp.

Description:
Diverse group composed of winter annuals and perennials. Perennials from rhizomes or long stolons. Leaves in basal rosettes or alternate on stems in some species. Many with heart-shaped leaves on long petioles. Other species with linear leaves or leaves palmately divided. Flowers range from purple to white to pink to yellow, usually with 5 petals. Flowers in spring to early summer. Fruit a three-celled capsule, splitting to release seeds. Found mostly in shady and wet open habitats.

Propagation:
Seed and when produced, by rhizomes.

Distribution:
Throughout the continental states except for the states in the High Plains. Also in Canada, the West Indies, Mexico, Central and South America, Asia, Europe, Africa, Australia, and Hawaii.

Control Strategies:
Repeat applications of two- or three-way mixtures of 2,4-D, dicamba, MCPP, or MCPA provide fair control. Other suggested options include atrazine/simazine, metribuzin, triclopyr alone or combined with clopyralid or 2,4-D, atrazine plus bentazon, and imazaquin. Refer to the Appendix for additional control information. Check the herbicide label for specific application rates and turfgrass tolerance before use.

Violet habit, many with heart-shaped leaves

Characteristic Violet flower

Violaceae (Violet Family)
Field Violet

Synonyms:
Wild Pansy, European Field-pansy

Species:
Viola arvensis Murr.

Description:
Winter annual with freely-branched stems. Leaves alternate, hairy, at least on veins on underside. Stipules hairy, divided into numerous segments. Stems hairy, often only on stem angles. Flowers light yellow to purple, stalked, produced in spring. Flowers in spring. Roots with wintergreen odor when crushed. Occurs along roadsides, in fields and pastures.

Propagation:
Seed.

Distribution:
From Alabama and Georgia north to Canada. Also found in Europe and Hawaii. Native to Europe.

Control Strategies:
Preemergence control with isoxaben. Postemergence control with repeat applications of two- or three-way mixtures of 2,4-D, dicamba, MCPP, or MCPA provide fair control. Other suggested options include atrazine/simazine, metribuzin, triclopyr alone or combined with clopyralid or 2,4-D, atrazine plus bentazon, and imazaquin. Refer to the Appendix for additional control information. Check the herbicide label for specific application rates and turfgrass tolerance before use.

Field Violet habit with hairy, rounded, toothed leaves

Field Violet flower

227

Violaceae (Violet Family)
Field Pansy

Synonyms:
Johnny-jump-up

Species:
Viola rafinesquii Greene; [*Viola bicolor* Pursh]

Description:
Winter annual with hairy, erect to spreading, branched stems, often in small colonies. Stems green turning dark purple. Leaves alternate, smooth, rounded with toothed margins. Stipules large, "leaf-like," divided into various segments. Flowers blue-violet to yellow, stalked with yellow centers. Flowers in spring. Occurs in fields, open woods, roadsides, and open grassy areas.

Propagation:
Seed.

Distribution:
From the Florida panhandle, Texas, Alabama, and Georgia north to Maine and west to Missouri, Nebraska, and Colorado. Native to North America.

Control Strategies:
Preemergence control with isoxaben. Postemergence control with repeat applications of two- or three-way mixtures of 2,4-D, dicamba, MCPP, or MCPA provide fair control. Other suggested options include atrazine/simazine, metribuzin, triclopyr alone or combined with clopyralid or 2,4-D, atrazine plus bentazon, and imazaquin. Refer to the Appendix for additional control information. Check the herbicide label for specific application rates and turfgrass tolerance before use.

Field Pansy habit with toothed margin leaves

Field Pansy flower

Zygophyllaceae (Caltrop or Bur Nut Family)
Jamaica Feverplant

Synonyms:
Punctureweed, Burnut, Puncture-vine

Species:
Tribulus cistoides L.

Description:
Prostrate summer annual with several stems radiating out from a single central crown. Leaves opposite, pinnately compound. Leaflets of each leaf even numbered, with some leaflets smaller than others. Stems and leaves with silky hairs. Flowers large, yellow, five-petaled, on stalks over 0.8 inch (2 cm) in length. Flowers in warm months. Fruit a spiny bur. Occurs in turf and vacant lots. Puncturevine (*Tribulus terrestris* L.) is similar but flowers on stalks less than 0.4 inch (1 cm) in length. Puncturevine is native to the Mediterranean area; it occurs in open disturbed sites and turf.

Propagation:
Seed and cut or broken stems.

Distribution:
Alabama, Georgia, Florida, and Texas. Also in the West Indies, Mexico, Central and South America, Hawaii, Guam, Australia, Asia, and west tropical Africa. Native to tropical America.

Control Strategies:
Repeat applications of two- or three-way mixtures of 2,4-D, dicamba, MCPP, or MCPA. Other suggested options include atrazine/simazine, metribuzin, triclopyr alone or combined with clopyralid or 2,4-D, atrazine plus bentazon, imazaquin, and metsulfuron. Refer to the Appendix for additional control information. Check the herbicide label for specific application rates and turfgrass tolerance before use.

Jamaica Feverplant flower

Jamaica Feverplant habit with pinnately compound leaves

Jamaica Feverplant fruit with spines

229

APPENDIX

Appendix Table 1A. Preemergence Herbicide Control Efficacy Ratings[a] for Various Turfgrass Weeds

Herbicide	Crabgrass	Goosegrass	Annual Bluegrass	Common Chickweed	Henbit	Lawn Burweed	Speedwell spp.	Spurges	Woodsorrel (Oxalis)	FL Pusley
atrazine (Aatrex)	F	P	E	E	E	G	E	G	P	G
benefin (Balan)	G-E	F	G-E	G	G	P	P	P	—	—
benefin+oryzalin (XL)	E	G	G	G	G	—	—	F	F	—
benefin+trifluralin (Team)	F-G	F	G	G	G	—	—	F	—	—
bensulide (Betasan, PreSan)	G-E	P-F	F	P	P	P	P	—	—	—
bensulide+oxadiazon	E	G-E	G-E	—	—	—	—	G	—	—
dithiopyr (Dimension)	E	G-E	G-E	G	G	—	G	G	G	—
fenarimol (Rubigan)	P	P	G-E	P	P	P	P	P	P	P
isoxaben (Gallery)	P-F	P	P-F	E	G	E	G-E	G	G	F
metolachlor (Pennant)	F-G	P-F	G	F	—	—	—	F	P	G
napropamide (Devrinol)	G-E	G	G	E	P	E	E	P	G	P
oryzalin (Surflan)	E	G	G-E	G	G	F	P	F-G	G	G
oxadiazon (Ronstar)	G-E	E	G-E	P	G	P	G	G	G	—
pendimethalin (Pre-M)	E	G-E	G-E	E	G	G	G-E	G	G	G
prodiamine (Barricade)	E	G-E	G-E	G	G	F-G	F-G	G	G	G
pronamide (Kerb)	P-F	P	G-E	E	F-G	P	E	P	P	—
simazine (Princep T&O)	P-F	P	E	E	E	G-E	E	F-G	P	G

[a]E=Excellent, >89% control; **G**=Good, 80 to 89% control; **F**=Fair, 70 to 79% control; **P**=Poor, <70% control; **L**=Listed on the label; — = Data not available.

These are relative ratings and depend on many factors such as environmental conditions, turfgrass vigor or health, application timing, etc., and are intended only as a guide.

Appendix Table 2A. Turfgrass Tolerance to Preemergence Herbicides *(Refer to Herbicide Label for Specific Species Listing)*

Herbicides	Bahiagrass	Bentgrass[a]	Bermudagrass[a]	Buffalograss	Centipedegrass	St. Augustinegrass	Zoysiagrass
atrazine (Aatrex)	NR[b]	NR	I (D)	NR	S	S	I-S
benefin (Balan)	S	NR	S	NR	S	S	S
benefin + oryzalin (XL)	S	NR	S	NR	S	S	S
benefin + trifluralin (Team)	S	NR	S	NR	S	S	S
bensulide (Betasan, PreSan)	S	S	S	NR	S	S	S
bensulide + oxadiazon	NR	S	S	NR	NR	NR	S
dithiopyr (Dimension)	S	S	S	S	S	S	S
ethofumesate (Prograss)[c]	NR	S	S(D)	NR	NR	I	NR
isoxaben (Gallery)	S	NR	S	S	S	S	S
fenarimol (Rubigan)	NR	NR	S	NR	NR	NR	NR
metolachlor (Pennant)	S	NR	I	NR	S	S	S
napropamide (Devrinol)	S	NR	S	NR	S	S	NR
oryzalin (Surflan)	S	NR	S	S	S	S	S
oxadiazon (Ronstar)	NR	NR	S	S	NR	S	S
pendimethalin (Pre-M)	S	NR	S	S	S	S	S
prodiamine (Barricade)	S	NR	S	S	S	S	S
pronamide (Kerb)	NR	NR	S	NR	S	S	S
siduron (Tupersan)	NR	I	NR	NR	NR	NR	S
simazine (Princep)	NR	NR	I (D)	NR	S	S	S

Appendix Table 2A. (cont.).

Herbicides	Overseeded Ryegrass	Perennial Ryegrass	Seashore Paspalum	Tall Fescue	Red Fescue	Kentucky Bluegrass
atrazine (Aatrex)	NR	NR	NR	NR	NR	NR
benefin (Balan)	NR	S	NR	S	S	S
benefin + oryzalin (XL)	NR	NR	NR	S	NR	NR
benefin + trifluralin (Team)	NR	S	NR	S	S	S
bensulide (Betasan, PreSan)	I-S	S	NR	S	S	S
bensulide + oxadiazon	NR	S	NR	S	S	S
dithiopyr (Dimension)	I	S	S	S	I	I
ethofumesate (Prograss)[c]	S(D)	S	NR	I	I	S
isoxaben (Gallery)	I-S	S	NR	S	S	S
fenarimol (Rubigan)	S	S	NR	S	S	S
metolachlor (Pennant)	NR	NR	NR	S	S	S
napropamide (Devrinol)	NR	NR	NR	S	NR	NR
oryzalin (Surflan)	NR	NR	NR	NR	NR	NR
oxadiazon (Ronstar)	I	S	S	S	S	S
pendimethalin (Pre-M)	NR	S	NR	S	S	S
prodiamine (Barricade)	I	S	S	S	S	S
pronamide (Kerb)	NR	NR	NR	NR	NR	NR
siduron (Tupersan)	NR	S	NR	S	S	S
simazine (Princep)	NR	NR	NR	NR	NR	NR

[a]Check herbicide label to determine if product can be used on golf course putting greens.

[b]**S**=Safe at labeled rates on mature, healthy turf; **I**=Intermediate safety - may cause slight damage to mature, healthy turf. Use only one-half the normal rate when temperatures are hot (>85° F) or if the turf is under water stress; **NR**=Not Registered for use on and/or damages this turf species.

[c]Ethofumesate is labeled only for Dormant (**D**) bermudagrass overseeded with perennial ryegrass.

These are relative rankings and depend on factors such as environmental conditions, turfgrass vigor or health, application timing, etc., and are intended only as a guide.

Appendix Table 3A. Established Turfgrass Tolerance to Postemergence Herbicides *(Refer to Herbicide Label for Specific Species Listing)*

Herbicides	Bentgrass Greens	Ryegrass	Tall Fescue	Fine Fescue	Kentucky Bluegrass	Buffalograss	Seashore Paspalum
Broadleaf Weed Control							
atrazine (Aatrex)	NR[a]	NR	NR	NR	NR	NR	NR
bentazon (Basagran T&O)	NR-I	S	S	S	S	S	S-NR
bromoxynil (Buctril)	NR	S	S	S	S	NR	NR
chlorsulfuron (Corsair, TFC)	NR	NR	NR	I-S	S	NR	S
clopyralid (Lontrel)	NR	S	S	S	S	S	NR
2,4-D	—	S	S	S	S	—	NR
MCPP (mecoprop)	S	S	S	S	S	—	S
dicamba (Vanquish)	—	S	S	S	S	I-NR	S
2,4-D + dicamba	—	S	S	S	S	NR	NR
2,4-D + dichlorprop (2,4-DP)	—	S	S	S	S	NR	NR
2,4-D + MCPP	—	S	S	S	S	NR	NR
2,4-D + triclopyr (Turflon)	NR-I	S	S	—	S	NR	NR
2,4-D + MCPP + dicamba	—	S	S	S	S	I-NR	NR
2,4-D + MCPP + 2,4-DP	—	S	S	S	S	NR	NR
MCPA + MCPP + 2,4-DP	—	S	S	S	S	NR	NR
halosulfuron (Manage)	NR	S	S	S	S	NR	S
imazaquin (Image)	NR	NR	NR	NR	NR	S-NR	NR
metsulfuron (Manor)	NR	NR	NR	NR	NR	S	NR
simazine (Princep T&O)	NR	NR	NR	NR	NR	NR	NR
triclopyr + clopyralid (Confront)	NR	S	S	I	S	S	NR
Grass Weed Control							
asulam (Asulox)	NR	NR	NR	NR	NR	I-NR	NR
clethodim (Envoy)	NR	NR	NR	NR	NR	NR	NR
diclofop (Illoxan)	NR	NR	NR	NR	NR	S-NR	NR
DSMA, MSMA, CMA	NR-I	S-I	—	—	—	—	NR
ethofumesate (Prograss)[d]	NR-I	S	S	—	S	—	S-NR
fenoxaprop (Acclaim Extra)	NR-I	S	S	S	S	NR	NR
fluazifop (Fusilade T&O)	NR	NR	S-I	NR	NR	NR	NR
metribuzin (Sencor Turf)	NR	NR	NR	NR	NR	NR	NR
pronamide (Kerb)	NR	NR	NR	NR	NR	NR	S-NR
sethoxydim (Vantage)	NR	NR	NR	NR	NR	NR	NR
quinclorac (Drive)	NR	S	S	I	S	S	S-NR

Appendix Table 3A. (cont.).

Herbicides	Bahia-grass	Bermuda-grass	Carpet-grass	Centipede-grass	St. Augustine-grass	Zoysia-grass	Overseeded Ryegrass/Blends
Broadleaf Weed Control							
atrazine (Aatrex)	NR[a]	S-I(D)	I[c]	S	S	—	NR
bentazon (Basagran T&O)	S	S	S	S	S	S	S-I
bromoxynil (Buctril)	S	S	S	S	S	S	S
chlorsulfuron (Corsair, TFC)	—	S	—	—	—	—	NR
clopyralid (Lontrel)	S	S	S	S	S	S	S
2,4-D	S	S	—	S-I	—	—	S-I
MCPP (mecoprop)	S	S	—	—	—	S	—
dicamba (Vanquish)	S	S	—	—	—	S	—
2,4-D + dicamba	S	S	—	—	—	S	S-I
2,4-D + dichlorprop (2,4-DP)	S	S	—	—	—	S	S
2,4-D + MCPP	S	S	—	—	—	S	S
2,4-D + triclopyr (Turflon)	NR	NR	NR	NR	NR	NR	S
2,4-D + MCPP + dicamba	S	S	—	—	—	S	S
2,4-D + MCPP + 2,4-DP	S	S	—	—	—	S	S
MCPA + MCPP + 2,4-DP	S	S	—	—	—	—	S
halosulfuron (Manage)	S	S	S	S	S	S	S
imazaquin (Image)	NR	S-I	—	S	S	S	NR
metsulfuron (Manor)	NR	S	—	S	S-I	S	NR
simazine (Princep T&O)	NR	S-I(D)	—	S-I	S-I	—	NR
triclopyr + clopyralid (Confront)	I	—	NR	S	NR	S	S
Grass Weed Control							
asulam (Asulox)	NR	S-I[b]	NR	NR	S-I	I-NR	NR
clethodim (Envoy)	NR	NR	NR	S	NR	NR	NR
diclofop (Illoxan)	NR	S	NR	NR	NR	NR	NR
DSMA, MSMA, CMA	NR	S-I	NR	NR	NR	S-I	NR
ethofumesate (Prograss)[d]	NR	D	NR	NR	NR	NR	—
fenoxaprop (Acclaim Extra)	I-NR	I-NR	NR	NR	NR	—	—
fluazifop (Fusilade T&O)	NR	NR	NR	NR	NR	—	NR
metribuzin (Sencor Turf)	NR	S-I	NR	NR	NR	NR	NR
pronamide (Kerb)	NR	S	NR	S	S	S	NR
sethoxydim (Vantage)	NR	NR	NR	S	NR	NR	NR
quinclorac (Drive)	NR	S-I	NR	NR	NR	S	S

[a]**S**=Safe at labeled rates; **I**=Intermediate safety, use at reduced rates; **NR**=Not Registered for use on and/or damages this turfgrass; **D**=Dormant turf only.
[b]Asulam is labeled for 'Tifway' (419) Bermudagrass and St. Augustinegrass.
[c]Carpetgrass tolerance to herbicides listed has not been fully been explored.
[d]Ethofumesate is labeled for use on dormant bermudagrass overseeded with perennial ryegrass.
These are relative rankings and depend on factors such as environmental conditions, turfgrass vigor or health, application timing, etc., and are intended only as a guide.

Appendix Table 4A. Guide to Grass Weed Control with Postemergence Turfgrass Herbicides (*Refer to Herbicide Label for Specific Species Listing*)

Herbicide[a]	Crab-grass	Goose-grass	Annual Bluegrass	Sandspur	Dallisgrass	Thin (Bull) Paspalum	Ryegrass	Smut-grass	Bahia-grass	Carpet-grass	Tall Fescue
atrazine (Aatrex)	P-F[b]	P	G-E	F	P	P	G-E	F-G	F	P	F
asulam (Asulox)	G	F	P	F	P	P-F	—	F	P	G	G
chlorsulfuron (Corsair, TFC)	P	P	P	P	P	P	G	F	P	P	G
clethodim (Envoy)	E	G-E	G	G	—	—	G-E	—	—	—	P
diclofop (Illoxan)	P	G-E	P	P	P	P	G	P	P	P	P
DSMA, MSMA	G	F	P	G	F	F-G	P	P	F	G	P
ethofumesate (Prograss)	P	P	F-G[c]	P	P	P	P	P	P	—	P
fenoxaprop (Acclaim)	G-E	G-E	P	G	P	P	P	P	G	—	P
fluazifop (Fusilade T&O)	G-E	G	F	G	P	P	G-E	P	G	—	P
metribuzin (Sencor)	F-G	G-E	G	—	F	P	F	P	P	—	F
metsulfuron (Manor)	P	P	P	P	P	P	G	P	G	P	F
pronamide (Kerb)	P	P	G-E	P	P	P	G-E	P	P	—	G
sethoxydim (Vantage)	G-E	G	P	G	P-F	P	P	P	G	P	P
simazine (Princep T&O)	P-F	P	G-E	P-F	P	P	G-E	F	F	P	F
quinclorac (Drive)	E	P	P	—	F	P	P	P	P	P	P

[a]Repeat applications usually 5 to 14 days apart are needed for most herbicides and weeds. This is especially true as weeds mature, producing flowers and seed-heads.

[b]**E** = excellent (>90%) control with one application;

G = good (80 to 90%) control with one application;

F = Fair to good (70 to 89%), good control sometimes with high rates, however a repeat treatment 1 to 3 weeks later each at the standard or reduced rate is usually more effective; **P** = poor (<70%) control in most cases.

— = Control unknown as all weeds have not been tested for susceptibility to each herbicide listed.

[c]Ethofumesate provides good to excellent control of most true annual biotypes of annual bluegrass but only poor to fair control of perennial biotypes.

Appendix Table 5A. Guide to Broadleaf Weed Control with Postemergence Turfgrass Herbicides

Weed	Lifecycle	Atrazine/ Simazine	2,4-D	Mecoprop (or MCPP)	Dicamba	Bentazon	Bromoxynil	Clopyralid	Imazaquin	Chlorsulfuron	Metsulfuron	Triclopyr	2,4-D + MCPP	2,4-D + 2,4-DP	2,4-D + MCPP + dicamba	2,4-D + triclopyr	Triclopyr + clopyralid	Quinclorac
Aster	P[a]	—	F	—	—	P	P	G	—	—	G	—	F	F	F	F	G	—
Bedstraw, smooth	P	—	P	P-F	P-F	—	—	—	—	—	P	F-G	F	F	F	G	G	—
Betony, Florida	P	F-G[b]	P	F	F	P	—	—	—	—	G	—	F	F	F-G	G	G	–
Bittercress, hairy	WA	—	E	F	E	—	—	—	G	—	E	—	E	E	E	—	—	E
Bindweed, field	P	—	E-F	F	E	P	P	—	—	—	—	F	E-F	E	E	—	—	E
Burclover	A	—	F-P	E	E	—	—	G	G	F	—	G	E-F	E	E	—	—	—
Buttercups	WA,B&P	F	E-F	F	F-P	P	P	—	G	G	E	F	F	E-F	E-F	F-P	E	—
Buttonweed, Virginia	P	—	F	P-F	F	—	P	F	—	F	F	F	F	E-F	G	F-P	G	—
Carpetweed	SA	E	E	F	F	—	—	—	—	—	P	—	E	E	E	E	—	—
Carrot, wild	A,B	—	F	F	E	—	—	P	—	F	E	G	F	E-F	E	E-F	E	—
Cat's-ear	P	—	E-F	F	E	—	—	—	—	—	E	—	E	E	E	—	E	—
Chamberbitter	SA,P	E	—	—	—	—	—	—	—	—	—	—	—	—	—	—	—	—
Chickweed, common	WA	E	P	E-F	E	F-G	P	—	G	G	E	—	E	E	E	E	E	E
Chickweed, mouse-ear	WA,P	F	F-P	E-F	E	P	P	P	G	G	E	P-F	F	E	E	E-F	E	E
Chicory	P	—	E	E	E	—	—	—	—	—	—	G	E	E	—	—	—	—
Cinquefoil, common	P	—	E-F	E-F	E-F	—	—	F	—	F	—	—	E-F	E-F	E-F	—	—	—
Clover, crimson	SA	—	E	E	E	—	—	E	—	—	E	—	E	E	E	—	E	E
Clover, hop	WA	E	F	E	E	—	—	E	G	F	F	—	E	E	E	E	E	E
Clover, white	P	E	P-F	F	E	P	—	E	G	F	E	F-G	F	E	E	E-F	E	E
Cudweed	WA	G-E	G-E	—	E	—	G	—	—	—	—	—	G-E	G-E	E	G-E	G-E	—
Daisy, English	P	—	P	F	E	P	P	F	F	—	F	—	E	F	E	F	F	—
Daisy, oxeye	P,B	—	F	F	F	—	—	F	F	—	—	—	E-F	F	E-F	—	—	—

Appendix Table 5A. (Cont.)

Weed	Lifecycle	Atrazine/Simazine	2,4-D	Mecoprop (or MCPP)	Dicamba	Bentazon	Bromoxynil	Clopyralid	Imazaquin	Chlorsulfuron	Metsulfuron	Triclopyr	2,4-D + MCPP	2,4-D + 2,4-DP	2,4-D + MCPP + dicamba	2,4-D + triclopyr	Triclopyr + clopyralid	Quinclorac
Dandelion	P	E-F	E	E	E	-	P	P-F	—	F	E	F	E	E	E	F-E	—	F
Dayflower, spreading	SA	G-E	F	F	F	G	—	—	G	—	P-F	—	F-G	F-G	F-G	F-G	—	P
Deadnettle, purple	WA	G-E	P-F	F	G	G	—	—	—	—	—	—	F	—	F-G	—	F	G
Dichondra	P	E-F	E	F	E-F	—	—	—	—	F	G-E	G	E	E	E	—	E	E
Dock, broadleaf & curly	P	F	F	F-P	E	P	P	G	—	F	G-E	G	E-F	E-F	E-F	F	E	—
Dogfennel	P	—	P	—	E	—	—	—	—	—	F	—	E	E	E	E	E	—
Doveweed	SA	G-E	F	F	F	—	—	-	—	—	P-F	—	F-G	F-G	F-G	F-G	—	—
Evening-primrose, cutleaf	WA	E	—	—	—	P	F	—	G	—	-	G	G	G	G	G	G	—
False dandelion, Carolina	WA,B	P	G	—	F	P	P	P-F	G	—	G-E	P	G	G	—	—	G	—
Filaree, redstem	WA	—	P-F	—	—	—	—	—	—	G	—	—	—	—	—	—	—	P
Garlic, wild	P	P	E-F	P	F	P	P	—	—	F	G-E	—	E-F	E-F	E-F	G	—	—
Geranium, Carolina	WA	E	E	E-F	E	—	—	—	—	F	F-G	—	E	E	E	E	E	—
Groundsel	WA	—	G	G	—	G	F-G	G	G	—	—	—	G	G	G	G	G	—
Hawkweed	P	P	E-F	P	E-F	P	P	P	—	—	G	P	E-F	E-F	E-F	E-F	—	—
Healall	P	—	E	P	E-F	P	P	P	—	—	E-F	—	E	E-F	E	E	E	—
Henbit	WA	E	F-P	F	E	—	F	—	—	G	G	P	F	E-F	E	F	—	F-G
Horseweed	WA,SA	E	F	—	E	—	—	G	—	—	G	—	G-E	—	G-E	—	E	F-G
Ivy, ground	P	—	F-P	F	E-F	—	F	G	G	G	G	G	F	F-E	E-F	F	G	—
Knawel	WA	—	P	F	E	—	—	—	G	F	F	—	E-F	E-F	E-F	E-F	—	—
Knotweed, prostrate	SA	—	P	P-F	G-E	—	F-G	—	—	F	F	—	F	F	F-G	F	E	—
Kochia	SA	—	G	—	—	—	G	—	G	G	G	—	G	G	E	G	—	—
Lambsquarters	SA	G	G	G	—	G	G	—	—	G	—	G	F	—	G	G	F	—

Appendix Table 5A. (Cont.)

Weed	Lifecycle	Atrazine/ Simazine	2,4-D	Mecoprop (or MCPP)	Dicamba	Bentazon	Bromoxynil	Clopyralid	Imazaquin	Chlorsulfuron	Metsulfuron	Triclopyr	2,4-D + MCPP	2,4-D + 2,4-DP	2,4-D +MCPP dicamba	2,4-D + triclopyr	Triclopyr + clopyralid	Quinclorac
Lespedeza	SA	E	F-P	E	E	—	—	E	—	—	E	—	E-F	F	E	—	E	—
Mallow	P	—	F-P	F	E-F	—	F	—	—	F	—	—	E-F	E-F	E-F	—	—	—
Medic, black	A	—	P	F	E	—	—	G	G	—	—	G	F	E	E	—	E	E
Moneywort	P	—	G	—	—	—	—	—	—	—	—	—	G	G	G	G	G	—
Mugwort	P	—	F	F-P	G-E	—	—	F-G	—	—	—	P-F	F	G	F	G	G	—
Mustard, wild	WA	E	E	F	E	G	F	—	—	G	F	G	E	E-F	E	—	—	—
Nettle, stinging	P	F-G	—	—	F	—	—	—	—	—	—	—	F	F	F	F	—	—
Onion, wild	P	P	G-E	P	E-F	P	P	—	—	F	G-E	—	F	E-F	F	—	—	—
Parsley-piert	WA	E	P	E-F	E-F	G	G	G	G	—	G-E	—	E-F	P	E-F	—	—	—
Pearlwort	WA	—	E-F	E-F	—	—	—	—	—	—	—	F	E-F	E-F	E-F	E	—	E
Pennywort (dollarweed)	P	E	E-F	E-F	E-F	P-F	P	G	—	—	G	F	E-F	E-F	E-F	—	—	—
Pepperweed, Virginia	WA	E	E	E-F	E	—	F	—	—	—	—	E	E-F	E-F	E-F	E	G	E
Pigweed	SA	G	E	E	E	P	F-G	G	—	G	E-F	F-G	E	E	E	G	E	—
Pineapple-weed	WA,SA	—	F	F	E	—	—	—	—	G	G	—	F	E	F	F	E	—
Plantains	WA, P	F-P	E	F-P	P	P	P	P-F	—	F	G-F	F-G	F	E	F	F-G	E	—
Purslane, common	SA	G	F	P	E	G	G	G	—	G	F	G	F	F	E-F	G	E	—
Ragweed, common	SA	G	G	G	G	G	F-G	G	G	F	G	G	G	G	G	G	E	—
Rocket, yellow	WA,B	—	F-G	F-G	F	—	G	F	G	G	G	G	G	G	G	G	F	—
Shepherd's-purse	WA	—	E	E-F	E	—	G	F-G	—	F	G	—	E-F	E-F	E-F	—	—	—
Smartweed	SA	G	G	—	E	G	G	F-G	G	G	G	G	G	G	—	G	F-G	—
Sorrel, red	P	—	P	E	E	P	—	G	—	F	G	F-G	E-F	F	E	—	E	—
Speedwell, common	P	F	F	P	P	P	—	P	F	G	—	F-G	P	P	P	P	F-G	E

Appendix Table 5A. (Cont.)

Weed	Lifecycle	Atrazine/Simazine	2,4-D	Mecoprop (or MCPP)	Dicamba	Bentazon	Bromoxynil	Clopyralid	Imazaquin	Chlorsulfuron	Metsulfuron	Triclopyr	2,4-D + MCPP	2,4-D + 2,4-DP	2,4-D + MCPP + dicamba	2,4-D + triclopyr	Triclopyr + clopyralid	Quinclorac
Speedwell, corn	WA	E	F-P	F-P	F-P	P	G	—	—	—	G-E	F-G	F-P	F-P	F-P	—	F-G	—
Speedwell, germander	P	F	P	P	P	P	—	P	—	—	—	F-G	P	P	P	P	F-G	—
Speedwell, purslane	WA	F	—	P-F	—	P	—	—	—	—	—	F-G	—	—	G	—	F-G	—
Speedwell, thymeleaf	P	F	P-F	P-F	P	P	—	P	—	—	—	F-G	F	F	F	P	F-G	E
Spurge, prostrate	SA	E-F	F	F	E	P	P	—	—	—	E	F-G	F	E-F	E-F	E-F	E-F	G
Spurge, spotted	SA	E	F-P	E-F	E-F	P	P	—	—	—	E	F-G	E-F	E-F	E-F	E-F	E-F	G
Spurry, corn	P	—	F	—	F-G	—	F-G	—	—	—	—	—	F	F	G	F	F	—
Spurweed (lawn burweed)	WA	F-G	F	E-F	E	E	F-G	—	—	—	G-E	F-G	E-F	F	E	E	E	—
Strawberry, Indian mock	P	—	P	F	E-F	—	—	—	—	—	—	—	F	P	E-F	—	—	—
Thistles	B,P	P	E-F	F	E	P-G	P	F-G	G	F	F	G	E-F	E-F	E	F	F	—
Vetch, common	WA, SA	E	P-G	G	G	—	—	E	G	—	E	G	G	G	G	G	E	G
Violet, Johnny-jumpup	WA	—	F-P	F-P	E-F	P	P	—	—	—	—	F	F-P	F	F-P	—	F-G	—
Violet, wild	P	—	F-P	F-P	E-F	P	P	—	—	F	—	F	F-P	F	F-P	F-P	F-G	—
Woodsorrel, creeping	P	F	P	P	P-F	P	P-F	—	—	—	F-G	F-G	P-F	P-F	F-P	F-G	F-G	—
Woodsorrel, yellow	P	F	P	P	F	P	P	P	—	—	E-F	F-G	F-P	F-P	F-P	F-G	E-F	—
Yarrow	P	—	F	F-P	E	P	P	—	—	F	E-F	F-G	F-P	F	E-F	—	E-F	—

[a] A = annual; B = biennial; P = perennial; SA = summer annual; WA = winter annual.

[b] E = excellent (>89%) control; F = Fair to Good (70 to 89%), good control sometimes with high rates, however a repeat treatment 1 to 3 weeks later each at the standard or reduced rate is usually more effective; P = poor (<70%) control in most cases. Not all weeds have been tested for susceptibility to each herbicide listed.

— = data not available.

Appendix Table 6A. Relative Sedge Control and Turf Tolerance to Various Herbicides *(Refer to Herbicide Label for Specific Species Listing)*

		Sedges			
Herbicide(s)[a]	Annual Sedge	Purple Nutsedge	Yellow Nutsedge	Annual Kyllinga Species	Perennial Kyllinga Species
Preemergence Control					
Metolachlor (Pennant)	G[b]	P	G	F-G	P
Oxadiazon (Ronstar 2G)	G	P	P	F	P
Postemergence Control					
Bentazon (Basagran T&O)	G	P	G	F-G	F-G
Imazaquin (Image)	G	F-G	F	G	G
Halosulfuron (Manage)	G	G-E	G-E	G	F-G
MSMA/DSMA/CMA	G	P-F	F	G	G
Image + MSMA/DSMA	G	G	G	G	G

[a] Repeat applications are necessary for complete control from all herbicides. This interval is from 5 days for MSMA/DSMA, up to 3 to 8 weeks for Manage or Image.

[b] **E** = excellent (>89%) control; **F** = Fair to Good (70 to 89%), good control sometimes with high rates, however a repeat treatment 1 to 3 weeks later each at the standard or reduced rate is usually more effective; **P** = poor (<70%) control in most cases.

These are relative rankings and depend on many factors such as environmental conditions, turfgrass vigor or health, application timing, etc., and are intended only as a guide.

Appendix Table 7A. Common and Trade Names of Turf Herbicides

Common Name	Trade Name(s)
Asulam	-Asulox 3.34L, Asulam 3.3
Atrazine	-AAtrex, Atrazine Plus, Purge II, Aatrex 90, Atrazine 4L, Bonus S, St. Augustine Weedgrass Control + others
Benefin	-Balan 2.5G. 1.5EC, Crabgrass Preventer, + others
Benefin + oryzalin	-XL 2G
Benefin + trifluralin	-Team 2G, Crabgrass Preventer 0.92%, Team Pro
Bensulide	-Betasan, Pre-San 12.5 & 7 G, Bensumec 4, Lescosan, Weedgrass Preventer, Betamec, + others
Bentazon	-Basagran T/O 4L, Lescogran 4L
Bentazon + atrazine	-Prompt 5L
Bromoxynil	-Buctril 2L, Brominal 4L, Bromox 2E
Cacodylic Acid	-Montar, Weed Ender
Chlorsulfuron	-TFC 75DG, Corsair 75DF
Clethodim	-Envoy 0.94 EC
Clopyralid	-Lontrel T&O 3L
CMA (CAMA)	-Calar, Ortho Crabgrass Killer - Formula II, Selectrol
Corn gluten	-Dynaweed, WeedzSTOP 100G
Dazomet	-Basamid
2,4-D	-2,4-D Amine & Ester, Weedone LV4, Dacamine, Weedar 64, AM-40, 2,4-D LV4, Dymec, Lesco A-4D, + others
2,4-D + clopyralid + dicamba	-Millennium Ultra 3.75 lb/gal
2,4-D + clopyralid + triclopyr	-Momentum
2,4-D + dicamba	-81 Selective Weedkiller, Four Power Plus, Triple D Lawn Weed Killer, Banvel + 2,4-D
2,4-D + dichlorprop (2,4-DP)	-2D + 2DP Amine, Turf D + DP, Fluid Broadleaf Weed Control, Weedone DPC Ester & Amine + others
2,4-D + dichlorprop (2,4-DP) + dicamba	-Super Trimec, Brushmaster
2,4-D + mecoprop (MCPP)	-2D Amine + 2MCPP, 2 Plus 2, MCPP-2,4-D, Phenomec, Ortho Weed-B-Gon Lawn Weed Killer + others
2,4-D + MCPP + 2,4-DP	-Broadleaf Granular Herbicide, Dissolve, Triamine, Tri-Ester, Jet-Spray 3-Way Weed Control + others
2,4-D + MCPP + dicamba + MCPA and/or 2,4-DP	-Trimec Southern, Three-Way Selective, Eliminate DG, 33-Plus, Dissolve, Triamine 3.9 lb/gal, TriEster, Triplet, Trex-San, Weed-B-Gon, 2 Plus 2, Bentgrass Selective Weed Killer, Trimec Bentgrass Formula, Strike 3, Broadleaf Trimec, MECAmine-D, Trimec 992, Weed-B-Gon for Southern Lawns, Formula II, + others

Appendix Table 7A. (cont.)

Common Name	Trade Name(s)
Dicamba	-Vanquish 4 L, K-O-G Weed Control, Bentgrass Selective, Banvel 4S + others
Dicamba + MCPA + MCPP	-Encore DSC, Tri-Power Dry, Trimec Encore
Diclofop	-Illoxan 3EC
Dithiopyr	-Dimension 1L
Diquat	-Reward LS, Watrol, Vegetrol, Aquatate
DSMA	-Ansar, DSMA Liquid, Methar 30, Namate, DSMA 4
Ethofumesate	-Prograss 1.5L
Fenarimol	-Rubigan 1AS, Patchwork 0.78G
Fenoxaprop	-Acclaim Extra 0.57EC
Fluazifop	-Fusilade II T&O, Ornamec
Glufosinate	-Finale 1L
Glyphosate	-Roundup Pro, Roundup ProDry, Gly-Flo, AquaNeat, Razor, Rodeo, Ortho Kleenup, Weed Wrangler, + others
Halosulfuron	-Manage 75WP
Hexazinone	-Velpar 2L
Imazapic	-Plateau 70 DG
Imazaquin	-Image 1.5L
Isoxaben	-Gallery 75DF
MCPA	-Weedar MCPA 4 lb/gal, MCPA-4 Amine, + others
MCPA + MCPP + 2,4-DP	-Triamine II, Tri-Ester II
MCPA + dicamba + triclopyr	-Eliminate, Three-Way Ester II
MCPP	-Mecomec 4, Chickweed & Clover Control, Lescopex, MCPP-4 Amine, MCPP-4K + others
MSMA	-Daconate 6, Dal-E-Rad, Crab-E-Rad, MSMA 6.6L, Drexar 530, Buano 6L, 120 Herbicide, Daconate Super, 912 Herbicide, MSMA Turf, Summer Crabicide, + others
MSMA + 2,4-D +MCPP + dicamba	-Trimec Plus (Quadmec)
Metribuzin	-Sencor 75DF
Metolachlor	-Pennant 7.8 lb/gal
Metsulfuron	-Manor 60 DF, Escort 60 DF

Appendix Table 7A. (cont.)

Common Name	Trade Name(s)
Methyl Bromide	-Brom-O-Gas, Terr-O-Gas, MB 98, MBC
Napropamide	-Devrinol 50 DF, Ornamental Herbicide 5G
Oryzalin	-Surflan AS 4 lb/gal
Oxadiazon	-Ronstar 2G, 50WP
Oxadiazon + bensulide	-Goosegrass/Crabgrass Control
Oxadiazon + dithiopyr	-SuperStar
Oxadiazon + prodiamine	-Regalstar II 1.2G
Paclobutrazol	-Turf Enhancer 50WP, 2SC, Trimmit 2SC
Pelargonic Acid	-Scythe
Pendimethalin	-Pre-M & Pendulum (60 DG, WP, 3.3EC, 2G), Turf Weedgrass Control, Halts, Corral
Prodiamine	-Barricade 65WDG, Endurance 65 WDG, Factor 65 WDG
Pronamide	-Kerb 50WP
Quinclorac	-Drive 75 DF
Sethoxydim	-Vantage 1.0 lb/gal
Siduron	-Tupersan 50WP, 4.6%
Simazine	-Princep 4 lb/gal, T&O, 80WP, Simazine, Wynstar, + others
Triclopyr	-Turflon Ester 4L
Triclopyr + 2,4-D	-Turflon II Amine, Chaser 3L, Chaser 2 Amine
Triclopyr + clopyralid	-Confront 3L
Triclopyr + MCPP + dicamba	-Cool Power 3.6 lb/gal, Horsepower 4.56 lb/gal, 3-Way Ester II
Xanthomonas campentris	-X-Po

GLOSSARY OF TAXONOMIC TERMINOLOGY

abaxial: located away from the axis side; for example, the underside of a leaf.

achene: a small dry, one-seeded fruit which does not open or split at maturity, such as sunflower seed.

acuminate: a tip gradually tapering to a point with the margins curving inward.

acute: sharply pointed.

adaxial: located toward the axis side; for example, the upper side of a leaf.

adventitious bud: a bud produced in an unusual or unexpected place; for example, near a point of stem injury or on a leaf or a root.

adventitious root: a root originating in an unusual or unexpected place such as from stem or leaf tissue instead of from another root.

aggregate: collected together in tufts, groups, or bunches.

alternate: an arrangement of a single leaf, bud, or branch attached singly at different points on the stem; appearing to alternate.

annual: a plant starting from seed and completing its life cycle and dying within one year.

anther: the sac-like portion of the male part of a flower (stamen) that bears pollen.

anthesis: opening of the flower bud; when pollination occurs.

apex: the tip of a stem, root, or leaf.

appressed: pressed flatly and closely against the surface.

aquatic: growing in water.

articulate: jointed.

ascending: sloping or growing upward or outward.

asymmetrical: lopsided; having two sides different in shape or area.

auricle: small, ear-shaped lobes or appendages at the junction of the leaf sheath and blade in grasses, or at the leaf base of broadleaf plants.

awn: a slender or stiff bristle, usually extending from a grass floret, specifically on the glumes or lemma.

axil: the angle between the leaf and stem.

axillary bud: a bud located in the leaf axil.

axis: the main stem of an inflorescence; a panicle is a good example.

basal rosette: a cluster of leaves radiating at the base of a plant at ground level.

beak: a hard point or projection, seen frequently on seeds and fruits.

bearded: having long hairs.

biennial: a plant that completes its life cycle and dies in two years. The first year, seed germinate and form vegetative growth. The second year, flowering, seed set, and death occur.

biotype: a population within a species that has distinct genetic variation.

bipinnate: two rows of lateral branches along an axis which are again divided into two rows; feather-like.

bisexual: flowers with male (stamens) and female (pistil) elements.

blade: the expanded, usually flat, portion of a leaf.

boat-shaped: leaf tips which are shaped like the front (or bow) of a boat such as *Poa* species.

brackish: somewhat salty.

bract: a modified, usually reduced leaf associated with a flower or flower cluster.

branch: a lateral stem.

bristle: a short, coarse, stiff hair-like part.

bud: an usually tightly bunched, undeveloped shoot or flower usually located at the tip of a stem or branch.

bulb: an underground short, thickened shoot where food is stored such as found in wild onion.

bur: a structure with spines or prickles that are frequently hooked or barbed.

calyx: the outer parts of a flower composed of leaf-like parts called sepals.

capitate: in a globular cluster or head.

capsule: a simple, many-seeded, dry fruit, splitting upon drying into two or more parts.

carpel: basal juvenile seed-bearing structure of the pistil.

caryopsis: the grass fruit, normally dry at maturity, consisting of a single seed within the ovary.

cespitose: tufted stems.

ciliate: fringed with hairs on the margin; hairy.

clasping: a type of leaf attachment where the leaf base partly or completely encircles the stem.

clavate: club-shaped.

clump-forming or **tufted:** grows in a compact cluster.

coleoptile: protective sheath covering the shoot tip and leaves of emerging grass seedlings.

collar: the outer side of a grass leaf at the junction of the blade and sheath.

composite: a member of the *Compositae* or *Asteraceae* family that has a dense inflorescence, usually composed of florets, a receptacle, and bracts.

compound leaf: a type of leaf composed of two or more distinct, similar parts often called leaflets.

compressed: flattened laterally.

conical: cone-shaped.

cordate: heart-shaped with the point at the tip.

corm: a stout, short, vertical, bulb-like underground food storage stem.

corolla: the flower petals that surround the stamens and pistil.

cotyledon: a seed leaf of the embryo, most often the storage sites of reserve food used by germinating seedlings.

crenate: a type of leaf margin that is shallowly round-toothed or scalloped.

crown: a meristematic growing point at or just below the ground where stems and roots join and new shoots emerge.

culm: flowering stem of a grass plant not including the leaves.

cultivar: form or type of a plant originating during cultivation.

cuneate: wedge-shaped.

cuticle: waxy outer layer of a leaf or stem.

cutin: a waxy substance found on the surface of certain seeds or leaves to conserve water.

cylindrical: cylinder-shaped.

day-neutral plants: plants with no daylength requirements for floral initiation.

decumbent: lying on the ground, but rising at the tip.

decurrent: a type of leaf attachment where the leaf base or margin extends down the stem beyond the point of attachment.

deltoid: triangular-shaped.

dentate: a type of leaf margin that is toothed, with the teeth perpendicular to the leaf margin.

denticulate: with very small, pointed teeth.

dicotyledon, dicot: broadleaf plants with two seed embryos (leaves) or cotyledons when it emerges from the soil; these also have netted leaf veins, showy flowers, flower parts in 4s or 5s, and often a cambium for secondary growth.

diffuse: loose and widely spreading.

digitate: branches arising from a common point. Resembling the fingers of a human hand.

dioecious: separate male (stamens) and female (pistil) plants; unisexual.

disc flower: a type of flower with a tubular shaped corolla that is found in a head as all or part of the complete flower of many members of the *Compositae* family.

dissected: divided into numerous narrow segments or lobes.

distichous: conspicuously two-ranked.

distinct: separate.

divaricate: spreading.

divided: cut to the base or to the midrib.

dorsal: on the back, away from the stem or axis.

ecotype: a strain or selection within a given species adapted to a particular environment.

elliptic: a narrow shape with relatively rounded ends that is widest at the middle.

elongate: narrow and long.

embryo: seed portion that develops into a juvenile plant.

endocarp: inner layer of the pericarp (fruit wall).

endosperm: seed portion containing food reserves.

entire: a type of leaf margin without teeth, lobes, or divisions; smoothed-edge.

epicotyl: young stem of a seedling or embryo just above the cotyledon(s).

epidermis: outer cellular layer of plants which helps prevent drying and mechanical injury.

exocarp: outermost layer of the pericarp (fruit wall).

extravaginal: growth from stem penetration through the basal leaf sheath such as rhizomes and stolons.

fascicle: a bunch or cluster.

fibrous roots: slender, branched roots of similar size arising from a similar point.

filament: anther-bearing stalk of a stamen (male part) of a flower; thread.

filiform: thread-like, long and very slender.

first leaf: the subsequent leaf produced after the cotyledons in seedlings.

flabellate: fan-shaped.

flaccid: without rigidity; limp or weak.

floret: a small flower or one of individual closely clustered small flowers (having both pistil and stamens) enclosed by bracts (lemma and palea).

folded: arrangement of the youngest leaf in the bud shoot where leafbuds are folded together lengthwise with the upper surface inside the fold.

fruit: a matured ovary with its enclosed seeds; a ripened pistil.

genotype: the hereditary makeup of a plant (or variety) which determines its inheritance.

genus (plural: genera): a group of related species.

glabrous: smooth, without hairs or bristles.

glandular hair: a small hair terminated in a small pinhead-like gland, frequently secreting resin, wax, or other substances.

glaucous: covered with a waxy coating that results in a whitish to blue-green color.

glume: one of the pair of bracts at the base of a grass spikelet that do not enclose flowers.

grass-like: leaves long and narrow, usually more than 10 times as long as broad.

gymnosperm: plant that produces seeds but not fruits. The seeds are not borne within an ovary and are said to be naked, hence the name. Example: pines.

habit: growth form of the plant.

habitat: natural environment where a plant grows.

halophyte: plant that grows in salty soil.

hastate: arrowhead shape with pointed basal lobes.

head: a dense cluster of stalkless flowers, as in dandelion.

herbaceous: nonwoody plant that may die back to the ground in winter.

hyaline: transparent.

hybrid: cross between two species.

hypocotyl: stem part below the cotyledons of a seedling.

immersed: growing under water; submerged.

imperfect flower: flowers lacking either male or female parts; unisexual flowers.

inferior: beneath.

inflorescence: the flowering portion of a plant.

intercalary meristem: meristematic area between two previously differentiated tissues of certain organs such as between the leaf blade and sheath or between a node and internode that accounts for stem elongation in grasses.

internode: the section of stem between two successive nodes or joints.

involute: rolled inward.

joint: node of a grass stem.

keel: a prominent ridge, often comprised of tissue on both sides of a midrib of a glume or leaf blade, for example, which has grown together.

lamina: the extended flattened portion of a leaf or petal.

lanceolate: a shape longer than wide, broadest below the middle; lance-shaped.

lateral bud: a bud originating in the leaf axil, on the side of the stem.

lateral shoot: a shoot originating from vegetative buds in the axil of leaves or from the nodes of stems, rhizomes, or stolons.

leaf axil: the upper angle formed between the axis of a stem and another structure such as a leaf.

leaf bud: an emerging grass blade.

leaflet: one of the divisions of a compound leaf.

legume: member of the pea or bean family having a dry fruit that splits open along two longitudinal sutures; pods.

lemma: lowermost of the two bracts enclosing a grass flower; the other bract is a palea.

ligule: projection at the inside junction of the grass leaf blade and collar, which may be membrane-like or a row of hairs.

linear: a long and narrow shape with parallel margins.

lobe: a segment of a simple leaf cut rather deeply into curved or angular segments.

lodicules: small, scalelike structures at the base of grass flower stamen that inflate at anthesis to force open the lemma and palea, thus opening the floret.

long-day plants: plants which initiate flowering under long day (short night) regimes.

membranous: thin, transparent, and flexible: membrane-like.

meristem: a cluster of dividing cells at the root and stem apices or tips.

mesocarp: middle layer of the pericarp (or fruit wall).

mesocotyl: that portion of the grass seedling separating sheath and cotyledon.

midrib: the main or central vein or rib of a leaf or leaflet.

midvein: the primary vein.

monocotyledon, monocot: grass and grass-like plants in which embryos (seedlings) have one cotyledon (seed leaf), parallel-veined leaves, inconspicuous flowers, flower parts in multiples of 3s, and no secondary growth.

monoecious: staminate (male) and the pistillate (female) flowers being in separate inflorescences but occurring on the same plant, such as corn.

252

nodding: hanging down.

node: the point or level of a stem at which one or more leaves and roots are attached.

obicular: circular-shaped.

oblanceolate: inverse of lanceolate, a shape where the terminal is half the widest.

oblique: a shape having sides of unequal length or form.

oblong: an elongate shape with approximately parallel sides, more or less rectangular; longer than wide.

obovate: inverted oval- or egg-shaped; widest above the middle.

obtuse: blunt or rounded at the end instead of being angular.

ocrea: a sheath or tube around the stem at a node, formed by a fusion of two stipules; common in the *Polygonaceae*.

opaque: dull, not transparent.

open: loose.

opposite: an arrangement of paired leaves attached opposite from each other at the same node.

orbicular: circular or round-shaped.

oval or **ovate:** a shape similar to a hen's egg; widest below the middle.

ovary: lower part of the pistil containing the ovules or later the seed.

ovoid: egg-shaped.

ovule: an immature seed.

palea: uppermost (inner) of the two bracts enclosing the flower of a grass floret; this bract is enclosed by the largest lower bract (lemma) and is located on the side opposite the embryo.

palmate: a type of leaf where leaflets or lobes originate from a common point, and diverge like the fingers from the palm of the hand.

palmate venation: three or more nearly equal veins extending out from the petiole like the fingers from the palm of the hand.

palmately compound: a type of leaf arrangement where leaflets arise from petiole-like fingers originating from a common point of attachment.

panicle: an inflorescence composed of several branches and sub-branches.

papilla: a minute nipple-shaped projection.

papillose: bearing nipple-shaped projections.

pappus: modified calyx of *Asteraceae* consisting of awns, scales, or bristles at the top of the achene.

pectinate: comb-like.

pedicel: the stalk of a simple flower or spikelet.

peduncle: stalk or stem of a flower cluster or individual flower.

peltate: a type of leaf attachment where the stalk is attached inside the leaf margin.

perennial: a plant that normally lives for more than two years.

perfect flower: flower with both functional pistils (female) and stamens (male); bisexual.

pericarp: the wall of a matured ovary when it becomes a fruit.

petal: an inner floral leaf that makes up a flower's corolla, generally colored or white.

petiole: the stalk or stem of a leaf.

pilose: hairy, the hairs being elongated, slender, and soft.

pinnate: a type of compound leaf with the leaflets arranged on either side of a central axis.

pinnate venation: venation resembling a feather with veins branching from both sides of the main vein.

pinnately compound: a compound leaf with the leaflets arranged along a central, common axis.

pinnatifid: pinnately divided to the middle or beyond (somewhat resembling a feather).

pistil: female flower composed of stigma, style, and ovary, and formed from one or more carpels.

pistillate: flowers bearing pistils but no stamens.

pith: the central soft tissue of a stem.

plumose: feathered, having fine hairs on each side.

prostrate: parallel to or lying flat on the ground.

pubescent: covered with hairs.

pyriform: pear-shaped.

raceme: an elongated inflorescence with each flower on individual stalks.

rachilla: central floral axis of a grass spikelet; a small rachis.

rachis: the main stem or axis bearing flowers or compound (pinnate) leaves.

radicle: embryo portion which grows into the primary root of the seedling.

ray flower: a type of flower with a strap-shaped petal, located around the margin of the flowering head found in many members of the *Compositae* family.

reclining: sprawling or lying down.

recurved: curved downward or backward.

reflexed: turned abruptly downward or backward.

reniform: kidney- or bean-shaped.

reticulate: a network pattern, netted.

rhizome: a creeping, horizontal underground stem, producing shoots above ground and root below; distinguished from a root by the presence of nodes, buds, or scale-like leaves; may originate from the main stem or from tillers.

rhombic: more or less diamond-shaped, having straight margins and being widest in the middle.

rolled: cylindrical arrangement of the youngest leaf in the bud shoot.

rosette: circular cluster of leaves usually appressed to or located near the ground level.

rudimentary: small, often incompletely developed.

runner: a slender stolon (or horizontal stem).

sagittate: arrowhead-shaped.

scabrous: rough to the touch with minute rough projections.

scale: any small, thin, dry membrane-like leaf or bract at the base of a shoot.

scarious: dry, thin, membranous, nongreen and translucent.

scurfy: covered with minute, membranous scales.

scutellum: a shield-shaped organ of grass embryos.

secund: arranged or turned to one side of the axis.

seed: a ripened ovule.

seedhead: a collection of flowers clustered upon a main stem; refers as used here to the inflorescence of the grasses, sedges, and rushes.

seminal root: root arising from the base of the hypocotyl.

sepal: a part of a flower which is usually petal-like in appearance and green in color.

serrate: a type of leaf margin with sharp teeth pointing forward; saw-toothed.

sessile: without a petiole, stem, or stalk; usually refers to a leaf being attached directly on the axis or stem of a plant.

sheath: the lower portion of a leaf which encircles the stem.

shoot: a general term for the aboveground portion of a plant.

short-day plants: plants which initiate flowering best under short day (long night) regimes.

simple: a type of leaf consisting of a blade not divided into individual leaflets; unbranched.

sinuate: a type of leaf margin that is wavy with regularly spaced indentations.

smooth: lacking hairs, divisions or teeth; not rough to the touch.

solitary: alone.

spatulate: a shape broadest at the rounded end, spoon- or spatula-shaped.

species: a group of individuals having certain distinctive characteristics in common.

spike: an unbranched inflorescence with the spikelets sessil (stalkless) on a rachis.

spikelet: the basic individual unit of the spike of grasses and some sedges; composed of one or more flowers and their subtending bracts (two glumes and one or more florets).

spur: a tubular projection from a petal or sepal.

stalk: any slender supporting structure such as a petiole for a leaf, a peduncle for an inflorescence, or a pedicel for a flower.

stamen: the male or pollen-bearing organ of a flowering plant consisting of the filament (stalk) and the anther.

stellate: star-shaped.

stem: plant organ for support, leaf production, food storage, and limited food production.

sterile: without seeds or pollen.

stigma: upper feathery part of the female flower pistil that receives pollen.

stipule: bract-like appendages at the base of some leaves.

stolon: a creeping, aboveground stem that roots at the nodes.

style: the stalk that connects the stigma to the ovary in flowers.

subtended: underneath, directly below, or close to.

subulate: awl-shaped.

succulent: soft and fleshy.

sucker: a plant shoot that arises from an adventitious bud on a root.

summer annual: a plant that germinates in spring, grows and flowers in summer, and sets seed in fall, after which it dies.

tapering: gradually becoming smaller toward one end; not abrupt.

taproot: a single enlarged vertical main root lacking major divisions.

tendril: a slender, twisting, thread-like structure of a leaf or stem that allows plants to climb.

terminal bud: bud located at the end or apex of a stem or branch.

three-ranked: diverging from the stem in three directions, as in the sedge family.

tiller: grass shoot, usually erect, originating intravaginally (grows upward within the enclosing leaf sheath) from axillary buds in the axis of a leaf or in the unelongated crown portion of a stem.

toothed: sawteeth-like projections (or 'teeth') on the margins of leaves.

trailing: prostrate but not rooting.

trifoliate: a type of compound leaf composed of three leaflets.

truncate: cut off square, very blunt, ending abruptly.

tuber: thickened storage portion of a rhizome or stolon (stem), bearing nodes and buds.

tufted: in compact clusters, forming clumps.

two-ranked: in two vertical rows on opposite sides of a stem or axis, as in the grass family.

ubiquitous: occurring everywhere.

umbel: an inflorescence with pedicels arising from a common point of attachment.

undulate: with a wavy or irregular surface or margin (edge).

unilateral: one-sided or turned to one side.

unisexual: flowers having only male (staminate) or female (pistillate) elements.

vaginate: sheathed.

vein: ribs of a leaf; one of the vascular bundles of a leaf.

vermiform: worm-shaped.

vernation: arrangement of the youngest leaf in the bud shoot; either rolled or folded.

verticillate: arranged in a whorl.

whorled leaves: three or more leaves attached in a circular arrangement at the same node.

winter annual: a plant that germinates in late summer, grows vegetatively during winter, flowers and sets seed in late spring to early summer, after which it dies.

woody: consisting or composed of wood or wood-like tissue.

zygote: a fertilized egg.